JULES
VERNE

JULES VERNE

A Biography by

JEAN JULES-VERNE

TRANSLATED AND ADAPTED BY ROGER GREAVES

AN ARNOLD LENT BOOK

TAPLINGER PUBLISHING COMPANY · NEW YORK

First published in the United States in 1976 by
TAPLINGER PUBLISHING CO., INC.
New York, New York

English translation copyright © 1976 by
MacDonald and Jane's, London, and
Taplinger Publishing Co., Inc., New York
All rights reserved. Printed in the U.S.A.

Originally published in France as *Jules Verne* by Jean Jules-Verne,
© 1973, Librarie Hachette

Library of Congress Cataloging in Publication Data

Jules-Verne, Jean, 1892–
Jules Verne: a biography

"An Arnold Lent Book"

Bibliography: p.
Includes index.
1. Verne, Jules, 1828–1905—Biography.
PQ2469.Z5J7813   843′.8 [B]   73-16958
ISBN 0-8008-4439-4

CONTENTS

ILLUSTRATIONS

TRANSLATOR'S NOTE

This biography of Jules Verne was originally published in French in 1973. For the English edition I have – with the consent of the author – adapted the text by making a number of excisions and rearrangements of material. I have also adjoined a bibliography of Verne's works listing English translations and other details not readily available elsewhere, together with a summary of critical books and articles.

Apart from the above, this edition differs from the French edition in that the *Voyage en Ecosse* is discussed and quoted for the first time, and the details on the life of Paul Verne and Herminie, as well as certain photographs, are also published for the first time. These additions to the work, along with several corrections, were made by Jean Jules-Verne. In order to situate Verne more fully in the contexts of Paris and Amiens I have compiled a number of biographical annotations concerning Verne's life in Paris around the Théâtre Lyrique and in Amiens around the town council.

Roger Greaves

Prelude

MY GRANDFATHER died on 24 March 1905, at eight in the morning. From the south of France, where we were still settling in after moving house, my elder brother and I were called north by telegram to join our parents and our other brother at Verne's bedside in Amiens. When he saw that we were all there, he gave us one fond look that clearly meant: 'Good, you are all here. Now I can die'; then he turned to the wall to await death bravely. His serenity impressed us greatly and we wished that we might have as fine a death ourselves when our time came.

According to Verne's sister Marie, he remarked to the priest who came to see him every day: 'You have done me good. I feel regenerated.' More significantly, it seems to me, he asked that any disagreements that might have arisen among the family should be forgotten.

When I was small, my parents sometimes left me behind in Amiens when they returned to Paris after one of our fairly frequent stays at my grandparents' home. On one occasion, when I was five, I lived with my grandparents for several months while attending the school next door. My grandmother liked to show me off to her friends and used to take me visiting with her; but I really preferred to stay at home in the Rue Charles-Dubois and play in the garden. It seemed enormous. Sometimes I would catch a glimpse of my grandfather strolling with his spaniel bitch, Follette, but mainly I saw him at mealtimes. His mornings were always spent in his study.

I cannot remember much about the house as it was then. I know that the little dining-room that we normally used was in the servants' wing giving onto the courtyard. The reception rooms that led off from a long glazed gallery all appeared very grand to me, although I never got more than a glimpse of them. In fact, they were not all that grand, just good-sized rooms furnished in an honest middle-class way: solid, and large enough for provincial family reunions. When I saw the house again, many years later, I was struck more by the number of the rooms than by their size: there were enough of them to sleep several generations of family and friends quite comfortably. On the other hand, the garden that had seemed so vast to me as a child turned out to be relatively small.

After 1901, our grandparents lived in a smaller house round the corner in Boulevard Longueville. My grandfather's routine remained the same. He spent all morning in his study on the second floor. This was a tiny room furnished with two ordinary tables (one to write on, the other for his reference books), a comfortable armchair and a camp bed. Up at five every morning, he was literally a mere step away from his work. I can vaguely remember a pipe-rack as well, hanging on the wall with a row of clay pipes. The place was more like a monastic cell than a study. Beyond it was a larger and more comfortable room arranged as a library, but Verne only went there to fetch books and return them. These two rooms were Verne's private domain where he could find silence and solitude. My grandmother's room was on the first floor; it overlooked the garden. It was unostentatious but comfortable, and contained a big soft bed that Verne used whenever he was ill; it was there that he died.

He was rarely downstairs, and then only at mealtimes. The dining-room had a large window through which my grandmother tossed breadcrumbs to the hordes of sparrows that lived in the tiny garden. On the street side there was a gloomy sitting-room crammed with furniture that was too big for it.

Because of his failing health, my grandfather had to follow a frugal diet. He ate before the rest of us, bolting his food while sitting on a chair so low that his plate was virtually on a level with his mouth. This habit had been acquired in the days when he suffered from what he thought was stomach trouble and when he needed to consume vast amounts of food in order to stave off abnormal hunger pains. He was by no means a gourmet – to my grandmother's dismay, for she was an excellent cook; indeed, he cared very little for what he ate, providing there was plenty of it to put a stop to his pain. However, towards the end of his life (and much too late) he was given medical treatment that involved a sudden curtailment of these many years of compulsive over-eating. I cannot help thinking that this huge hunger of his – which, incidentally, is reflected in his books: he is always concerned about getting his heroes enough to eat – may have had something to do with the diabetes that killed him.

JULES VERNE

1828–1848

V ERNE is derived from the Celtic word *varna*. It is fairly common
as a family name in France, in one form or another; presumably it
goes back to a family or settlement of Gauls who lived on the banks of a
river sheltered by *vernes*, or alder trees, and who kept a Celtic form
of their name after the Roman conquest. I have met a good many
Vernes in my time and have been struck by the fact that they can
generally trace their family origins to the Beaujolais region, which
would seem to confirm the tradition that a member of our family
emigrated from the Beaujolais to Paris in the eighteenth century. At all
events, it is possible to trace the paternal line of my family to a certain
Fleuri Verne, who may have been the son of one Mathieu Verne,
bourgeois of Lyons, but who definitely lived in Paris at this time.
Pierre, Jules Verne's lawyer father, was Fleuri Verne's great-grandson
by way of Gabriel, a magistrate, and Antoine, who was a judge.

So much for the insane legend that Verne was an émigré Jew from
Poland who changed his name from Olchevitz! I would have thought
that Edmondo Marcucci (in *Bulletin* No 2, 1936) had finally disposed
of that one, but no: I still get letters from American 'cousins' née
Olchevitz. Not that I object to this kind of thing; on the contrary: the
fact that over the years Verne has been 'naturalized' by nation after nation, including the Poles, the Italians and the Hungarians, strikes me as
a singular tribute to his universality.

On his mother's side, Verne is known to be descended from one
'N. Allott, Scotsman', who came to France to serve in the Scots Guards
of Louis XI and rose to earn a title (in 1462). He built his castle, complete with dovecote or *fuye* (a privilege in the royal gift), near Loudun
in Anjou and took the noble name of Allotte de la Fuye. Quite a few
generations later, we reach Sophie Allotte de la Fuye, Jules Verne's
mother, whose ancestors – as befitted the descendants of a Scottish
bowman – were mainly military.

1

Verne's parents met in Nantes in 1826. Pierre Verne was twenty-seven. He had been called to the bar the year before, after studying law in Paris; and on promptings from his uncle, Alexandre Verne, who lived in Nantes as a naval supplies officer, he had just bought the Paqueteau law practice at 2 Quai Jean-Bart. Within weeks of arriving in Nantes, Pierre fell in love with a girl whom he first noticed strolling through the dead autumn leaves, 'gold and ruddy and light as the leaves themselves', in the words of his son's biographer Marguerite Allotte de la Fuye. He easily discovered who she was and got himself introduced to her family. Sophie was twenty-six.

The couple were married in the parish of Sainte-Croix on 19 February 1827. Having little means of their own, they set up house at 4 Rue Olivier-de-Clisson, in the apartment of Sophie's parents. (Her father, Jean Isaac Augustin Allotte, was a wanderer. He was so rarely at home that his absence was eventually formalized by a legal separation.) Sophie's and Pierre's first child, Jules-Gabriel, was born on 8 February 1828, a year after their marriage. A few months later they moved to a place of their own in the same building as the law practice.

Pierre was a good lawyer; and I am told that there used to be a saying in Nantes: as honest as Verne. Maurice Allotte de la Fuye and Raymond Ducrest de Villeneuve, members of the family who knew him well, have written that he was 'highly intelligent, charming, a passionate music lover' and 'charming and kind if rather severe-looking . . . a respected jurist, a very erudite scholar, a gifted and witty poet, but also very interested in science and the latest discoveries'. My own feeling is that in fact Pierre's severe looks were just the badge of his profession. But they may have been something else as well. Everyone agrees that Pierre was extremely pious. Actually, religion was the most important thing in his life, almost to the point of mysticism; and according to my father he practised self-flagellation. In a series of pensées scribbled on slips of paper, apparently as a distraction between files, he harks on the efficaciousness, in the face of doubt, of material and corporal penitence. How much of this interior struggle got through to his children is a subject for conjecture; it probably went no further than a few severe looks. Of course, the example he set ensured that his children acquired proper Christian feelings and a clear moral sense, but he was not a forbidding man in the sense that his children might fear him: in his own inner dialogue between the harshness of the Old Testament and the sweetness of the New, it was the spirit of charity that gained the upper hand. This ardent, jansenistic Christian was kindness itself; he was inflexible only in matters of morality.

Sophie was equally pious, thanks to her careful upbringing. But she doubtless did not share her husband's metaphysical anguish, and felt no compulsion to follow him in his parsings of St Thomas Aquinas. More relaxed than her husband, she was a gentle person and brought into the home the sparkle of a lively imagination.

In this happy home Jules found the circumspection, the love of music, the literary tastes, and the keen lawyers' wits of the Vernes together with the rather tumultuous imagination of the fanciful Allottes. He found much love as well, both from his parents and from his brother Paul and his sisters, Anna, Mathilde and Marie. Jules's uncle, Francisque de la Celle de Châteaubourg, Sophie's brother-in-law by a second marriage, was an artist like his father before him; he has left some delightful miniatures and some good pencil drawings. As a child, Jules Verne was fond of listening to Châteaubourg tell him stories brought back from America by Châteaubriand, who was the brother of Châteaubourg's first wife, Pauline.

Around the age of five or six, Jules attended a school kept by a Mme Sambin, the widow of a sea captain, who never tired of telling her pupils the story of how Captain Sambin had left her many years before to undertake a fateful voyage from which he had never returned. Was one of those pupils so moved by her hopes and fears that fifty years later, as an ageing writer, he built the story into his book *Mistress Branican*, as Mme Allotte de la Fuye, the author of *Jules Verne* (1928), would have us believe? Maybe; he had a good memory.

According to Mme de la Fuye Jules and his younger brother Paul were sent at nine and eight respectively to the junior seminary of St Donatian in Nantes. In fact, they were enrolled at St Stanislas, a junior school whose present headmaster has discovered their names on the honour rolls for the years 1837–8, 1838–9 and 1839–40. The one for 1836–7 is missing from the archives, so it cannot be known whether Jules Verne was enrolled in that year. In 1837–8, Jules was in the seventh class (according to the French count-down system, i.e. the year before the first form in an English grammar school). That year, he obtained prizes for composition, geography and singing, and won the first prize in recitation. The following year, he gained third prize in geography, first prize in Greek prose and second prize in Greek composition, as well as a prize for singing. The year after that, in the fifth class, he won first prize for Latin composition and second prize for singing. These results speak for themselves, whatever his prowess as 'king of the playground' (in Marguerite Allotte de la Fuye's phrase); and even if he did work after his own fashion he worked well.

At St Stanislas, the fifth class was the highest. Very probably, Jules moved to St Donatian's Seminary at this point to start secondary school in the fourth class. All we know about his year at the seminary derives from the rather vague information given by Mme de la Fuye. In the following year, however, he moved again, this time to the Lycée Royal, where he was far from brilliant. In his penultimate year he could manage only a fourth in French speaking and a fifth in Latin composition – though he is said to have won a prize for geography. All the same, he passed the baccalauréat the following year without difficulty.

Writing to his father on 14 March 1853, he was perhaps remembering his dilatory schooling: 'I agree, it's a great pity when children don't work at school. But it's always like that. Fortunately, studious children invariably turn into blockheads as adolescents and fools as adults.' (A remark that should not be taken too literally, needless to say!)

In 1840, when Jules was thirteen, Pierre Verne decided to move his family to a larger house. Fourteen years of work had built his law practice up into the busiest in town, so he must have been very satisfied to find a suitable house halfway between the Chamber of Commerce and the lawcourts: 6 Rue Jean-Jacques-Rousseau. His children were just as pleased with their new home, since it was right by the river Loire and the tip of the Ile Feydeau. (This branch of the Loire has since been filled in to form a boulevard; the Ile Feydeau is consequently no longer an island.) The docks were close by; and it was an easy matter for the children to walk up the Rue Kervegan, spinal column of the Ile Feydeau, to visit their maternal grandmother in the Rue Olivier-de-Clisson. In those days, before the Loire silted up, the harbour at Nantes was an active seaport: Cape-Horners and other large vessels docked with exotic merchandise from the four corners of the world, bringing a whiff of the South Sea and many a mariner's tale virtually into the Vernes' back yard. Compared with the harbour, the docks on the Ile Feydeau were small beer; but they were crammed with little boats from Le Croisic and Guérande laden with fish and shell-fish and besieged by haggling fishwives, and the masts of the big ships lying in the harbour proper were enticingly visible above the house tops. Undoubtedly, it was in Nantes that Verne's love for the sea made its first mark on him, a real love that many years later led him to remark: 'I cannot see a ship leaving port but my whole being goes with her.'

At Chantenay, a village near Nantes, Pierre Verne had acquired a country cottage around 1838. Today, Chantenay is an industrial suburb; the little house stands miserably disfigured between its neighbour and a school which has finally devoured what garden remained. However, in Jules's boyhood, the house was surrounded by fields and copses, with the Loire river glinting in the sunlight below.

In an article written for *The Youth's Companion* (Boston, Mass.) when he was past sixty, Jules Verne recalled his boyhood at Chantenay. Already, he and his brother Paul were mad about boats. For a franc a day they hired leaky old tubs from a yard at the harbour, teaching themselves the art of sailing and gradually progressing from one to three masts:

What hopeless sailors we were! Tacking down river on the ebb-tide against the westerly breeze, how many times we capsized disgracefully owing to a misjudged shove at the helm, a botched manoeuvre, an ill-advised tug on the sheets when a swell arose to ruffle the broads of the Loire off our Chantenay! We generally set out with the descending tide and returned on the flood-tide a few hours later. And as our hired boat floundered along between the shores we cast looks of envy on the pretty pleasure yachts skimming past and around us.

In the summer of 1839, Jules had somehow discovered that an ocean-going vessel called the *Coralie*, a three-master, was due to sail for the Indies. In imagination, he saw himself sailing with her, visiting foreign parts, sailing for days on end beneath the proud swell of canvas, with infinite possibilities for adventure and discovery. The very name of the ship was like an invitation: *La Coralie*. What a romantic adventure it would be to sail to the Indies on the *Coralie* and bring back a necklace of coral for Caroline, the lovely cousin with whom he was madly in love.

A plan soon took shape in his head. At eleven and a half he was not one to let difficulties stand in his way. He *might* get a job as a cabin boy, but that wasn't easy; and in any case his father would never agree to it. The first thing to do was to ask around. Luckily, he hit upon a boy of his own age who had been signed on as a cabin boy aboard the *Coralie*.

For a small sum, the boy agreed to let Jules take his place. But how could they avoid raising the captain's suspicions? They decided that Jules would go aboard at the last minute, along with another cabin boy.

This hare-brained scheme must have been agreed in advance, since there is no other way that Jules could have crept out of the cottage at six in the morning, and crossed Chantenay while the dew was still fresh on the ground, to meet his two accomplices with their dinghy at La Grenouillère, a ferry point on the Loire. Everything went as planned and the swap was not noticed in all the bustle of the ship's departure.

Back at home, the house was waking up. Jules was missed, but his mother probably thought he had gone out for a walk. When he had not returned by half-past twelve, however, Sophie panicked and asked Colonel de Goyon, who lived in the nearby château, to set off on horseback to warn Pierre Verne. It turned out that Mathurine Paris, Jules's old nurse, who now kept the pork-butcher's shop, had noticed Jules crossing the church square. Then a second piece of information arrived that left no room for doubt: a waterman from the Grenouillère ferry, who had retired momentarily to the *Homme qui porte trois malices*, a tavern run by Jean-Marie Cabidoulin (later to crop up as an old salt in Verne's novel *Le Serpent de Mer*), had seen Jules in a dinghy with two cabin boys rowing out to the *Coralie*, which had started out for the Indies but which was to call that evening at Paimbœuf. Fortunately, Pierre was able to catch the steam ferry that plied down the river and reach Paimbœuf in time to recover his son.

According to Mme de la Fuye, whose book recounts this escapade, Jules was 'scolded, thrashed and put on bread and water' and was made to promise his mother that from then on he would travel only in his imagination.

Some time ago, wondering whether Mme de la Fuye had not been somewhat carried away here, I took the trouble to check her story. I already knew, of course, that at the age of twelve my grandfather had run away from home to join a ship, and that his father had caught up with him. But what about the rest? It would seem that Mme de la Fuye's account is mainly correct. Colonel de Goyon was indeed the Vernes' neighbour at the time. His château still exists; it is now a private college. There really was a three-master called the *Coralie*, which was owned by the firm of Le Cour Grand-Maison. And the pork-butcher's shop was indeed run by Mme Paris. However, the reference to the boy's wanting to give Caroline a coral necklace, and the statement that Pierre thrashed his son, seem to me to remain open to question.

There can be little doubt that Jules was scolded and indeed punished in some way. But was he really thrashed – and if so, how severely – or even put on bread and water? We cannot know; but with a bit of imagination the words that flowed from Mme de la Fuye's lively pen can gradually take on sinister overtones. We can safely dismiss Bernard Frank's blithe assertion in *Jules Verne et ses Voyages* (1941), that the 'thundering good hiding' administered to Jules cured the enterprising lad for ever not only of the sea but of things feminine. Of much more consequence, however, is the thesis propounded by Marcel Moré, the author of *Le très curieux Jules Verne* (1960).

Moré takes Mme de la Fuye at face value and affirms that Jules, an ultra-sensitive boy who was already living in secret dread of his father's house (as shown by his running away), received a beating from his father that left a permanent mark on his unconscious; and that from then on Jules was unconsciously in revolt against his father, who became a symbol of threat, with the result that the boy retreated into himself and became impervious to other people. Now, fair punishment is not likely to modify any twelve-year-old's image of his father. At the very most, unfair and clearly excessive punishment might be a motive for (conscious) resentment – which leads to voluntary revolt rather than to a complex.

True, the hypothetical beating is supposed to have been a punishment for running away, and running away is regarded as a sign of maladjustment. Yet, there are exceptions to the rule: there can be other motives for running away besides the wish to escape from the environment to which one cannot adjust. In my work as a judge, I have frequently had to deal with young runaways; and I have found that in some instances the motive was not to get away from the home environment but simple curiosity – a wish to see the sea, in particular.

I do not believe for a moment that there was ever a breach of trust between father and son; nor do I believe that the latter bore his father the faintest shadow of a grudge. Their letters to one another are open and friendly; indeed, I doubt whether many sons in those days would have written to their fathers as freely as Jules did: they would have been too shocked. Pierre understood his son and trusted him, even though many of his schemes seemed hare-brained enough to a staid provincial lawyer – rational, precise and traditionally-minded – for whom the calendar tended to mark the year 1830. Occasionally, Pierre quarrelled with his son's plans out of worry about his future; but in the end he always gave in, apparently without much of a struggle. He had always intended Jules to be his successor in the law practice in Nantes, and sent him to qualify in Paris with that specific aim in mind. But when Jules turned around the minute he had passed his examinations and announced that he wanted to be a writer, Pierre backed him to the hilt, sending him money, encouragement, and even ideas for plays (which Pierre found reprehensibly frivolous). And when Jules took it into his head to buy a small share in a stockbroking firm, Pierre once again disapproved, hemmed and hawed, and then finally gave in. No, Pierre was a model of understanding, not a symbol of threat.

Pierre never doubted that his son knew where he was going, even though he did tend not to look before he leaped. As for Jules, it is perfectly obvious from the tone of his letters that he was completely at ease with his father: no awe here, no dread, but fun and games as with a friend of his own age. One example will suffice (15 November 1852):

By the way, I've turned over a new leaf. I'm as level-headed as an oc-togenarian, I think on crutches, I perceive in spectacles. I'm as old as the world, as wise as the Greeks, as profound as a well, as keen-sighted as Arago [the astronomer], as rational as the moralist in a classical comedy: you won't recognize me – my heart is bald!

How figurative I'm being today! It must be because I've got colic. What a nasty stomach my mother gave me; yet my way of life is exemplary, and St Simeon Stylites, who spent ten years on the top of a column to be accep-table to heaven, is far from attaining my virtuous conduct.

I live in philosophical solitude. I don't exactly eat bird droppings, but it wouldn't take much to make me, and the meat that sustains me must have drawn many an omnibus through the good city of Paris. I'm greatly tempted to become as misanthropic as Alcestis and as silent as a Trappist – better still, as silent as the statue of silence that Clésinger wanted to sculpt for an Englishman. This fellow came to see Clésinger one day and offered to commission an emblem expressing the ultimate in taciturnity. Clésinger turned the matter over in his mind for some time and then came up with the idea of a man with one finger in his mouth and the other up his backside. The idea wasn't bad at all – and it wouldn't have been hard on the model, because when he got tired of having his finger in his mouth he could have changed hands. I regard that as a touch of genius.

Not surprisingly, considering that no two generations can share the same points of view, Jules and Pierre were by no means always in agreement – particularly in matters of religion. Throughout his youth, Verne's religious views naturally coincided with his father's: intelligent but orthodox Roman Catholicism. Up to around 1870, indeed, his hackles rose whenever anyone attacked the Catholic religion, whose dogma he accepted and felt he should defend. On such occasions, his views could be remarkably blinkered, as his publisher did not fail to point out to him around 1868 when Verne made some denigrating remarks about the lapsed Catholic historian Renan: 'Silly fool! Isn't he a *very distinguished* writer, to say the least? Pocket your prejudices and read what he has to say.' After about 1870, Verne was less and less subservient to the discipline of the Church: his wife went to Mass without him and his views broadened into a kind of Christian-based deism. Pierre, on the other hand, remained pious and orthodox to the end. If he had lived longer, there can be no doubt that the gap between father and son would have grown wider than it did.

All the same, disagreements of this kind do not need to be explained in terms of hypothetical childhood traumas. On the contrary, there is every reason to believe that the influence of Pierre, old-fashioned as he was, led his writer son to cast his progressive and potentially shocking ideas in an anodyne form that made them universally acceptable.

On holiday and during the weekends, at Chantenay or nearby at his uncle Prudent's house at La Guerche, the 'king of the playground' was in his element, sailing with Paul or roaming the fields with his sisters and cousins. With one of these cousins, Caroline Tronson (daughter of his aunt Lise), he fell head over heels in love. He had good taste: she was very pretty. A year older than Jules, she was already a flirt; smilingly, she accepted his extravagant protestations of devotion. For her, then aged twelve, it was a kind of game, flattering and amusing at the same time. Unfortunately, her dreamer of a cousin was in earnest: he became increasingly obsessed with her and convinced himself that one day he would marry her.

As they grew up, Caroline became a very lovely young lady with scores of suitors, whereas her adoring cousin lingered in adolescence. By the time of her first ball, she could take her pick of any number of marriageable young men infinitely more attractive than Jules. One of them, Jean Cormier, became particularly solicitous and Jules grew

violently jealous of him; but Cormier was spurned as well as Jules when
Caroline's choice finally settled on a certain Dezaunay. Jules was heart-
broken. His childhood crush had developed into a mature love with a
depth of feeling that necessarily left its mark, perhaps for life. Several
years later, as a budding writer in Paris, he wrote to his mother:

> Tell me about Mlle Caroline Whatshername, who turned me down. Is she
> married, or about to be? I'm very interested in this young lady, as you
> know. She has been in my dreams more than once and had the privilege of
> being the sole object of my thoughts for several months. I would like to be
> kept informed about her life and loves. The wretched girl doesn't realize
> what a brilliant match she turned down in me in order to marry, some day,
> a snail like Jean Cormier or another of that ilk. But it was not to be! (*15
> November 1853*)

Quite possibly, his parents were secretly pleased that his plans for
Caroline were frustrated. They seem to have disapproved of marriages
between first cousins, for when a similar marriage was projected
between his sister Marie and an Allotte de la Fuye the obstacle of con-
sanguinity appeared insurmountable. (Ironically enough, the Allotte de
la Fuye in question subsequently married Marie's daughter, Edith
Guillon.) In any case, an early marriage for Jules was not really part of
his parents' plans for him. Once he had obtained his bachelor's diploma
in 1846, his future was all laid out: as the elder son, he would naturally
take over his father's law practice, whereas his younger brother would
go into the Navy and his sisters would be married off.

In accordance with this family scheme, Jules began his law studies in
late 1846, working at home in Nantes with the standard textbooks. He
studied all winter, but was unable to keep his mind off Caroline. Her
engagement was announced, with the wedding set for the spring of
1847. In April, either to spare him the shock of the wedding or for other
reasons, his father decided to send him to stay with his great-aunt
Rosalie Charruel, née Verne, who lived in Paris. It was in Paris that he
took his first-year law examinations and put the finishing touches to a
five-act tragedy in verse entitled *Alexandre VI* on which he had been
working during the winter. (The manuscript of this play is dated 8 May
1847. This date, together with the unusually small format of the paper
and considerations of handwriting and signature, enables us to date the
subsequent manuscripts.) Immediately after the exams, he went to
Provins: a small town about fifty miles south-east of Paris, the
residence of his widowed paternal grandmother and her two unmarried

daughters, Augustine and Alphonsine. Presumably, it was hoped that the warm family atmosphere in Provins would help him to recover from his disappointment. But such hopes were in vain. All the rest of that summer, which he spent working fitfully and dully at his law books in Chantenay, he remained moody and silent.

Little is known about his life during the winter of 1847–8. However, just before the publication of the French edition of the present work, I came across a notebook containing poems in Verne's hand dating from this period and containing references to a girl called Herminie. However, I fell seriously ill and was unable to do more than communicate my findings to another biographer of Verne, Charles-Noël Martin, who has subsequently traced the girl in question. She was a Herminie Arnault-Grossetière, who married one Terrien de la Haye in Nantes on 18 July 1848. It would seem, then, that a second disappointment followed upon the one that Jules Verne underwent with Caroline, or even coincided with it. At all events, there can be no doubt that the famous letter inspired by a fateful marriage in 1848 (see page 12) refers to Herminie and not, as previously supposed, to Caroline.

Whether or not he was love-sick again, as it would seem, there can be no doubt that at the end of 1847 Jules was chafing for a broader vision of life than he could obtain within the necessarily confining family circle in Nantes. Even the pleasure of listening to his sister Anna at the piano – she was something of a prodigy – or taking part in piano duets with Paul, and singing or acting sketches with the rest of the family could no longer console him for the absence of the larger universe that he had glimpsed in Paris in the spring. Nantes was too small for him. Paul himself, his truest friend, having failed the stringent medical for the École Navale, sailed from Nantes on 23 December as a novice pilot aboard the three-masted merchantman the *Regulus*, bound for Reunion and not due back until the following autumn. Stuck in Nantes with his law books, Jules had every reason to feel sorry for himself.

Fortunately for him, there was a political coup d'état that winter, shortly after his twentieth birthday in February 1848. King Louis-Philippe was forced to abdicate and the Second Republic was proclaimed, with a parliament elected for the first time by universal suffrage. This triumph of liberal republicanism over the royalists, which was followed by a backlash of conservatism and social unrest, inspired Verne to write a tragedy in verse entitled *La Conspiration des Poudres* about Guy Fawkes's attempt to dispose of James I and his parliament by blowing up the Palace of Westminster. (Interestingly, the Catholic Fawkes is depicted more as a religious hero than as a political figure. Even at twenty, Verne gave more weight to moral values than to purely political ideals.) The writing of this play, together with the political debate that raged in Nantes as everywhere else in France that winter, provided him with a much-needed distraction.

In June, Paris suffered from a severe bout of rioting. Nonetheless, Pierre allowed him to go up to the capital as soon as things quietened down. In a letter dated 17 July 1848 Jules accounts to his father for his use of his allowance — seventy-five francs for thirty days' food, forty francs for lodging, one hundred francs for the journey — and describes the damage caused by the rioting. He adds:

> I see that in the provinces you are still afraid. You're much more scared than we are in Paris. The much-heralded fourteenth of July went off without anything happening. Now it's on the twenty-fourth that Paris is for burning, but that's not stopping the city from being as gay as ever.

At the end of a further letter, dated 21 July, he refers to Herminie:

> Good heavens, I was forgetting: there is something else I can't get out of my mind in the midst of my preoccupations with Paris. What has happened about the wedding of a certain young lady you know well that was supposed to take place on Tuesday? I would be quite glad to know for sure what the situation is.

Writing back to his mother on 30 July, he is more open about his bitter disappointment:

> Alas, dear mother, life is not all roses, and fellows who build shining castles in the air just don't get to them, try as they might. So it's true that the wedding has taken place!

Then he describes a 'fateful dream' in which a wedding is being celebrated in sumptuous halls illuminated by expensive candles, overseen by the figure of death — a motif found in several of his books and discussed by Marcel Moré, Verne's self-appointed latterday psychoanalyst.

> The bride was in white, the symbol of purity of soul. The groom was in black, symbolizing the true colour of her soul . . . The bridal chamber opened to admit the trembling couple and the joys of heaven filled their hearts . . . and all night long, all that dark night long, a man in rags and tatters had sharpened his teeth on the door knocker. Ah, my dear mother,

this dreadful idea woke me up with a bound – and now your letter informs me that my dream was true! What misfortunes I foresee! Poor fellow! But I shall always say: Forgive him, father, for he knows not what he does. Personally, I shall console myself by killing the first black cat I meet! . . . This funereal ceremony, this funeral, required to be recorded on paper . . . (*30 July 1848*)

Even allowing for literary heightening, this dream may well have psychoanalytic significance. At all events, it reveals that the young Verne remembered his early frustrations with bitterness; in itself, that is sufficient to explain his later tendency to compare marriage to a funeral!

However, his mood after his jaunt to Paris was joyful. He seems to have spent much of the summer writing: a one-act farce called *Une Promenade en Mer*, two synopses entitled *Le Coq de Bruyère* and *Don Galaor*, and a one-act comedy, *Le Quart d'Heure de Rabelais*. In addition, he managed to convince his father, after some discussion, that for his third year of law studies he should attend regular law school in Paris, arguing that working at home had not been very satisfactory, since the examinations were always geared to topics covered in lectures, which the home-based student could not, of course, attend. Paul, who returned to Nantes from his first voyage on 9 September, full of stories, backed him as did his mother and sisters. Consequently, on 10 November 1848, a few days before Paul embarked on the *Lutin* for a second voyage to Reunion, Jules and his friend Edouard Bonamy took the stage-coach to Tours and from there the train to Paris, where they rented a room in the Latin Quarter at 24 Rue de l'Ancienne-Comédie, sufficiently close to the Law Faculty and the solid bourgeois parish of Saint-Sulpice to satisfy their parents; but just around the corner from the bohemian Beaux-Arts and quite literally surrounded by bookshops and cafés. For Verne, the only inconvenience of his new address – which disappeared to make room for the Boulevard Saint-Germain towards the end of the century – must have been that it was quite a long way from the fashionable theatres north of the Seine.

1849-1856

V ERNE'S allowance, at the start of his student days in Paris, was one hundred francs per month. Mme de la Fuye suggests that by keeping him poor Pierre intended to keep him out of trouble, but this seems to me to be a slight exaggeration: it is more likely that around 1850 tight budgets were intended merely to teach their recipients the value of money, not to keep them from enjoying themselves. At that time, room and board were available at sixty francs per month; allowing for the cost of breakfast, which had to be eaten out, students could still get by on one hundred francs and have something to spare. But it was not easy, and not infrequently Jules was obliged to ask his father for a little extra. Eventually, his allowance was raised to one hundred and twenty-five francs per month, which undoubtedly gave him slightly more leeway but still left him essentially dependent on his own ingenuity for the organization of his social life.

He was not alone, of course. Apart from Bonamy, with whom he shared not merely his rooms but also a set of evening dress, he had recourse to his cousin, Henri Garcet, thirteen years his senior and a teacher of mathematics at the Lycée Henri IV; to his childhood friend Charles Maisonneuve who had a job in finance; to the Conservatory student Aristide Hignard whose family lived in the same street as the Vernes in Nantes; and above all to his uncles Châteaubourg and Prudent Allotte de la Fuye who on their seasonal visits to the capital introduced him to influential friends, no doubt on promptings from Sophie Verne back in Nantes. These initial contacts enabled Verne to get to know a great many people in a very short space of time; and this wide circle of acquaintance compensated for the shortcomings in his budget — notably in the form of invitations to dinner and complimentary tickets to the theatre.

The importance of the Nantes connection in Verne's Parisian début, and in particular Sophie's role in exploiting that connection, cannot be overstressed. For the fact is that, within weeks of his arrival in the capital, his associations brought about a fundamental change of key in the duet for law and literature that he had been playing for the past couple of years. In a letter to his parents dated 21 November we find his usual refrain: a career in law would give him the security that he desired in order to indulge in a life of letters. But a month later, when he was seeing none but the musicians, writers and artists made accessible through Sophie's connections, the tone of his letters had changed altogether:

> It is really a pleasure, excessively misunderstood in Nantes, to be in immediate contact with literature, to sense it taking a fresh turn and to witness the different phases through which it passes in its constant oscillations between Racine and Shakespeare, Scribe and Clairville. Profound studies could be made of the present age and above all of the literature of the future. Unfortunately, infernal politics casts its drab mantle over the beauty of poetry. To the devil with ministers, president and chamber as long as there remains in France one poet who can stir our hearts. Politics, as history has shown, is purely contingent and ephemeral. I for one think and repeat with Goethe: Nothing that makes us happy is illusion. (*12 December 1848*)

This not entirely innocent quotation was not to the liking of Pierre Verne, because to his mind it had overtones of epicureanism – the antithesis of his own moral standpoint founded on penitence – and because it smacked of a bohemianism not wholly in keeping with a future career in law. He promptly fired a moral broadside across the bows of his eccentric son, telling him that his associations with dissolute artists in Paris were destroying his hopes of salvation. Verne answered this diatribe with a model of cool legal argument. On 24 January 1849 he begins:

> Thank you very much for your excellent advice . . . To this very day I have followed the line of conduct that you mention . . . I myself was the first to recognize the good and the bad in these artistic societies, which are really not so bad as you make out . . .

Further on, he states reassuringly:

> I'm due to sit for my examination next Tuesday and I can assure you I'm losing my wits over it. I think I can promise that I will pass, though I

wouldn't swear to anything; I've been working a lot and still am, and that's
why I wish it were done with. But that doesn't mean that afterwards I'm
going to sit back and drop law altogether ... I *know* that a third of my
qualifying exam depends on the *Institutes*. I *know* that I have to submit
this thesis around August in order to qualify ... If I had some other career
in view, would I have come this far only to drop out of school or delay my
qualifying? Surely that would be utter madness ...

Thus comforted, his father probably did not seize the full significance
of what followed:

You know how irresistibly appealing Paris is to everybody, young people
in particular. I would much sooner live in Paris than in Nantes ... But
there would only be one difference between the two life styles: in Paris, I
don't miss Nantes, but in Nantes, I will miss Paris a little – but that won't
stop me from living there peacefully . . .

Having said so much, Verne quickly tries to remove some of the sting
from his remarks:

It's alarming what wrong ideas people in the provinces have about the
world of letters . . . I never stop saying that what I have seen of it is as like
our society in Nantes as two peas in a pod . . . It's no dafter, dizzier, dir-
tier nor danker than Nantes is! After all, if the women are prettier here,
you can hardly blame them for that . . . I was the first to recognize my
high standing in Nantes due to you, and I was proud of it, and have had
reason to thank you, as I always will, for having made things so. But I've
always said I'll be a barrister!

His father must have been thoroughly confused by now, as Verne no
doubt intended him to be. At this point, sheltering behind his welter of
verbiage, he slips in his knock-out blow:

You're absolutely right in saying that literary studies are useful in every
position in life. If my studies in this field led me to envisage an attempt in
this direction, it would merely be an adjunct, as I have frequently repeated,
and would not divert me from that aim we have set ... Yet, you say this:
'Do you mean that you will be an Academician, a poet, a renowned
novelist?' If I were fated to become any of those, my dear father, you
would be the first to urge me towards this career. And you'd be the first to
be proud of it, because it's the finest position any man can hold! And if I
were fated to become such a man, my vocation would urge me towards it
irresistibly. But that is not the case.

Here, there should no longer be any doubt in his father's mind. 'My vocation would urge me towards it irresistibly': law has taken second place, and Jules Verne's heart is set on something far removed from the staid existence of a provincial lawyer.

> Family life . . . the gentle emotions stemming from a peaceful occupation are completely incompatible with the life of letters. Well, if that were so, politics itself, which no one disdains and which you say starts with law, would surely be even more subversive of any form of domestic bliss.

This letter, bitter-sweet and to say the least ambiguous, must have left the provincial lawyer quite perplexed.

Shortly after his arrival in Paris, Jules was introduced by his uncle Châteaubourg to an old friend of Sophie's called Mme Barrère. (Châteaubourg had come up to Paris for the Salon, the annual exhibition of works by living artists.) This lady was something of a literary hostess, whose callers included, if not the great themselves, some not insignificant friends of the great. Many of these literary figures struck Jules as being very dull, but he was delighted to get into the good graces of the Comte de Coral, editor of *La Liberté*, who promised to take him to see Victor Hugo. A further acquaintance that he made at Mme Barrère's was a decisive one: the Chevalier d'Arpentigny, an expert on palmistry and a friend of the elder Dumas. D'Arpentigny was glad to oblige his hostess by introducing Jules Verne to the author of *The Three Musketeers*, and through him to the circle of young writers who gravitated around him, around his son (who had just become famous overnight thanks to his novel *La Dame aux Camélias*) and around the Théâtre Historique.

At the time Verne met him, Alexandre Dumas *père* was forty-seven, a popular hero, and at the height of his powers. Since 1846 he had been the effective director of a brand-new theatre on Boulevard du Temple, next to the Cirque Olympique, which opened on 20 February 1847, under the name Théâtre Historique. After a very prosperous start, this theatre, in common with others in Paris, was affected adversely by the revolution of 1848. Despite reductions in prices in an attempt to boost his houses, Hippolyte Hostein, the theatre's nominal director, was obliged to close at the beginning of June and take his company to the Drury Lane Theatre in London – where they were heartily booed and chased off the stage after vain attempts to defend themselves with their costume swords. The Théâtre Historique reopened, thanks to a

27,000-franc subvention from the government, but ended the year with a considerable deficit.

In an effort to restore its fortunes, Dumas and his collaborator Auguste Maquet cooked up a lavish show called *La Jeunesse des Mousquetaires* (*The Youth of the Musketeers*), which opened in a flurry of publicity on 17 February 1849. Among those in the author's box on the opening night was Jules Verne. 'Old Dumas watching his play was incredible. He couldn't help telling you everything that was going to happen next. While I was there, a lot of well-known people came into the box.' Among the people that Verne met on this occasion were Emile de Girardin, playwright and republican journalist; Théophile Gautier, romantic poet and novelist, art and theatrical critic, travel writer, literary critic, journalist, polemicist, and personality; and Jules Janin, the drama critic of the influential *Journal des Débats*.

Dumas seems to have adopted Verne immediately, warming to his quick wits and his gift for repartee. Very possibly, Verne may have acted as a kind of unofficial secretary for Dumas in his relations with the Théâtre Historique. Be that as it may, the two became quite close, and there can be no doubt that Verne sought Dumas's professional advice concerning the plays that he continued to write while working on his law thesis. In 1849, he produced a five-act tragedy entitled *Un Drame sous Louis XV*, a two-act farce called *Abdallah* and a one-act comedy, *Les Pailles rompues*. But the situation in the theatre that year was so bad that any thought of getting one of his plays on to a stage was out of the question. In addition to the political difficulties, the weather was suffocatingly hot and there was an outbreak of cholera. Audiences stayed away from the theatres, many of which, including the Opera, the Vaudeville and the Porte Saint-Martin, went bankrupt. At the Théâtre Historique, Hostein was losing nearly 20,000 francs per month.

At the end of the summer, having completed his law examinations, Verne stayed on in Paris, determined to make a name for himself in the theatre, apparently without his father raising any serious objections. He continued to frequent the Dumas circle and the various salons to which his kind uncles took him; he also saw a lot of the musical set that gathered around the pianist Adrien Talexy, to whom he was introduced by Aristide Hignard.

He seems to have written little during 1850: a libretto for Hignard and a two-act comedy appear to have been his total output. But in June Dumas put on *Les Pailles rompues*, written the year before, as a curtain raiser at the Théâtre Historique. It opened on 12 June and was quite well received. It achieved twelve performaces and earned Verne a total of fifteen francs. Although not much of a play – the theatre historian L. Henry Lecomte calls it 'an old-fashioned trifle' – it is quite neatly done; obviously, Dumas worked on it closely with Verne. This fact is borne out by the verse dedication to the printed text, which was paid for by Charles Maisonneuve.

Over the ten years that followed this far from considerable theatrical event, Verne wrote some eight or nine comedies, a drama, and six libretti. Of the plays, only two actually reached the stage, although a third was published for home performance in the *Musée des Familles*, a monthly magazine. The libretti did somewhat better; four out of the six were performed, fairly successfully – though it may well be that their success owed more to the quality of the music than to any intrinsic merit. Four of the plays and all but two of the libretti were written in co-authorship – a very common practice at that time. For the two plays that were actually produced, and for a third that wasn't, Verne's co-author was Charles Wallut, a rather obscure figure in finance and publishing whose only other theatrical endeavours appear to have been a couple of short comic operas and a few lyrics for a vaudeville comedy. By contrast, the co-author with Verne of three of the successful libretti was the extremely professional Michel Carré, who together with Jules Barbier, whom he met in 1849, formed a team that, from the mid-fifties to Carré's death in 1872, was in constant demand for libretti for the major composers, as well as for boulevard comedies. Verne met Carré, who was nine years his senior, through Aristide Hignard, for whom the joint libretti and Verne's solo efforts were written.

Aristide Hignard took the Second Prix de Rome in 1850 after studying at the Paris Conservatory under Halévy; he made his public début as a composer in Nantes, his home town, on 18 January 1851, with a comic opera entitled *Le Visionnaire*. Besides his five comic operas (one unperformed) with Verne, he wrote an operetta on a libretto by Scribe, a musical joke in collaboration with Délibes, Erlanger and Offenbach, songs (some with words by Verne), two drawing-room operettas, piano duets, choral music and (his magnum opus) a full-scale opera, *Hamlet*. According to Rollo Myers, the biographer of Emmanuel Chabrier who studied composition with Hignard in the sixties, Hignard's *Hamlet* 'was considered by many to be superior to Ambroise Thomas's opera – though that in itself perhaps would not constitute a certificate of the highest merit, since, as Chabrier himself said, there were three kinds of music: good, bad, and Ambroise Thomas's.'

Despite the protection of Dumas and the collaboration of Carré and Hignard, the fact remains that Verne's early attempts to make his mark in the theatre led him virtually nowhere. Nonetheless, his sense of vocation remained undiminished. As we shall see, he pursued other forms of literary composition alongside his activities in the theatre. In the meantime, he realized that he was a heavy burden on his father, who was only moderately well-off: he got a job in a law office for fifty francs per month, but had to give it up because it left him no time for writing. He tried working in a bank, but soon tired of that and took to giving private law lessons. How much easier things would have been for him if he had just gone home! His father could not understand why he had stooped to giving private lessons and tried in vain to persuade him to take up a career in law. Verne replied (March 1851):

> You tell me to think before answering; but meditation has its source in the polar mountains of uncertainty and discouragement. The land I live in is not so far north; it is closer to the torrid zone. True, it is bordered on all sides by work, ennui, sadness, fame and so on. But it is a land of perpetual hope; hence, my thinking is all done.
>
> My only aim in undertaking to give private lessons was to reduce my allowance. It is unpleasant for me not to be able to keep myself – as it is for you to have to support me . . .
>
> As for my working as a barrister, remember your own dictum about not trying to do too many things at once; a job in a law practice means starting at seven-thirty in the morning and finishing at nine at night. How much time do I have left for myself?
>
> With respect, you're quite wrong about why I'm acting as I am. To begin with, literature matters more to me than anything else, because that is all I can succeed at, since my mind is made up on this point . . . If I practised law for a couple of years at the same time as my writing, one of these two careers would stifle the other; and the stronger of the two would not be law!
>
> To leave Paris for two years would mean losing all my contacts and allowing the enemy to dig himself in all over again. You just can't work an eight-hour day as a law clerk in Paris. When you're a clerk, you're a clerk and that's it.

Meanwhile, the Théâtre Historique, after struggling on through the difficult summer of 1850, had been forced to close down. The actors and stage staff had not been paid for several weeks. On October 16, after a series of warning strikes, the entire company walked out until such time as the management could find their wages. Dumas preferred to hold a benefit gala for them on 27 October, after which he withdrew his support, reserving his rights on the use of the name Théâtre Historique. On 2 November the licence was taken over by a former collaborator of Dumas's, the author Adolphe d'Ennery, who, when he looked at the accounts, became instantly convinced that the Théâtre Historique was not for him after all; in its four years of operations, it had managed to cover its enormous costs only twice and for two years running had lost over 200,000 francs. Other efforts to save the theatre came to nought, and it was declared bankrupt on 20 December 1850. The report to the receiver revealed many instances of gross mismanagement, which Dumas vainly attempted to explain away as 'manifestations of artistic fraternity'. (Was *Les Pailles rompues*, hardly a paying proposition, one such manifestation?) Debts totalled over 200,000 francs, for which Dumas was held personally responsible and which he had great difficulty in paying off.

The magnificent, virtually brand-new building on the Boulevard du Temple, with its 2,000 seats arranged in five tiers, its enormous stage running almost the whole length of one side of its elliptical auditorium, its rich red and gold hangings, remained empty until 27 September 1851, when Edmond Seveste, who had acquired the opera licence from Adolphe Adam and Achille Mirecour, reopened it as the Opéra National.

In December the Second Republic fell, shortly to be replaced by the Second Empire under Napoleon III. Consequently, Jules Seveste, who had taken over the theatre after the death of Edmond in February, felt the need to change its republican-sounding name to something more anodyne. Hence, on 12 April 1852, the Opéra National became the Théâtre Lyrique. (Ten years later, the Théâtre Lyrique was moved to a new building on the Place du Châtelet now known as the Théâtre de la Ville. A scratch company formed by the dramatist Edouard Brisebarre used the old building on the Boulevard du Temple for just over a year until its demolition on 21 October 1863, as part of the rebuilding of the boulevard.)

At some point in these political and theatrical convolutions, in early 1852 Jules Verne got himself appointed secretary of the Théâtre Lyrique, possibly through the good offices of Dumas, who was aware of his financial problems. If the subsequent careers of two later secretaries of the Théâtre Lyrique are any guide, the job was an important one and could be expected to carry significant financial rewards as well: both Charles Réty in the sixties and Emile Rochard in the seventies became owner-managers. In effect, Verne was responsible for the whole running of the theatre along lines laid down by Seveste; typically, he took on this huge task for nothing, intent as he was on earning a living from his pen and only from his pen. He explained the situation to his father (2 December 1852):

> Let me assure you that I am anxious to wean my Muse as soon as possible, because I can't afford all these months of wet-nursing. In spite of what you think, and in spite of your grousing, I assure you that this is absolutely true. But let's get straight to the point: the secretary job and what it's worth. What fool went and told you it was worth *anything*? . . .
>
> The Playwrights Guild, to which I belong, will not allow a theatre director to produce plays by himself or his employees. If, then, I get an opera accepted by my theatre, it is because I'm only an amateur; and if I'm only an amateur, I don't get paid . . .
>
> Indeed yes, dear father: tit for tat. The director needs me, I need him: I give him some of my time, he gives me an acceptance on one of my plays. It is certainly true that others get their plays accepted without all this; but I'd hang myself rather than still be at this game at forty!

Of course, he never had to hang himself, but he was well over forty by the time the huge success of the dramatized versions of *Around the World* and *Michael Strogoff* more than made up for his early struggles in the theatre. In the meantime, he had to live meagrely. He was glad to get his mother's food parcels, but even gladder when she helped him with his linen. The following is a good example of the jaunty good humour of his letters to her at this time; it is dated 14 October 1852; Verne was twenty-four:

> Ma chère maman:
>
> I *promise* I'll go and see Mme Delaborde, honest I will. I have no reason not to. [Sophie had asked this Nantes lady with supposed Parisian connections to help him meet people. She was on a visit to the capital.]
>
> So my shirts are giving you nightmares, are they? You advise me to buy a false front but, dearest mother, they haven't even got a real back. But I know what your reply to that will be: Her Ladyship will never notice. Catch me saying she will! But I, too, lie awake at nights worrying about

this lack of clobber. I'm not pursued by ghosts any more, but I *am* pursued by shirts. Only pretty women are fit to be seen, *I am told*, in such undress. Anyway, I've decided to end my suffering by having a shirt made to measure here in Paris and sending it to you to be copied. That *is* the best thing to do, isn't it?

Anyway, I must have shirts. I'm even out of handkerchiefs as well. Just think, dearest mother, what a mess I'm in: I can't even blow my nose on my shirt tails! In the words of Shakespeare: how sad, how sad!

I renewed father's subscription four days ago, so there should not be any gaps in the delivery of his newspaper.

How exceedingly happy I would be if you came up to Paris to furnish your drawing-room! It would be so much more fine and artistic. You would really save by making the trip; as you know, I've seen lots of fine furnishings in the best of taste, and I'd be able to give you first-rate advice. On Saturday we shall be regaled by the Solemn Entrance into Paris of His Imperial Majesty Napoleon III. I find the whole thing most entertaining. We shall see what happens.

The weather is beginning to get cold. Now's the time when fires are lit in honest homes, and when poor devils like me do without. But I've put on my woollies and am keeping as warm as I can. I expect you will soon be moving back to town; the trees are beginning to lose their hair. The Chateaubourgs will doubtless stay on in the country to enjoy the last fine weather. Brrrr! the very thought of it makes me shiver.

Well, I must leave you, dearest mother. My love to you all: father, my little sisters, and the whole family. I call those young ladies 'my little sisters' because I'm convinced it annoys them!

> Your loving son,
> Jules Verne

Verne's optimism was not in the least affected by such minor problems. After all, he was poor by his own choice. In addition, his appointment at the Théâtre Lyrique had given a fillip to his self-confidence; he celebrated it by founding a bachelor's dining club, the Onze-sans-femme, with ten friends, all young and struggling like himself: writers, musicians and painters. Adrien Talexy, the pianist, had been a friend of Verne's since 1850. Charles Delioux's comic opera on a Breton theme, *Yvonne et Loïc*, had been produced at the Gymnase in 1851. Louis-Philippe-Gabriel-Bernard Morel-Retz, known appropriately as Stop, had come up to Paris from Dijon in 1850 to study painting with Gleyre; he was to become famous as a cartoonist and caricaturist on *L'Illustration* and *Charivari*. Philippe Gille was a sculptor, born in Paris; he

exhibited at the Salon in 1851 and 1852, but later turned to journalism
and the stage, and eventually found his niche as literary editor of *Le
Figaro*. Eugène Verconsin was known as a wit; in the 1860s he was to
make an ephemeral mark as an author of sketches and one-act comedies
for salons, casinos and charity fêtes. Ernest L'Epine, a lifelong civil servant, wrote an operetta with his boss, the Duc de Morny, in 1861, and
comedies with Alphonse Daudet and others thereafter. Henri Caspers
wrote the music for several comic operas. Of the remaining three listed
by Mme de la Fuye, Charles de Becchenec seems to be as good as
anonymous; David Pitford sounds English or American but seems
likewise unknown; while Ernest Boulanger was probably Jules Verne's
old schoolmate from Nantes who died while fighting as a volunteer in
the American Civil War (1861–65). Aristide Hignard, Charles
Maisonneuve and the composer Victor Massé also dropped in at the
Tête Noire restaurant from time to time. The Onze-sans-femme were
not exactly misogynous, for according to Mme de la Fuye none of them
remained unmarried four years later. But at the time, Verne, for one,
may well have been resigned to remaining a bachelor; the thought of
marriage reminded him of his frustrated wooings, about which he was
still bitterly hurt.

It is said that the only cure for a broken heart is to fall in love all over
again. Did Verne remember this of his own accord, or did someone
prompt him?

His mother certainly thought that what he needed was a wife. She
began to look around for prospective daughters-in-law. To begin with,
Verne made fun of her (14 March 1853): 'What have I done to you to
merit this? You must be mortally offended without my knowing why.'
Since his rejection by Caroline and Herminie, he had become convinced
that all women were fickle and unreliable: at the end of an amusing
letter home (17 April 1853) about a ball that his parents were planning
for their daughters, he adds a few disillusioned lines of verse ending
with what is probably an echo of his own misfortune: 'None but he was
in my thoughts throughout the ball/None but he and many more
besides!'

In July, Paul completed a three-year stint with the war navy, which
he had joined as an unlisted midshipman in March 1850. On one of his
berths, the *Milan*, he went virtually round the world (January 1851 to
March 1853); in all, he served on five different classes of vessel and had

ten separate berths. With this experience behind him, he returned to the merchant navy with the intention of earning his master's ticket. (He qualified as a *capitaine au long cours* in 1854.) In December 1853, learning that Paul was due home for a few days after a voyage to Martinique, Verne planned a trip to Nantes. Anxious to avoid displeasing Seveste, he asked his father to send him a letter requesting him to go to Nantes on urgent family business. By February 1854, he was in Nantes, and we find him attending a fancy-dress ball given by M. Janvier de la Motte, chief justice at the county court. Mme de la Fuye reports that Verne turned up at the ball dressed in the tight-fitting costume of an *Incroyable* (a late eighteenth-century dandy) once graced by the brother of his grandfather, the late wanderer Augustin Allotte. Marcel Moré deduces from this that Verne liked to conceal his personality beneath a disguise, and finds particular significance in the fact that Verne chose to cut a dash as a dandy. Yet, surely, there was nothing unusual about going to a fancy-dress ball in fancy-dress; and his particular choice of costume was presumably dictated more by what was available in the family attic than by any special fantasies of his own.

More importantly, Verne seems to have gone to this ball determined to try the cure for a broken heart suggested by his mother. Casting around for a girl with whom he might fall in love, he was very taken with the gracious figure of Laurence Janmare, the daughter of a local notable and the close friend of Ninette Chéguillaume (who was to be to Paul Verne what Caroline had been to Jules). Laurence was dressed as a gipsy; her beautiful dark eyes more than made up for what her loyal friends described as 'excessive slenderness'. Be that as it may, Verne decided to pay his court to her. Unfortunately, he forgot that there was a big difference between the freedom of speech to which he had become accustomed in Paris and the rather narrow ideas of society in the provinces. Overhearing Laurence confess to Ninette that her whalebone corset was digging into her ribs, he bowed deeply and remarked, 'One might have a whale of a time fishing for that bone!' In Paris, where a farce called *La Pêche aux Corsets (Fishing for Corsets)* had opened at the Théâtre de la Gaîté a few weeks earlier, the joke would have passed for a bit of harmless nonsense.

Laurence herself probably laughed. But others at that provincial ball were shocked; the word got around, and when it reached the ears of her worthy father he was not amused. Nonetheless, Pierre Verne was duly despatched to M. Janmare to request his daughter's hand for his son.

He was turned down: Janmare considered that Jules Verne's position at the Théâtre Lyrique was far too uncertain and that a young man capable of making unseemly jokes about his daughter's corset would not make a suitable son-in-law. In point of fact, Laurence had already made her choice: she eventually eloped with a certain Duverger and was married secretly in a convent chapel.

It was during this visit to Nantes that Verne finally convinced his father that for nothing in the world would he take over the family law practice and settle in the provinces. 'Anyone else would be mad not to jump at your offer', he had written earlier (17 January 1852). 'But my mind is made up: the career that suits me best is the one I am already engaged in . . . I know what I am, I can appreciate what I will become. How could I take over a practice that you have built up so well and that in my hands could not improve but only regress?' Pierre gave in. Although only fifty-five, he was anxious to retire. Consequently, to his great sadness, the practice to which he had given so much of his time and energy was sold out of the family on 19 April 1854.

In the meantime, Verne had returned to Paris, and had gone back to work at the Théâtre Lyrique. He was unhappy and somewhat embittered, not with Laurence but with the people in Nantes who refused to take him seriously. It is surely exaggerated to suggest, as Mme de la Fuye does, that Verne was in love with Laurence: he barely knew her, and it is unlikely that even he would fall in love as the result of a few words exchanged at a ball.

In April, he was at Mortagne, a market town south-west of Paris, ostensibly to repair his health. This trip was his mother's idea: she doubtless hoped that a period of rest in the country would give him a taste for the quiet life and turn his thoughts towards marriage. But it seems improbable that he went there to meet a specific young lady, the 'daughter of colonial gentry' referred to by Mme de la Fuye. In a letter to his mother dated 7 April 1854, and written at Mortagne, he jokes about marriage in a way that she must have found rather offensive:

> . . . I am quite well again. It's the perfect moment to marry me off, dearest mother. I accordingly request that you start your campaign: arm yourself with all it takes to serve me up as succulently conjugal, piping hot and cooked to perfection; cry me as your ware ('Try my fine son') and put me in the hands of some nice young lady with plenty of money. If necessary, I'll move to Mortagne, which I've never given as much thought to as now and which strikes me as an ideal place to dream in. I can just see my rich rolling

acres basking in the sun. The father-in-law is a reactionary old fool but a good fellow at heart, with the right amount of belly for one to give him a friendly dig in the ribs without embarrassment. The mother-in-law makes pickles, harvests her chickens, breeds her jams and goes in for all the occupations of a humdrum country household. As for the daughter ('the missus'), she's neither pretty nor ugly, stupid nor clever, amusing nor disagreeable, and gives me a son or daughter every nine months as regularly as clockwork.

Isn't that the way things look for me? Since it would seem that the only happiness in this life lies in being an utter blockhead and living like the ducks on a pond, let us at least try to make the pond as clean as possible. I hope that I'm finally on the road to married bliss. Don't think I'm joking: I love the country life, I adore domesticity, I worship children. Remembering Mortagne, I forget Laurence; and I find Fernand [F. de Bouillé, a family friend, his host] to be a right noble fellow who has a fine flair, a very fine flair, a very very fine flair, tralala, for music. In fact I am told, though I don't believe a word of it, that the day his carriage overturned and his wife broke her nose the horses bolted because he started to sing one of his prettiest bits of opera. I cannot believe this calumny, preferring to think that what made those noble beasts bolt was having read their master's account of his journey to Mont-Blanc!

So you see I am wise and well-disposed: if you agree to lend a hand, I swear you'll be a grandmother by the end of the year.

Back in Paris, he tried to resign from his job at the Théâtre Lyrique, finding that his duties left him no leisure for his own work, but Seveste refused to let him go. However, he was set free unexpectedly when Seveste contracted cholera and died on 29 June 1854. 'I was very fond of him', Verne wrote the next day; 'and he had a great affection for me. But since there is always some good in misfortune, I am at last free of the theatre.' Not as free as he thought, however, for he was obliged to stay on at the Théâtre Lyrique until November 1855. Writing to his father around this time, he says:

I'm expecting the appointment of the new director [Pellegrin, who went bankrupt almost immediately and was succeeded by the great Carvalho] from one day to the next. Then I'll be free. In the meantime, I'm still on excellent terms with M. Perrin [the director of the Opéra-Comique who had taken over the Théâtre Lyrique as well on Seveste's death]. Perrin has been doing all he can to persuade me to take over the management of the Théâtre Lyrique, even on a non-paying basis and with a long-term contract. I refused. He even offered to make me sole director of the theatre,

under his nominal supervision and with a share in the profits. Again I
refused, because I want to be free and give proof of my capacity.

Coming from a young man of twenty-six who a few months before had
been obliged to write to his father for a loan of sixty francs, this decision must have seemed distinctly rash. Pierre probably accused him of
not knowing his own mind. In fact, however, Verne had a very clear
idea of what he wanted: all his decisions, however negative they
seemed, led him in the same direction. 'I want to be free and give proof
of my capacity.' His feet were set firmly on the stony road of literature,
with no thought of turning back.

Fortunately, his early efforts at prose fiction were more promising than
his activities in the theatre. As the resounding tinkle created by *Les
Pailles rompues* faded into a definitive silence, he wrote a novella entitled *Les Premiers Navires de la Marine mexicaine* which was good
enough to be republished – as *Un Drame au Mexique* – twenty years
later, at the height of his fame. (An English translation, *The Mutineers*,
was published in 1877.)

The Mutineers was first published in 1851 by the journalist Pitre-
Chevalier in the *Musée des Familles*. P.M.F. Chevalier, born in Paimbœuf in 1812, had connections in Nantes; he befriended Verne quite
early on via the Sophie connection, and Verne looked to him much as he
looked to Dumas: as a mentor. In fact, by giving him space in the
Musée, an illustrated family magazine of great repute of which he was
chief editor, Chevalier ultimately helped him almost as much as Dumas
did, insofar as he gave him the means to discover his gift for narrative
fiction, a gift which might otherwise have gone by default. This did not
prevent Verne from complaining to his father (29 July 1859) that
Chevalier, with his fondness for explanatory titles, had headed his
story 'South America: an historical study'. 'It should be North
America,' said Verne.

Chevalier may have been responsible also for introducing Verne to
Jacques Arago, the brother of the great astronomer François Arago. An
inveterate traveller, Jacques Arago had led an expedition to the
Sacramento gold fields in California. Although blind, or almost so, he
had sailed from the north of China to the Antarctic, the southernmost
reaches of the Pacific and Cape Horn. 'I love these daily, hourly
struggles against the passions of nature,' he wrote to Chevalier in 1852.
Arago's *Voyage autour du Monde* was one of the biggest publishing

successes of his day, but he had also written plays, directed a theatre, and written many articles. Keen-witted, burning with enthusiasm and originality, Arago could not fail to make a strong impression on Verne. The two men became good friends; and Verne listened avidly to the tales told by this enterprising old traveller, who was as good a talker as he was a writer. Besides factual information, Arago gave Verne a fresh taste for adventure: listening to him, although in Paris and very much a *boulevardier*, he could renew his boyhood dreams of sailing on expensive delicate ships to faraway islands – whereas in reality he had never been anywhere. In particular, it is probable that Arago talked to him about his elder brother Jean, something of a black sheep, who left the Imperial Mint in Perpignan under a cloud and went to America. After an adventurous début he went to Mexico and joined the revolutionary army under Mina and Santa Anna, who rewarded his efforts with the rank of general. He died in 1836 at the age of 48, penniless.

Jaques Arago was adventure personified. (In 1855 he was to lead yet another expedition – his fifth – to Brazil, where he died, aged 56.) But he was also François's brother and his house was a meeting place for scientists as well as for geographers and travellers. Their conversation stimulated Verne to take a special interest in science, and the world unfolded in his mind as an infinite series of questions. He was only twenty-two, yet this period of his life seems to have been the turning point in his career. He was still a would-be playwright; but he had enough sense to realize that his narrative fiction was better than his plays. (All the same, his skill in the construction of plots was learned in the theatre.) His letters at this time reveal that he was thinking of trying 'something else' in his writing. Yet he had everything to learn. In itself, imagination was not enough. What he needed was facts, and he sat down to learn them with the dogged conscientiousness that he had inherited from his lawyer father.

In *The Mutineers*, a novella, Verne tries out several of the techniques and motifs that are characteristic of his novels. Indeed, the seafaring theme itself is typically Vernian; and already the novella form seems too small for the scale of Verne's plot.

For the opening, Verne uses a device to which he frequently resorts later on: a date, a place, and a ship. 'On 18 October 1825, the *Asia*, a rated vessel out from Spain, and the eight-gun brig the *Constanzia* were lying in harbour at Aguijan, one of the Marianas . . .' Aboard the

Constanzia, once she is sailing free on a quartering wind that we can positively taste, so vivid are Verne's descriptions and his use of nautical terms, the crew mutinies with the aim of selling the ship to the rebels in Mexico. The captain is killed by the spanker-boom when the villain, his lieutenant, cuts its sheets; whereupon the two heroes appear to turn their coats and join the mutiny. At this point, the action moves on to dry land in Mexico and the reader is treated to a few notions of local geography, botany, economy and orography that are integrated into the narrative and the dialogue – a favourite device, didactic no doubt, but also serving to increase the reader's sense of the story's immediate setting. The superstitious leader of the mutiny is pursued by remorse for his crime. After escaping from an avalanche and having climbed the slopes of Popocatepetl, he has hallucinations in a raging thunderstorm and kills his accomplice. He goes stumbling off through the storm but meets his doom when a rope bridge that he is crossing is cut loose by the two faithful sailors intent on avenging their captain. (They had only pretended to join the mutiny.) On this moral note, with good triumphing over evil (as it had to in the rather moralistic *Musée des Familles*), the story ends. It prefigures Verne's later work in many ways: his attention to factual detail; his fascination with volcanoes, storms and gales; his skill with dialogue; his rapid style making for directness and immediacy; his plots constructed like plays and staged in successive scenes; and so on. Yet it was not until quite a few years later that these qualities were allowed to come to the fore and reach the attention of a publisher who was enough of a writer himself to recognize them at their true worth.

At this time Verne was reading the *Tales* of Edgar Allan Poe. Poe had died in 1849, leaving two volumes of *Tales*, the first of which, *Tales of the Grotesque and Arabesque*, was translated by Charles Baudelaire after 1848. The copy of Poe's works found in Verne's library is a fourth edition dated 1862; but it is certain that Verne read the first volume of *Tales* in the years following 1848. Two of the stories in particular, *The Balloon Hoax* and *The Unparalleled Adventure of One, Hans Pfaal*, most likely gave him the idea for a story of his own, *Un Voyage en Ballon*, first published in the *Musée* in 1851, a month after *The Mutineers*, and republished in 1872 as *Un Drame dans les Airs* (English translation in *Dr Ox's Experiment and Other Stories*: 1874). Neither of Poe's stories is in the least bit convincing: the first, as its title suggests, is an avowed hoax from the start; the other is a tongue-in-cheek fantasy. Verne was struck by the bizarreness of Poe's stories but criticized their lack of verisimilitude. His own story owes little to Poe's: it deliberately sets out to make the fantastic appear convincing. The *Musée* printed it under the editorial heading 'Science for the Family'. This time, Pitre-Chevalier got it right, because when Verne came to write his essay on Poe thirteen years later a point that he made was that Poe could so easily have made his tales convincing, 'had he respected a few elementary laws of physics'.

In 1851 it was still the theatre that was absorbing most of Verne's time, despite these attempts at a new kind of writing. The Théâtre Lyrique was keeping him busier than he would have liked; in between his secretarial duties, he found time nonetheless to write a verse comedy, *De Charybde en Scylla*, and a *commedia dell'arte*, *Quiridine et Quidinerit*, and fretted at being kept by other work from completing a further verse comedy, *Monna Lisa*, to which he was particularly attached. He was harrassed and ill, but could not resist going to stay with his uncle Auguste Allotte de la Fuye in Dunkirk. That trip cost him his last five-franc piece, but he could write: 'I have seen the North Sea.' He was never to forget it.

In 1852 he was in better shape and managed to work with Charles Wallut — who appears to have been the publisher of the *Musée* at one time — on a drama entitled *La Tour de Montléry*. *Les Châteaux en Californie*, subtitled *Père qui roule n'amasse pas mousse*, written in collaboration with Pitre-Chevalier, was published in the *Musée*. The rest of his free time was taken up by his five-act play in verse entitled *Les Heureux du Jour* and a libretto for Hignard written with Michel Carré called *Le Colin Maillard* (which opened in April of the following year at the Théâtre Lyrique and was a great success: forty performances, good notices and a revival promised for the following season). Yet he did not neglect his new-found genre: in the second half of the year the *Musée* published his novella *Martin Paz*, with which he was quite pleased. 'Most people like it and the ending comes out just right', he wrote on 22 August 1852.

The opening pages of *Martin Paz* set the scene theatrically. We are in Lima: the Plaza Mayor, women wrapped in mantillas, elegant señoras in their coaches, Spaniards, half-breeds and Indians, all going their way in an atmosphere of mutual scorn and hatred. Immediately, our attention is drawn by the beautiful Sarah, the daughter of an immensely rich Jew called Samuel. She seems strangely different from her father, who has scurrilously sold her in marriage to an opulent merchant, a half-breed, named André Certa. However, Sarah is loved by the noble Indian Martin Paz, who cannot hope to marry her because he is too poor. Certa and Paz fight a duel with knives: wounded, Certa is borne to Samuel's house whereas Martin Paz is forced to flee. Trapped on a bridge, he dives into the tumultuous waters of the river and is given up for lost. Sarah goes off in despair to pray at the church of Santa Anna.

However, Martin Paz has survived his plunge. A nobleman, Don Vegal, has given him refuge in his magnificent dwelling on the banks of the river. A member of an ancient and illustrious family, Don Vegal is nonetheless on the verge of ruin; but having never recovered from the loss of his wife and daughter in a catastrophe at sea, he is facing his imminent downfall with equanimity. Indignant at the incompetence of the Spanish administration and the cupidity of the half-breeds, he takes up the cause of Martin Paz and the Indians.

A revolt is planned under the leadership of El Sambo, the father of Martin Paz. In the meantime, Paz overhears a secret conversation between Certa and Samuel and learns that Sarah is really the daughter of a nobleman: having saved her from a shipwreck, Samuel has passed her off as his own daughter. By marrying her and then proving her noble origins, Certa will get himself admitted into the high society of Lima. The two men strike a bargain: one hundred thousand piastres. Just as the contract of marriage is about to be signed, Sarah runs away to join Martin Paz, who entrusts her safety to Don Vegal and goes off to lead the revolt.

Things go wrong, however. When the Indians invade Lima, they attack the house of Don Vegal. Martin Paz is obliged to fight his own people. El Sambo contrives a conflict between his son and Certa: the latter is killed, and Martin Paz discovers in his wallet a receipt revealing that Sarah is the daughter of Don Vegal. In the meantime, the unlucky girl has been abducted by El Sambo and set loose in a canoe on the Madeira rapids. As the canoe is dashed towards the thundering waterfall, Martin Paz arrives and with a mighty fling catches the canoe with his lassoo. But an arrow hits him: he falls into the canoe and the young lovers are swept over the falls to their death. A second arrow pierces the heart of Don Vegal.

Despite its melodramatic ending, *Martin Paz* is quite a good novella.

Verne's biographer and editor, Charles-Noël Martin, has called it a decisive development in Verne's career. Personally, I believe that the 'decisive development' was *The Mutineers*, since it was Verne's first published effort at prose fiction. But Martin makes a further point about *Martin Paz* with which I concur entirely. This is that *Martin Paz* reveals one of Verne's major attributes as a writer: his visual approach to narrative. It seems that Verne wrote this story from a series of watercolours by the Peruvian painter Merino, a friend of Arago's. As Charles-Noël Martin says: 'Like Victor Hugo, Jules Verne was a visionary, in that his inner eye perceived scenes which he afterwards described with remarkable accuracy, an accuracy not unlike the gift of observation in a painter. His secret lies in his having succeeded in causing tens of millions of readers to see what he had seen himself in his imagination.' I would add that Verne's letters, which are full of such phrases as: 'I'm down on the eightieth parallel and it's eighty below zero; I'm catching cold just to write about it' and 'I'm in New Zealand . . .' confirm that Verne was imaginatively present in the scenes he described. However, at this time he did not appreciate this gift; instead of cultivating it, he wasted his time and energy writing comic operas and insipid comedies. In his letters, he seems to have cared little for *Martin Paz* whereas he enthuses (5 November 1853) about a second comic opera by himself and Hignard. 'Both the music and the book are tremendously gay.' (*Les Compagnons de la Marjolaine*, as it was called, was accepted by the Théâtre Lyrique in 1853 and produced two years later.) Pierre Verne showed more discernment than his son: he urged Verne to submit *Martin Paz* for an award from the Académie. His hot-headed son give the idea short shrift (22 August 1852) 'No thanks. You have to lobby for the things like you do for the stupid puffs of the Institute and unfailingly the best are not accepted; and if lobbying is required I prefer to serve a more useful purpose.'

Pierre, his rhymester father, had accompanied his compliments with a reproach that might have diverted his son from his newfound vein: why was he not writing verse any more? 'Oh, but I am: a whole lot; and right now my *Leonardo da Vinci* is taking up all of my time.' This play, which he eventually entitled *Monna Lisa*, seems to have preoccupied him for many years. Yet it was never performed or printed. (It was published in 1974 in *L'Herne*.) It has a certain charm, nonetheless, and I shall discuss it later when I come to consider the extent to which Verne may be regarded as a misogynist.

Verne continued to consider himself first and foremost a man of the theatre. Nonetheless, he spent much of his time learning scientific facts – an activity that is rarely mentioned in his letters home, as if he were shy of drawing attention to what might have been regarded as useless labours. The first science that he studied closely was geography, which necessarily led him on to physics and mathematics. His intellectual quest was stimulated by the circles that he frequented: at Arago's he encountered minds trained in the most diverse disciplines, from literature to astronomy, geography and painting; at Talexy's, too, he met men of distinction drawn together by a common interest in music.

He began the study of mathematics with the help of his cousin Henri Garcet. Garcet was thirteen years his elder, the son of Pierre Verne's sister Mathie, and it was he who held the money sent by Pierre Verne for his student son's allowance. A professor of mathematics at the Lycée Henri IV and the Ecole Polytechnique, Garcet published textbooks in cosmography (1853) and mechanics (1856). Verne read both these books, and had the advantage of discussing them with their author in the course of their frequent conversations.

Verne had an enormous capacity for work. He never stopped, whatever activity he was engaged in: playwright, secretary of the Théâtre Lyrique, or (later on) stockbroker and novelist. He grudged the eight hours per day that he sacrificed to his social functions, which he regarded as a waste of time. His real work began at home at five in the morning and continued in the reading-room of the Bibliothèque Nationale, which he frequented assiduously. This bookworm approach, together with his excellent memory, enabled him to forge a tool for his work, a tool which he used for the first time in *The Mutineers*.

If he had had any basic scientific training, he would doubtless have opted for some speciality. As it was, his literary ambitions exposed him to the danger of becoming a scientific jack of all trades, had he not discovered a way to crystallize his knowledge through his writing. In 1895 his files contained over 20,000 data cards abstracted from his reading: this immense labour would have been sterile if he had not realized, in the 1850s, that the general public knew little of what was happening in the world of science and that this virtual ignorance would stop the scientific movement in its tracks, for lack of funds and cooperation, if nothing was done about it. At the same time he could not employ the tactics that Diderot had used a century earlier. (Diderot had promulgated the scientific spirit by addressing himself to the cultivated minority in power.) The social climate had changed, and so had the scope of science. Thanks to the broadening of educational opportunities there had been an increase in the numbers of intellectuals and para-intellectuals: hence, any appeal in the name of science in the nineteenth century must perforce be addressed, not to an élite, but to the educated masses.

Reading Edgar Allen Poe, Verne saw what could be done by mixing fantasy and reason. Yet in Poe science plays a secondary role: it is merely a pretext, a frame for Poe's own anguish. His stories are personal fantasies that enable him to depict human behaviour in highly abnormal situations: he cultivates the bizarre for its own sake. He is interested in moral deviation; but the mainspring of his inspiration remains his crushing scorn for the idea of progress and American society. Verne's approach to fantasy is quite the opposite. He is essentially a realist. His essential belief is that men can achieve consciousness and fulfilment by working on their environment, which is both real and hostile, and not by subscribing to the escapist cult of Truth, Beauty and even Progress, which for him are entities that are emanations of reality and not transcendentals.

Science makes its first appearance in Verne's fiction in the novella *Maître Zacharius ou l'horloger qui a perdu son âme*, originally published in the *Musée* in 1854 and republished in the *Docteur Ox* volume twenty years later (English translation in *Dr Ox's Experiment, and Master Zacharius*: 1876). With its amalgam of positivism, poetry, moralism and the bizarre, *Master Zacharius* is reminiscent of the manner of Poe, but its fantastic elements are, properly speaking, Hoffmanesque.

Zacharius is a Genevan clockmaker, the inventor of the escapement mechanism, who belives that his invention has enabled him to 'discover the workings of the union of body and soul' – the soul being the spring of life and the body its regulator. Having regulated time, he must therefore be immortal, because if he died time would die with him. Unfortunately for him, his clocks start going wrong one after another under the mischievous influence of a bizarre gnome, whose job it is to regulate the sun. Even the church clock stops when Zacharius, dragged unwillingly to mass by his daughter Gérande, refuses to bow his head at the elevation of the host. (In the 1874 version, at any rate. In the 1854 version, he does bow his head.) Only one clock is left in working order: the one at the castle of Andernatt, which marks the hours with Catholic mottoes that appear in a panel above the dial. Zacharius goes off to keep it working, because if it stops his life will end. Eventually, he finds the clock and its owner, who is none other than the gnome. Zacharius winds the clock for a century, but instead of pious mottoes the clock starts to display blasphemies. Gérande calls in a hermit to exorcise the clock, which explodes after producing one last adage: 'He who would be equal with God will be damned for ever.' The spring goes bouncing around the room chased by Zacharius who, exclaiming 'My soul! My soul!', fails to catch it and duly expires.

Verne's later fiction contains quite a few similar reminders that science has its limitations. But the relative violence of *Master Zacharius* suggests that at the time he was writing it Verne was himself in two minds about the role of science. His admiration for science clashed with his religious convictions. Consequently, he felt almost guilty about attaching so much importance to human knowledge. As his studies progressed, however, this inner conflict sorted itself out, and he came to realize that research can have a moral value of its own. Indeed, man's obligation to dominate nature, which otherwise oppresses him, was to become his major theme.

In the spring of 1854 he was tired of the theatre, 'this burdensome Théâtre Lyrique', and was looking forward to the end of the season. He was doing more studying than working, he wrote to his father (19 April 1854); 'I am beginning to perceive a different approach.' He sent his father a one-act play in verse – probably *De Charybde en Scylla* – and informed him about his hopes to fill in part of his time during the annual closure of the Théâtre Lyrique with work at the Odéon and the Gymnase. But he did not lose sight of the imminent publication of 'another story about a winter in the Arctic ice'.

Un Hivernage dans les Glaces (*Musée*, 1855 and *Docteur Ox* volume, 1874; *A Winter amid the Ice:* 1876) is the story of an engaged couple from Dunkirk, the 'very Dutch little seaport' in northern France where Verne had visited his uncle Auguste Allotte de la Fuye in 1851. The flat drab landscape around Dunkirk and above all the North Sea had made a strong impression on him. ('I love the sweet sadness of misty landscapes and regard the sun as my enemy,' he wrote much later. For Verne, the North was an obsession.) *A Winter amid the Ice* is a transposition of his memories of his short stay in Dunkirk and the thoughts prompted by his contemplations of the North Sea. Several of its themes recur later on in *Captain Grant's Children* and *Twenty*

Jules Verne (left) and his younger brother Paul as children (painting by Châteaubourg, an uncle of Verne's)

Jules Verne's mother, Sophie

His father, Pierre

A family gathering at Provins, in about 1861. Jules (bearded) plays the fool at the back; he stands next to his father, below whom his mother is seen peering over the shoulder of one of cousin Henri Garcet's children. The old lady sitting at the front is Mme Gabriel Verne, Jules Verne's grandmother

Jules Verne's sisters Mathilde and Marie

Honorine, the young widow of 26 (with two children) whom Jules Verne wed in 1857

Jules Verne's brother Paul, with the latter's son Gaston (who, much later, was to fire a revolver twice at Verne in a fit of madness)

Michel, Jules Verne's only child, aged about eleven

Michel as a young man

Michel's second wife Jeanne, known as 'Maja'

Jules Verne, aged 25

Alexandre Dumas *père et fils*, who befriended Jules Verne soon after his arrival in Paris in 1848

Pitre-Chevalier, editor of the magazine *Le Musée des Familles*. He was the first to publish a story of Jules Verne (in 1851)

Jules Hetzel, Verne's chief publisher and closest friend and adviser

(Above left) Nadar, as seen by himself. *(Left)*
Hetzel, as seen by Nadar. *(Above)* Jules Verne
(aged about 50), photographed by Nadar

Thousand Leagues under the Sea. In particular, it looks forward to the powerful Hatteras novels.

Skipper Jean Corbutte has handed over the command of his brig to his son, Louis, who is due to marry his cousin Marie on his return to Dunkirk at the end of the fishing season. As soon as the ship is sighted, the whole town turns out to accompany the bride and her uncle to the quayside, with the priest leading the way. But a cruel shock is in store: the ship is flying her flag at half mast, her skipper having gone overboard near the Maelstrom while attempting to rescue a ship in distress, and the Corbutte boat has been brought back to harbour by the mate, André Vasling. Immediately, Jean Corbutte decides to sail his boat back to the place of the accident. The gallant Marie contrives to stow away in order to help in the search — which Vasling loudly proclaims to be pointless. The search is pushed so far north that the ship is forced to sit out the winter amid the ice. After many mishaps, including a mutiny led by Vasling, who wants Marie for himself, Louis Corbutte is discovered safe and sound on the pack ice. Vasling dies, and all ends well except for the unfortunate death of brave Jean Corbutte, the father, who has worn himself out in the search.

From 1 July 1854 Verne was theoretically free to use his time as he pleased, because the death of Seveste had terminated his agreement with the Théâtre Lyrique. In fact, he was obliged to continue in his functions for a year more, as we have seen. During this period he wrote several comedies which were never performed, a lost libretto for Hignard entitled *M. de Chimpanzé* (produced at the Bouffes-Parisiens in 1858) and the comedy *Onze Jours de Siège* (1861). From November 1855 he was totally free. It is therefore surprising to find him spending almost as much time as ever on the theatre at the expense of his prose fiction. His letters to his parents at this time rarely mention his stories for the *Musée*, whereas they are full of references to his plays. 'My whole day is spent working,' he wrote to his mother on November 20, 1855. 'I go out when I have to.' His play about Leonardo da Vinci was going to have a new title; and he was doing a lot of work on his five-act comedy. An undated letter to his father mentions that *Les Compagnons de la Marjolaine* (1855) had gone into rehearsals at the Théâtre Lyrique and that *Le Colin Maillard* (1853) was to run for another season; his verse comedy, just completed, was going to be staged at the Gymnase by the younger Dumas. (It wasn't.)

This comedy must be *Les Heureux de Jour*. It is more serious than

the insipid comedies and farces that preceded it. A financier, Montbrun, plans to triple the capital of Madame de Gorr by playing on a fall,
and then to grab the proceeds by marrying the lady's daughter,
Laurence. Pierre, a young Breton, seems likely to spike Montbrun's
guns, so the financier challenges him to a duel and compromises the girl
to make the marriage inevitable. Whereupon his plans are thwarted by
an unexpected French military victory, which sends share prices up instead of down as he had hoped. 'Why didn't they lose, dammit!' he
exclaims. He promptly repudiates the marriage, since it is no longer
lucrative. The duel takes place. Contrary to all expectations, Pierre kills
the more experienced duelist; and as the play ends we are left hoping
that Laurence will marry him.

This comedy, which turns to tragedy in the last act, is an attack on
the Paris of Verne's youth – a society of pleasure-seekers, straw men
and hypocrites. It is quite a good play, and suggests that in time, with
more maturity, Verne could probably have succeeded as a playwright.
However, it is doubtful that the theatre would ever have brought him
the international fame that he won as a novelist.

On 19 April 1854, Verne wrote to his father that he had had 'a very
pleasant interview with the formidable Judge Janvier' during the
latter's visit to Paris. Judge Janvier de la Motte, at whose fancy-dress
ball in Nantes Verne had made his unfortunate joke about Laurence's
corset, told him that Laurence had asked him to speak to her father in
support of Duverger, whom she hoped to marry. According to Verne,
the judge scolded her on this occasion for 'having let a poor young man
like Jules Verne die of love for her while she was really planning on
marrying Duverger, and so forth.'

Around this time, Verne was affecting to feel left on the shelf.
Everyone seemed to be getting married, except him. He became touchy
and self-conscious: when he had to shave off his beard to treat an attack
of facial neuralgia (a malady that dogged him throughout his life
henceforth), he complained to his mother that he looked 'horribly like
[his sister] Mathilde'. Yet a contemporary photograph shows him to
have been a very handsome young man, with firm features and large
dreamy eyes. To his mother, who had written to wish him 'you know
what', he replied in December 1855: 'Is "I know what" a loving wife?
Heavens, I won't say no.' Two months later, writing about the 'superb
match' made by his friend Victor Marie, he says (19 February 1856): 'I

can't see why I too shouldn't get myself a society bride – for instance, a girl with money who has made a mistake (or would be preprared to make one with me). I'd be in for that like a shot!'

For all his fooling, it is obvious that he was seriously considering finding himself a wife. He was beginning to feel distinctly lonely in Paris, where at first he had felt so gloriously free. The harshness and indifference of the society that he had castigated in *Les Heureux du Jour* left him with a growing need for companionship and tenderness. Furthermore, his provincial's dream of taking Paris by storm had resulted in many a disappointment; and as time went on his chronic poverty became increasingly hard to put up with. Also, he had been ill, and was still not in the best of health: in times of sickness, a woman's presence could be very useful. As he was to write later on: 'Misfortune is kinder to two than to one.'

His failure with Laurence Janmare in 1854 had not pained him, because she was already set on marrying someone else. (As it turned out, her marriage was not a happy one.) He *had* been hurt by the lack of consideration shown him as a budding playwright by her people in Nantes; but his flop as a suitor had not affected him in the least. Things were different with Caroline. There, he had been totally ingenuous and madly in love. The hurt caused by her turning him down went very deep and ultimately affected his whole mental outlook. He consciously repressed his love for her and hid his sorrow, deliberately lowering the emotional tone of this personal tragedy by presenting it as a farce in which he was the clown and she the coquette. At the same time, he recognized that she had never committed herself to him in any way and that if he felt betrayed it was because he had believed she loved him as much as he had convinced himself she did. With Herminie, too, he had been forced into the role of the rejected suitor. Justifiably or not, his experiences led him to the conclusion that women are wily creatures who are not worthy of being loved.

Nor was he likely to be favourably impressed by what he saw of fashionable marriages in Nantes at this time. The sincerity of the maidens led to the altar certainly mattered less than social conventions – which is understandable, but which a passionate young man like Verne could not accept. Laurence was not one for these settlements, as she proved by kicking over the traces to marry the man she loved. She and Verne were undoubtedly of the same stamp; unfortunately, by the time they might have fallen in love with one another the hearts of both belonged elsewhere: Laurence's to the man she intended to marry, Verne's to his memory of Caroline.

As his mother pestered him to get married, Verne accustomed himself to the idea of a marriage of convenience, which would at least put an end to his poverty and loneliness. On 23 August 1852 he told her: 'I'll marry any woman you can find for me – with my eyes closed and my pockets open.' The bitter cynicism of this jest is too blatant for him to be believed. But it reveals that his mind was made up on marriage: his friends had shown him that it was the normal thing to do and he envied them a little; but he still could not take marriage altogether seriously. For him, it was 'the burial of one's bachelor days'; and when he attended the wedding of his friend Victor Marie in April 1856 he was 'extremely moved when the funeral procession went by – in other words, I nearly choked with laughter, and I haven't stopped laughing yet.' He went on: 'I can't see myself ever seriously playing a part in a ceremony of that kind. I find it comical in the extreme. And yet . . .' That 'and yet . . .' is revealing: his cynical jesting is only so much bluster. There could be no marriage of convenience for him unless its advocate was Cupid.

At the beginning of May 1856 Verne took the northern line train to Amiens, where he was to be best man at the wedding of a college friend (who was also Henri Garcet's brother-in-law) Auguste Lelarge to Mlle Aimée du Fraysse de Viane. Unexpectedly, this sad and unlovely town proved to be his Capua.

He felt at ease there immediately, for there was nothing in the solid provinciality of Picardy to make him feel self-conscious. On the contrary, as someone up from Paris, he had a distinct edge on the people he met, an edge that was denied him in Nantes where he was regarded as a local boy. In Nantes he always felt hampered by the social conventions, or in other words by his own prejudices; in the new surroundings of Amiens he felt infinitely more free, because he was a stranger there.

He was the guest of the de Vianes, unpretentious provincial gentry who made him feel at home. Several days after the wedding, he wrote: 'I'm still in Amiens, the charming solicitations of the de Viane family having forced me to stay longer than I intended.' The household was *en fête*, the parents having decided to marry off their daughter with due ceremony: in this atmosphere of merry-making, banqueting and feasting, Verne felt happy and relaxed, and his ready wit made him a welcome guest. What is more, Caroline was there, his adored forgotten Caroline, looking as pretty as ever, if not prettier, beautifully dressed and laughing gaily – except that this Caroline was called Honorine. She was the sister of the bride, she was a widow, and she had two children. Not that that mattered!

He fell for Honorine as he had fallen for Caroline, without realizing why. Both were pretty, Honorine possibly more so than Caroline. Both liked to laugh. And both were what Mme de la Fuye, perhaps a little unfairly, calls Caroline: silly. In other words, both of them were feminine and trivial – which in no way detracted from their more important qualities, as their lives proved. They corresponded to Verne's image of womanhood, at any rate, even if that image bore little relation to the real person on whom it projected its aura.

Verne was euphoric:

> I shall have spent a week here finally, a week of galas, kisses, handshakes, embraces, tears of joy and pleasure, wedding feasts, conjugal effusions, Amiens pâtés, stuffed chitterlings, spicy hams, luncheons lasting for three hours, dinners beginning at six and ending at eleven. Oof! I shall be lucky if I don't die of indigestion. But in point of fact I'm in the pink of health: I sleep, eat, laugh – and have more definite views on marriage than ever. I want to marry, I need to marry, I have to marry. It isn't possible that the woman who is to love me hasn't yet been born, as Napoleon said.

Using a well-tried tactic, he begins by dropping hints, like the opening bidder in a game of bridge:

> This Deviane [sic] family that Auguste is marrying into is a charming family, made up of a delightful young widow who is the bride's sister, the bride herself who seems very happy, and a young man of my own age who is a stockbroker in Amiens, making a lot of money at it too, and who is certainly the most charming fellow ever to walk this earth. The father is an old retired military man, several cuts above the general run of such pensioned-off warriors, and the mother is a woman of great intelligence.

Sophie would be surprised, he knew, by this unwonted eulogy of an entire family. In fact, it was a feint to enable him to admit that there were other attractions for him in Amiens besides the duck pâté:

> Your natural perspicacity will have told you that there is more here than meets the eye. Indeed, I think I am in love with the young widow of

twenty-six. Oh, why does she have to have two children? I'm always running up against impossibilities of one sort or another. She lost her husband seven or eight months ago . . .

A day or so later, he followed this up with a letter to his father:

As you can see, I'm back in Paris . . . Auguste's marriage and the family that he has married into gave me much food for thought . . . In this Devianne [*sic*] family there is a brother of my own age who is the most charming fellow on earth. He has gone into partnership with one of his friends as an intermediary between shareholders . . . and the stockbrokers in Paris . . . This is a good position for a young man, and it is absolutely safe. The point is that what he can do in Amiens, one could do even more easily in Paris on a smaller scale . . . M. Devianne is very well in with financiers and brokers; he could easily get a friend of his involved in a large firm in Paris, even for a small amount . . . So what I need to know, father, is whether (if the need arose) you would be prepared to buy me a share in a firm like this, which is just as official as a law firm. I need to change my way of life, because this precarious existence of mine cannot go on . . . When I go for a year without earning anything, my allowance is only half enough to keep me, what with prices going up the way they are . . .

Pierre must have leapt when he learned of this latest whim. His son was decidedly full of surprises. The worthy lawyer found it increasingly difficult to consider him seriously. After refusing to take over his law practice in order to devote himself to writing, yet having produced nothing but a few slight comedies, and after turning down an offer to become the director of an important theatre, here he was wanting to dabble in finance! The financial world was potentially more dangerous for him than the world of books: he knew nothing about finance and could barely manage his own affairs, let alone other people's. Since he had started out to be a writer, let him remain a writer!

The least one could say for his son was that he would not take no for an answer. He argued back at his father, cleverly choosing his words and knowing that eventually Pierre would give in out of sheer lassitude (29 May 1856):

On the one hand, I can see that you ask nothing better than to help me get established. On the other hand, I can clearly see that you take me for a thoughtless boy chasing the latest idea to pass through his head and wanting to get involved with the '*Change* for *change's* sake' alone.

I don't intend to throw the baby out with the bathwater. Far from it: my determination to continue writing is firmer than ever. Writing is an art with which I have identified myself and which I shall never abandon . . . I am determined not to write vaudeville sketches and similar lightweight stuff; my ambition is merely to write one big, well-wrought comedy per year . . . But I need to have a position . . .

His final argument was irresistible, and he knew it. It was also the only true one:

Furthermore, I intend to marry at the earliest opportunity. I am fed up with the bachelor life, as all my friends are also . . . It may strike you as funny, but I need to be happy, it's as simple as that. And if a position as a broker can improve my prospects and still enable me to live in Paris . . .

In other words: I want to marry the pretty widow of twenty-six, children and all; she consents, but her charming family quite rightly object that my situation is not stable enough; if the equally charming son contrived to find me a position, the pensioned-off warrior would be delighted to have such an agreeable son-in-law.

There is every reason to believe that Verne had really fallen for this pretty young woman whose laughter reminded him of Caroline, and equally that she had fallen for him. She did not doubt that this handsome young man, so witty and quick, would make her a pleasant husband. Everything was getting off to a good start; all that was needed was for Pierre to chance a small sum of money in an enterprise that he thoroughly disapproved of.

Verne played his next card in a letter dating from June. M. De Viane (*sic*: Verne seems to have been unsure of the spelling) was to enquire about the possibilities in Paris. Pierre Verne was wrong to mistrust this young man's motives: he had nothing to gain personally from the steps he was taking. 'And once again, father, it has *nothing* to do with speculation.' Pierre asked why his son did not just get himself employed by a stockbroker in the normal way. Verne retorted (27 June 1856):

I want to have a *presentable* position, because . . . I am at the age when the urge for union, for cohabitation, is stronger than anything else, and legitimacy is such matters is better than the alternative . . . As long as I am merely a would-be writer, parents will turn their backs on me, and quite rightly so.

The arguments back and forth went on until September, by which time

de Viane had done his work and Verne felt strong enough vis-à-vis his
father to lead his trumps (9 September 1856):

> I have seen M. De Viane . . . One of his friends is negotiating to buy a
> stockbroker's firm. I have the option of buying one fortieth of the firm for
> 50,000 francs. Once I have my share, I can either work in the firm or work
> on my own; M. De Viane greatly prefers the latter course, because in his
> opinion there would not be a position in the firm's office that would either
> suit me or be sufficiently lucrative. As you can see, dear father, it's a matter
> of 50,000 francs or thereabouts.

His 'dear father' cannot have been convinced by this mass of argumen-
tation, since three days later Verne wrote: 'My letters must be un-
intelligible, since you ascribe to me ideas that I do not have. Gambling
has nothing to do with it, nothing at all.' And he followed this up with
eight paragraphs demonstrating the rightness of it all.

Even though his parents were not entirely convinced by his
arguments, they had to allow that he was set on marrying the young
widow. Undoubtedly, Sophie and his sisters were on his side. Pierre's
resistance weakened, and he asked a friend in Amiens for information
about the de Viane family. By November, after his son had disposed of
his final objection ('I swear that I am not going to give up my writing'),
he had given in and his son had got his own way once again. 'Silverware
doesn't seem right . . . What does mother think? If I took along
silverware, it would look like a present for myself.' (22 November 1856)

Sophie was thrilled, and wrote to say so. Her letter was so affectionate that it was 'read again and again' at the de Vianes' and
delighted everyone. Amiens was under a foot of snow that November,
but Verne was reluctant to leave 'this beloved town'. As a mark of
respect for the dead husband's family 'in the interests of the children', it
had been decided to wait out the year. Consequently, the wedding had
been set for 10 January 1857. ('The husband died in July 1855 but one
has to observe the common decencies.') The presents would be quite
modest:

> I gave a gold and jasper chatelaine, very pretty, that cost me 235 francs. I
> won't buy any earrings or diamonds: she already has some fine ones that
> we'll have remounted. She won't need a dress, she has plenty. Perhaps a
> muff. As regards the cashmires, we can't decide: she already has a long
> French shawl and a plaid one. We may have her diamonds mounted as a
> bracelet . . .

Honorine cannot have been very impressed. Yet it seems that this recycling of what doubtless represented the *spolia opima* of her marriage to the late M. Morel did not dampen her enthusiasm. She accepted, and probably suggested, these arrangements with good grace; as she agreed to the skimpy wedding ceremony held at the Town Hall of the third arrondissement in Paris and the church of St Eugene. I, for one, find that admirable; and I am greatly pleased to think that my grandmother laughingly accepted this mediocre way of life which was so different from what she would have wished.

However, Sophie and Pierre were shocked. Bourgeois, and provincial into the bargain, they could not understand. The Bohemian style of the wedding breakfast for a dozen people held in a second-rate restaurant upset them: they would have preferred something more like the copious feasts that had marked the marriage of Aimée. All the same, the younger members of the family soon made the room ring with laughter. Hignard, who was best man, was the only friend of Verne's present. 'No fuss, no expense – we're paying!' Pierre warmed to the proceedings; over the dessert, he smilingly read the lines of verse that he had written for the occasion, in accordance with the family tradition.

1857–1865

T HE YOUNG COUPLE duly set up house in Paris, five floors up at 18 Boulevard Poissonnière, near the Bourse. To avoid any unnecessary upheavals, they probably left Honorine's two little girls, Valentine and Suzanne, with the grandparents in Amiens. Honorine cannot have wished to have her honeymoon disturbed by the presence of two small children and it was preferable, in any case, for the children themselves to have a little time to get used to the fact that they were no longer alone with their mother. Verne himself was determined that the children should not suffer on this account; and he rapidly came to regard them as his own. By April, at all events, Valentine (aged four) and Suzanne (two) had joined their mother in Paris, and the little family moved into more comfortable lodgings. Within the space of a few years, they moved five times, from Boulevard Poissonière to the Rue Saint-Martin, Boulevard Montmartre and thence to Boulevard Magenta, Passage Saulnier and Carrefour de la Croix-Rouge — each move corresponding to an improvement in Verne's finances. The moving itself cannot have been very trying, because — to begin with, at least — their entire worldly goods could be fitted on to a handcart.

Verne went back to his old routine: up at dawn, he worked until breakfast and then went off reluctantly to earn his living, which was now provided by Eggly & Co, stockbrokers, Rue de Provence, in which he had a fortieth share. Not that the Bourse displeased him. On the contrary, in those days the exchange seems to have been a kind of club for a crowd of young financiers like Verne who spent more time discussing literature than actually doing business — young men such as Félix Duquesnel, the future impresario; Frédéric de Cardailhac, the owner of the Vaudeville; Charles Wallut, Philippe Gille and Charles Delioux; Feydeau, the novelist (father of the playwright); Zabbah, who was on the staff of the magazine *Charivari*; and many others.

Mme de la Fuye quotes Duquesnel: 'Our group was well-known, and Jules Verne became our ringleader. Verne did better with his witticisms than he did with business. He was quick at answering back, mocking, sarcastic, and sceptical in every respect but one: from his Breton background he retained a Catholic mentality that stayed with him all his life. But oh! what fun we had together at the exchange!'

Fortunately, Verne had the backing of Charles Maisonneuve, his childhood friend, who was also with the Eggly firm. But Verne had no money sense: despite Maisonneuve's help, he only just made enough to support his family. Honorine, who spent a large part of her time cooking complicated meals that he gulped down unappreciatively, must have felt that all the time he spent scribbling would have been put to better use at the stock exchange – but then, she did not know what went on at the exchange! I doubt that she ever nagged him for more money; but I am sure that she felt that the hours spent in study and writing were unnecessary and pointless. Verne's intellectual life escaped her entirely: she did not understand his interests, could not follow his conversation, and indeed felt excluded from this aspect of her husband's existence. Fortunately, her quick wit was equal to his: she could still make him roar with laughter; and on this level their relationship was unstrained and happy. Yet I have heard my family mention more than once that she could not prevent herself from disturbing Verne while he was working. Having no intellectual life of her own, she could not comprehend his need for isolation and silence: she would go into his study repeatedly to ask if he needed anything, if she could do anything for him and so on, intending to be kind and affectionate but succeeding only in being a nuisance. This need of hers to mother Verne – or perhaps to interpose herself between her husband and his work – was surely one of the reasons behind their perpetual migrations in search of larger quarters.

A few months after their marriage, Paul Verne, whose life paralleled that of his beloved brother to a quite remarkable extent, went through an unfortunate experience not unlike Verne's disappointment with Caroline. After a spell in the merchant marine Paul had joined the war navy in March 1855, at the height of the Crimean War, with the rank of ensign. Thus, at the age of twenty-five, serving on the *Cassini*, he was given command of the landing squad, in which capacity he took part in the battle for Kinburn and Sebastopol. In the course of a leave spent in Nantes, at about the time that his big brother was waxing lyrical from

Amiens over Honorine de Viane, a plan materialized to marry him off
to Ninette Chéguillaume, the confidante of Laurence Janmare at that
fancy-dress ball in 1854. To judge from a letter of Jules to Pierre in
1855, Ninette's father's heart was set on having 'one or t'other' of the
Verne brothers as his son-in-law; having lost Jules to the de Vianes, he
asked for Paul. He almost got him: the engagement was announced
with appropriate provincial pomp towards the end of 1856, and Paul
went off to serve a final stint on the *Tartare*, having promised his
fiancée to resign the service as soon as possible; but when he returned
to Nantes as a civilian in May 1857, his bride-to-be confessed to
doubts, and the engagement was broken off. (Ninette must have been
less enthusiastic about marriage than her father thought, because she
went through exactly the same performance with another navy man a
few months after Paul's *débâcle*.) Jilted and jobless, Paul was forced to
cast around for a way to earn his living. The fact that he eventually
decided to set himself up as a stockbroker, like his brother, cannot be a
coincidence; but a stockbroker he remained until his retirement, first in
Nantes and then, from around 1870, in Paris. In 1859 he married a
Mademoiselle Meslier from Blois, who made fairly frequent stays with
her mother and three sisters at the appropriately-named Hôtel des
Quatre-Soeurs in Bordeaux, where Paul may have met them during one
of his business trips. It is more likely, however, that plans for a
marriage were initiated in Nantes; the Vernes and the Mesliers must
have known each other quite well, because Mme Meslier was related to
the Ducrest de Villeneuve family, and a Ducrest de Villeneuve married
Paul's sister Anna in 1858.

On 15 July 1859, Verne wrote to his father:

> Honorine and I have just got back from the country, where we spent three
> days with Auguste Lelarge near Essonnes along with Valentine, Hignard,
> Delioux and Lerois [a friend from the Bourse]. We had a lot of fun, despite
> temperatures up near the hundred mark . . . In a week or so, I've got a
> chance to go to Nantes, alone this time . . . Alfred Hignard has offered his
> brother and me a free trip to Scotland and back on one of his ships. So I'm
> grabbing the chance to make such a lovely trip . . . I'm doing well on trips
> lately. I took the opportunity to go to Rheims while in Essonnes and
> visited the wonderful cathedral from top to bottom. While I'm away in
> Scotland, Honorine will go to Amiens.

This trip to Scotland impressed him greatly. Later on, he used it for a novel (*Les Indes noires*) and it was perhaps the source of his affectionate regard for the Scots that is apparent in many of his novels. Verne wrote a slightly fictionalized account of the journey that makes for very entertaining reading: Hignard and himself, disguised behind invented names, react naively to the strangeness they encounter; their utter inexperience of travel and foreign *mores*, together with their schoolboyish sense of fun, gets them into scrapes that are related in Verne's best manner; and the descriptions of Victorian London are particularly fine.

The account of this journey is the manuscript *Voyage en Ecosse*. Verne and Hignard joined the *Hamburg* in Bordeaux. After an uneventful voyage, they reached Liverpool, where Verne was struck by the poverty of the working class, a poverty which seemed inexplicable considering the obvious prosperity of the harbour. He was also astonished by the apparent freedom of speech and manners that he encountered among the English, who seemed to be much less inhibited than the French. (Interesting comments on this difference between the two peoples are found throughout the narrative.)

Arriving in Edinburgh by train in torrential rain, the two tourists took a cab to Lambret's Hotel, whence the following morning they set out to explore the city:

> Apart from the hotels, there are few places in Edinburgh where one can get something to eat: there are no restaurants as in Paris, and the few taverns that exist have no signs outside them. Eventually, the famished tourists discovered a sort of coffee-house where they were served very cheaply with cold meat and Scotch ale. Jonathan [i.e. Hignard] would have liked to have a few fresh eggs as well; but he could not make himself understood; he lacked the word for *à la coque*.
>
> After this substantial breakfast, Jacques [i.e. Verne] again suggested that they climb the hill that he had seen from his window that morning . . . The long street took them past the house of the great reformer John Knox, the only man who ever resisted the smiles of the Queen of Scots – and who consequently died peacefully in his bed on 24 November 1572. Netherbow ends at the Canongate, an ancient street that was once the whole extent of the town. Canongate is Edinburgh's street of shame – and it leads to the royal castle! Naked children, barefoot women and girls in rags, beggars holding out hats, all collide, pass, stumble, limp and sidle with famished faces beneath the tall house-fronts. Surrounded by this poverty-stricken crowd, in this pestilential atmosphere, on the heavy, muddy cobblestones of the foul, dark, damp little streets called 'closes' that lead to vile slums

stumbling down into the nearby ravines, one yet encounters the terrible poetry of old Scotland. It was here that Waverley lived on his arrival in Edinburgh; here that the tailor made him his battle tartan; here, probably, the highlanders fired into the air to celebrate the victory of Bonnie Prince Charlie and Flora was almost hit by flying shot. The Canongate is incomparable; it is unique, *sui generis*. Its stalls and shops, its signboards creaking in their iron rungs, its overhanging roofs, its prison clock looming in mid-street, its ancient hostelries – all this cries out for the brush of a Delacroix. In this street, as almost everywhere else, women seem to be more numerous than men, owing to the fact that there are very few male servants in Edinburgh, whereas the streets are flocked with chambermaids scurrying to and fro, crowned with the cast-off millinery of their mistresses.

After climbing Arthur's Seat, Verne and Hignard went out to Portobello, where an amusing incident occurred, typical both of their inexperience and of their schoolboyish sense of fun (and of the tone of Verne's narrative):

Portobello is a cluster of houses fronting a pretty fine beach – but why the Italian name among the harsh Gaelic names of the rest of Edinburgh? (The only explanation that Jonathan could think of was the presence at Mary's court of the singer Rizzio and his companions.) Here, on the yellow sands, they discovered the bathing activities that they had seen depicted in English prints and magazines. Numerous families spent the greater part of the day on this beach: the children played under the watchful gaze of their nurses and governesses while the mothers and charming young misses vanished into the sea. Mobile huts carried them out beyond the first waves. The men bathed about thirty feet from the women.

'There's English prudery for you,' said Jacques. 'Separations of that sort don't happen in France.'

'It's a great pity, I agree,' answered Jonathan. 'But when in Rome . . .'

They entered their huts on wheels.

'Jonathan!' Jacques cried after a few moments. 'Get the proprietor to bring us bathing costumes.'

'Heavens, yes. But it won't be easy. I don't know the word in English.'

'Use signs.'

Jonathan called for the attendant, but try as he might he could get nowhere with the fellow.

'Here's a nice state of affairs,' Jacques said. 'Why didn't he understand?'

'Obviously, he doesn't speak English.'

'That's all very well, but we can't . . .'

The words froze on his lips. Through the half-open door of his cabin he had just perceived a magnificent specimen of the English bather, a true thoroughbred, emerging from the water slowly and gracefully, stark naked.

'Jonathan! Do you see what I see?'

Jonathan was stupefied to see other bathers wading towards the beach in the same state of undress as the first, quite oblivious of the misses, mistresses and ladies on the shore.

The two friends hesitated no longer. They ran towards the first breaker and dived in without a glance to right or left.

'There's real English prudery for you,' said Jacques, shaking his wet hair. 'I expect they'd be shocked if we had costumes on.'

The temperature of the water seemed rather low, considering that a few days earlier they had been swimming at Arcachon. Consequently, after understandable hesitations as to how to return to their cabins in such a primitive state, they waded out backwards, braving the laughter of the girls at their modesty and their hasty retreat.

After this pleasant dip, they made their way to the neighbouring vault, where a glass of excellent ale cheered them considerably. The omnibus plying between Portobello and Edinburgh passed at that moment: they jumped on to the platform and managed to find two seats on the top deck: children, old folk, women, dogs — it was a regular free-for-all on this swaying contraption whose every square inch was occupied by a passenger; the coachman, a dignified fellow in a black frock coat and a top hat, seemed to be constantly on the point of being toppled from his perch. At last they reached the terminus, via Calton Hill and Regent Road, where the new prison stands: a cluster of small Saxon buildings laid out over a little hill, with battlemented walls, stone turrets, windows with enormous iron bars, and innumerable fortifications — a medieval town in miniature, kept extremely clean and gleaming.

The omnibus stopped in front of the theatre — a monument about which the less said the better — almost opposite the archives building with its graceless dome.

From Edinburgh, the two friends went to Newhaven, accompanied by Hignard's cousin by marriage, the charming Miss Amelia, and her parents. It was Miss Amelia who helped them to plan their tour of Scotland; and a family friend invited them to spend some time at his brother's castle. One evening after dinner, Hignard and Verne performed some of the songs they had written together, Hignard singing and playing the piano, accompanied by Verne at the organ; and then Verne learned some highland melodies from Miss Amelia, harmonizing them at the piano and remarking that Scottish music was easy – all one had to do was stick to the black keys.

Crossing the Forth on the steam ferry *Prince of Wales*, they were caught in a storm and had to land at Cramby Point in a rowing boat, sick and wet. A few hours at Oakley Castle enabled them to recover, however, and they set out in good heart for Stirling, Bannockburn, Castlecary and Glasgow, travelling by rail. Glasgow left them unimpressed, despite the aurora borealis that was visible on 30 August. From Glasgow by train to Balloch was their next stage; and they crossed Loch Lomond on the *Prince Albert* to Inversnaid, where they took the stagecoach over the hills to Loch Katrine. Appropriately enough, in the eyes of these two admirers of Walter Scott, the Katrine ferry was called the *Rob Roy*; during the short crossing, a highland piper played in the stern of the boat and Hignard transcribed the melody in his notebook, just as he had recorded the peal of the bells in Edinburgh – whither the two friends returned by train via Callender and Stirling.

Their train from Edinburgh to London was an excursion train and they were kept awake all night – fortunately for Verne, who was thus able to observe the industrial regions of the north of England, where factory chimneys belched flames in the pitch of night and one could imagine men working underground in the collieries that fed them.

Verne's record of the two days that they spent in London is a remarkable piece of writing, full of detailed observation and comment. Clearly, his admiration for the English and their way of life dates from this visit, along with his loathing for their cruelty and pursuit of profit. Paradoxically, however, Verne seems to have been more impressed by the Blackwall Tunnel and the *Great Eastern* being built in Greenwich than by a performance of *Macbeth* at the Princess Royal; and it would seem that what he most warmed to in the English was their energy, their desire for improvement, their determination, and above all their extreme logicality in the pursuit of apparently irrational and unconventional deeds and forms of behaviour. It was not by chance that *Five Weeks in a Balloon*, Verne's first novel, published four years later, begins in London before soaring over Africa; nor was it fortuitous that Dr Fergusson, the first in a long line of Vernian eccentrics, is an Englishman.

Undoubtedly, *Voyage en Ecosse*, which presumably dates from the winter of 1859–60, was originally written with an eye on eventual publication: its novelized narrative, its disguised names, its careful descriptions and its style set it quite apart from the general run of personal travel notes. But it was not published during Verne's lifetime and it remains unpublished today. Considering its biographical importance and its interest as a sharply-observed and keenly-written piece of social history, its absence from the bookshelves seems inexplicable. One reason is that Verne himself considered it in later life to be an unimportant work of his youth; and this opinion seems to have been shared by Michel Verne, his son, when he came to publish the works left behind at Verne's death.

After this, his first trip outside France (which itself was for him at that time a little triangle fanning out from Paris to Nantes and the North), Verne seems to have entered a period of literary incubation. Apart from the *Voyage en Ecosse*, apparently, he wrote comparatively little over the next two years, possibly because he was attempting to become more serious in his attempts to earn money from the Bourse. Honorine's two daughters were reaching the age when girls need to feel pretty; Honorine herself was constantly tempted by the world of fashion; and her feelings of insecurity cannot have been lessened by her discovery, as the lanterns and tinsel emerged in the shops for the Christmas season of 1860, that she was pregnant. All the same, *L'Auberge des Ardennes*, a comic opera by Hignard for which Verne wrote the book in collaboration with Michel Carré, received its first performance at the Théâtre Lyrique on 1 September 1860; and *Onze Jours de Siège*, a three-act comedy by Verne and Charles Wallut, written in 1854–5, opened at the Vaudeville on 1 June of the following year.

The latter is worth a short aside, because in spite of its recourse to the hackneyed comic conventions of the day it throws some light on Verne's attitude towards female sexuality. (At the same time, its very coyness suggests that the licentious poem ascribed to Verne and supposedly dating from 1854 is of doubtful authenticity. In common with most of his generation, Verne could be freely scatalogical at times; but his sense of fun stopped short of the brutally ribald. The poem published by P. Pia seems therefore to be apocryphal.) In brief, *Onze Jours de Siège* is about a couple who learn that their marriage is not legally valid. The wife, horrified to think that she is living with a man as his concubine, refuses to sleep with him, and the fellow goes out of his wits while besieging her resistance, which lasts for eleven days. Of course, she succumbs in the last act, once the situation has been clarified.

On 3 August 1861 the lights went up on a different kind of comedy: Verne's first and only child, Michel, came bawling into the world, and from the start utterly fouled up all his father's plans. Verne had gleefully accepted the offer of another free trip on one of the Hignard brothers' ships. The trip was to last for six weeks and take them to Scandinavia, notably to Norway. Despite the imminence of the birth, Verne decided to go. He and Hignard sailed on 15 June and enjoyed themselves thoroughly until they reached Denmark, where Verne reluctantly left Hignard sniffing out inspiration for his opera on Hamlet and returned to Paris. (A later trip to Scandinavia in 1881 was transposed into his novel *Un Billet de Loterie*, 1886.) By the time he got back, it was all over: mother and child were both well and all he had to do was feel paternal. Nonetheless, we should not conclude, as some people have done, that Verne lacked the usual fatherly instincts. If by 'fatherly instincts' we mean irresistible urges to dandle and coo, he undoubtedly lacked them; but if, on the other hand, we mean a propensity to care for and worry about one's child, there is no reason to find him lacking: Michel worried him stiff for most of his life. Fond fathers deserve praise; but that is no reason to criticize Verne for not being fond. It was not in his nature to be effusive. Nor should we forget that he had to do his work in spite of the disturbance caused by the child's crying.

The noise bothered him particularly because he was at that time working under great pressure on a subject that required close attention and much research: a 'balloon story' which Honorine belittled, complaining that her husband was 'forever in his balloon' – an activity that to her mind verged on the absurd. When the story was eventually finished, she exclaimed: 'Thank heavens! At last he's through with his balloon!'

Yet that same balloon was to make her a wealthy woman. Verne showed his manuscript to Dumas, who liked it enough to put Verne in touch with the novelist Bréhat. And Bréhat introduced him to Hetzel.

Pierre-Jules Hetzel, known as Jules Hetzel, was born on 15 June 1814. His father came from a long-established Alsace family, and while he was stationed in Chartres with the Premier Régiment de Lanciers, he married a local girl, as calm as he was fiery, who gave him the son who was to become one of the greatest publishers France has ever known.

It was soon realized that the boy was very bright, and he was sent as a boarder to the Collège Stanislas in Paris, where he succeeded brilliantly. At twenty-one, determined to cease being a burden on his parents, he took a job as a clerk with the Librairie Paulin in Paris, where he found great scope for his talents. Paulin was a publisher of some note and an active polemicist: he had founded *Le National* (an opposition newspaper) with Thiers and Mignet and in 1843 he started *L'Illustration*. Paulin soon saw that Hetzel could be very useful to him and after two years made him a partner in the firm. At the same time, he encouraged Hetzel to write for *Le National* and thereby embark in Republican politics.

Politics and publishing became Hetzel's twin concerns. In 1843 he succeeded in founding a publishing house of his own at 33 Rue de Seine by acquiring the list of a publisher of books on religion. His own list came to include Balzac, Musset, George Sand and other famous writers; and he himself wrote under the pseudonym of Stahl. Through Bastide, the director of *Le National*, and Marrast, the founder of the Republican Party, he became closely involved in the revolution of 1848. It was Hetzel who was sent to ask Lamartine to lead the movement against the royalists; and it was he who burst into parliament to stop the debate on the continuation of the monarchy. After the proclamation of the republic, Hetzel became Bastide's *chef de cabinet* at the Ministry of Foreign Affairs, where he remained until Louis-Napoleon Bonaparte was proclaimed president on 10 December 1848. In the years that followed, he built up his publishing firm; but the coup d'état of 2 December 1852 forced him into exile in Brussels. During his exile, he remained in contact with his political allies, among them Victor Hugo languishing in the Channel Islands, and continued his publishing activities in secret. When the amnesty came, he returned to Paris and expanded his list to include, besides Balzac, Sand and Lamartine, such significant authors as Proudhon, Louis Blanc, Rochefort and Reclus.

This, then, was the man to whom in 1862 Verne timidly submitted the manuscript of his *Voyage en Ballon*. Their first meeting was not as picturesque as Mme de la Fuye would have us believe. Verne did not call on Hetzel at home and find him in bed; he just went to his office on the Rue Jacob. However, there can be no doubt that the two men hit it off. In many respects their views were identical: Verne had come up to Paris as a student at the time when Hetzel was joining the provisional government, and had cheered on the progress of a republic that the older man had helped to create. At the time of their first meeting Verne was thirty-four, whereas Hetzel was forty-eight. Neither of them lacked enthusiasm and both had learned to look before they leaped.

Hetzel had a particular interest in children's books. His list already included several titles for children, notably his own version of *Tom Thumb*. For some time, however, he had been seeking to expand this interest by starting a quality children's magazine to be called the *Magasin d'Education et de Récréation*. (It ran monthly from March 1864 to December 1906, then appeared sporadically until it petered out a few years before the First World War.) At its title indicates, it was to be both instructive and entertaining. Hetzel had already got together a team of specialists under the editorship of Jean Macé, one of his authors. But Hetzel saw at once that Verne was ideally suited to set the tone of his new venture. Macé was a good writer, but he had a weakness for overt didacticism. Verne, on the other hand, married fact with fiction as naturally as he breathed. Hetzel leafed through the manuscript, made a few suggestions for improvements, and told Verne to come back in a couple of weeks.

Verne went home elated. No doubt to her chagrin, Honorine saw him spread his 'balloon story' all over his desk and set to work on the revision. This cannot have been a complete rewrite, as has been suggested: time was too short. Probably, Hetzel recommended a few cuts and additions and, as a great stylist himself, gave some advice on matters of style. At all events, two weeks later Verne was back at Hetzel's with the manuscript of *Cinq Semaines en Ballon* (1863; *Five Weeks in a Balloon*: 1870). It was on this occasion that Hetzel, who was often ill, received him in bed. With only one further cut, to which the author readily agreed, the manuscript was accepted. But Hetzel did not stop there: thinking of the *Magasin*, he offered Verne a contract under the terms of which Verne would provide Hetzel with three volumes per year, which the latter would buy outright for 1,925 francs per volume. In modern money, this was about $2,300 or £1,000 per volume, which may seem very little until one remembers that Balzac and George Sand sold their books for 2,000 francs, only a few francs more than the price Hetzel was offering Verne. One may suppose that authors short of funds were liable to being exploited by their publishers. At the same time, Hetzel could scarcely have offered a beginner like Verne more than he paid an established author like George Sand. And Hetzel himself was sometimes in difficulties to the point where he had to ask his friends to bail him out. (Verne himself helped him more than once, as we shall see.) At all events, Verne jumped at the chance to earn a guaranteed 500 francs per month and live off his writing, confident that his capacity for work would enable him to assume the enormous burden that he was taking upon himself. What he did not realize at the time was that by linking his fate with that of the *Magasin* he was limiting himself as a writer; but later on he came to regret having to edit his work to avoid shocking his young readers.

In point of fact, his first books were not serialized in the *Magasin* but were published directly in book form. *Five Weeks in a Balloon* came out in 1863. It was an immediate best-seller in both the adult and the children's markets, helped by its intrinsic merits and by a much-publicized venture that it had in some sort helped to promote.

In 1863 aeronautics was in its infancy. No satisfactory solution had yet been found for steering a balloon. After studying the problem, Verne concluded that all the current experiments with dirigibles were doomed to failure and that a far better solution would be to invent a balloon that could climb or descend at will to take advantage of the different wind directions at different altitudes. The hero of his novel, Dr Fergusson, has invented such a balloon, the *Victoria*, using the principle of a heated coil causing the hydrogen to expand in varying degrees within a sealed envelope; and with the backing of the Royal Geographical Society he sets out to cross Africa from Zanzibar to Senegal accompanied by his friend Kennedy and his manservant Joe. Many adventures befall them on the way.

Verne's original solution to the basic problem of air travel met with an enthusiastic response from his friend Nadar (Félix Tournachon), whose ebullient and mercurial personality led him to espouse novelty in all its forms. He had been a political cartoonist for the Republicans (having offered his services to Bastide as a secret agent), and was now a fashionable photographer. Verne may have met him through Hetzel, but it is more likely that the two men knew each other already — Nadar knew practically everybody. When his interest in aeronautics was sparked, perhaps by Verne, Nadar rushed to form a Society for Aerial Locomotion with the aim of developing a heavier-than-air flying machine. Verne became the secretary of the Society; and two other friends of Nadar's, Gabriel de la Landelle and Ponton d'Amécourt, who had been experimenting with various models of rudimentary helicopters, were co-opted as technical advisers. All Nadar needed was money. To attract funds, he decided to build a large balloon called *The Giant*, which would be launched in a blaze of publicity. Verne's book appeared in the midst of the preparations for this event, which aroused much public curiosity. Surprisingly, all went ahead as planned: the huge balloon, about as tall as Notre-Dame, rose majestically from the Champ-de-Mars in Paris carrying crates of champagne, food, guns, a princess or two, other famous people (at a thousand francs per head) and a Negro — who was presumably there to act as interpreter in case the balloon came down in Africa. (In fact it came down a few miles away, in Meaux. On a subsequent flight it crashed on Hanover and Nadar and his wife were lucky to escape with their lives.) Of course, all this helped Verne's book enormously. In the eyes of the public, the *Giant* and the *Victoria*, the real and the imaginary balloons, were one and the same: Nadar could not have publicized Dr Fergusson's adventure more if he had tried.

The success of *Five Weeks in a Balloon* heralded a new kind of fiction: the science novel. A mass of facts are skilfully incorporated into the narrative — facts that by themselves would have remained unattractive or even inaccessible to the general readers that Verne had in mind. In this respect alone, Verne shows himself to be a consummate storyteller. Furthermore, his facts turn out to be scrupulously accurate and up to date, as Edmondo Marcucci has shown (*Bulletin*, 1935): his description of the source of the Nile is correct, as are other details such as the curdled milk diet of the womenfolk of the tribes living west of Lake Victoria — none of which was generally known until Speke's return in 1863, after the novel had been published. Evidently, Verne had access to information provided by one of Speke's companions who returned earlier than his leader.

Verne kept this respect for accuracy throughout his life. Indeed, on many occasions Hetzel used his influence to get Verne introduced to specialists whose brains he wished to pick. Yet getting the facts would in itself have been pointless, had it not been for Verne's genius for translating facts into elements of fiction, not so much by a process of pure imagination à la Poe as by a process of hypothesis, the power of which was such that Verne's inductions frequently surpassed the facts upon which they were based. In *Five Weeks in a Balloon*, he says already: 'Africa is perhaps where the peoples of the future will move when the regions of Europe have been exhausted.'

The year 1863 was a turning point in Verne's life: it brought him success and it laid the foundations for his confident collaboration and close friendship with Hetzel. He worked with renewed enthusiasm. 'I've just given a mighty heave worthy of a cart horse,' he wrote to Hetzel in June, announcing that he would send in the first part of *Voyage au Pôle Nord* in about two weeks. This was to be *Les Aventures du Capitaine Hatteras*, a long novel about polar exploration. In September Verne was working at the second part of this novel, having already completed *Voyage au Centre de la Terre* which was published the following year.

This prolific output coincided with another change of address – to Auteuil, a 'superior' suburb on the outskirts of Paris. He was evidently better off, having decided to continue with the stockbroking firm for the time being. All the same, he was unable to come up with twenty to forty thousand francs to help Hetzel – who was going through one of his money crises – owing to a few mishaps on the exchange.

On 10 September Verne took the proofs of the first part of the Hatteras novel to the printer's by hand. It was published under the title *Les Anglais au Pôle Nord* (*The English at the North Pole*: 1874) in the first number of the *Magasin d'Education et de Récréation* on 20 March 1864, at a time when public interest in the Northwest Passage had been reawakened by reports of McClure's unsuccessful search for Franklin. This first part of the novel is essentially an enjoyable geography lesson, as the enigmatic Captain Hatteras steers the *Forward* through a succession of Arctic straits in the wake of the great explorers.

The second part of the novel, *Le Désert de Glace* (*The Field of Ice*: 1876), was not published until 1866, also in the *Magasin*. Verne was still working on it in 1864, judging from a letter (25 April 1864) in which he accepts Hetzel's suggestion that he should not have a duel between Hatteras and his American rival, as he had originally planned.

Both parts of the novel are remarkable for what Hetzel called Verne's 'sense of the perpendicular' – his ability to extrapolate from fact into fiction. The sum of knowlege contained in the novel is staggering. But nowhere does it stand out from the narrative: it *is* the narrative. Charcot, the French explorer, once told me that the Hatteras novel gave the most accurate picture of life on board ship that he had ever encountered, and claimed that he could vouch for the authenticity of the events described from personal experience. Charcot pointed out to me also that the latitude of the *Porpoise*, the ice-bound American ship discovered by Hatteras, is that of Cape Columbia, the point at which

Peary established his base camp for his succesful trek to the Pole in 1905. All this goes to show that not only did Verne know his facts, he also knew them well; and he could appreciate the situations that he was writing about as if he were involved in them himself.

By piling on detail after detail, he succeeds in creating an atmosphere of threat and mystery that is most unnerving. I have never been able to read without a shiver the passage describing the appearance of the Devil's Thumb, or the bit about the dog transformed by a refraction effect into an apocalyptic monster. I have just been reading the book again, and I confess that I felt the cold endured by these polar explorers as if I were one of them, and shared their emotion in their immense prison of ice. Verne cleverly plays on our emotions, interspersing his scenes of violent or fantastic action with episodes of dreamy calm: after the battle with the icebergs in the storm, we get a vision of an Arctic arcadia; and before he embarks upon his terrifying description of the cyclone that seems to guard the Pole from intruders, he describes the astonishing waters of the Arctic Ocean, whose transparency reveals a teeming population of marine monsters — Verne derived this from the explorer Penny — while overhead fly innumerable flocks of birds, some of them with a wingspan of up to twenty feet. These monsters of the air are reminiscent of the 'many gigantic and pallidly white birds' screaming *Tekeli-li!* that retreated from the vision of Arthur Gordon Pym as he rushed into the embraces of the cataract of white ash. The influence of Poe seems indubitable here.

It so happens that the April (1864) issue of the *Musée des Familles* carried an article on Poe by Verne, at a time close to when he was working on the Hatteras novel and on *Voyage au Centre de la Terre*. Verne begins by noting that in France Poe was famous despite the fact that few people had actually read his works.

> Even so, Poe occupies an important position in the history of the imagination, because he has created a genre of his own which owes nothing to anyone else . . . One might say that he is the leader of the school of the strange.

In Poe, imagination can become delirium.

> Ann Radcliffe made full use of terror, employing situations that could always be explained by natural causes . . . Hoffman went in for pure fan-

tasy unjustified by physical causes . . . The characters in Poe are just about feasible: they are eminently human, yet endowed with a highly nervous, supercharged sensibility. They are exceptional individuals, *galvanized* (if I may use that word) like people fed with air that has more oxygen than it should have and whose lives are one long combustion. If they are not mad, they must inevitably become mad through abuse of their minds . . . They push reflection and deduction to their furthest limits. They are the most fearsome analysts: starting from the merest trifle, they reach absolute truth.

Verne goes on to examine some of the most famous of Poe's short stories, including *The Murders in the Rue Morgue, The Purloined Letter* and *The Gold-Bug*. The last was a particular favourite of his. In his article, he revels in the warming of the manuscript that finally reveals a skull and lines of unspaced figures. He concludes:

This strange, disturbing story grips us through the use of techniques that no one tried before. It is crammed with observation and infallibly logical deductions; and it alone would suffice to make the writer worthy of his fame. To my mind, it is the most remarkable of all the *Tales*, the one in which is revealed to the highest degree the literary genre now known as Poe's own.

Among others, Verne studies also a little-known story called *Three Sundays in a Week*, in which Poe demonstrates that for three different individuals a week can have three Sundays. If one man sails west around the world, he will gain a day with regard to a second person who stays put. But if a third individual sails east around the world and joins up with the other two, he will be one day behind the person who never left and two days behind the person who sailed west. Thus, with one *yesterday* will be Sunday, with another *today* will be Sunday, and with the third *tomorrow* will be Sunday. 'As you can see', says Verne in his article, 'it is a cosmographic oddity recounted in a curious way'. It is evident from the way Verne writes up this story that he liked it; and of course he was to remember it when he wrote *Around the World in Eighty Days*.

Moving on to *The Narrative of Arthur Gordon Pym*, Verne remarks that this novel, while more human than the *Tales*, 'is nonetheless of the same stamp'. He analyses the story at length and quotes the last entry in Pym's journal ('Many gigantic and pallidly white birds flew continuously now from beyond the veil, and their scream was the eternal *Tekeli-li! . . .*') before concluding his essay as follows:

> And so the story ends, unfinished. Who will ever complete it? A bolder man than I, and one more bent on venturing into the domain of the impossible.
>
> Yet, we must believe that Pym survived, since it was he who made this strange tale public, only to die before he completed his work. Poe appears to regret this keenly, and declines to fill in the gap . . .
>
> If we ignore his incomprehensible side, what we must admire in Poe is the novelty of his situations; the discussion of little-known facts; the observation of the sick side of human nature; the choice of themes; the invariably strange personality of his heroes; their unhealthy and nervous temperaments; their way of expressing themselves in bizarre interjections. Nonetheless, in the midst of so much that is impossible there is sometimes a verisimilitude that grips the reader's credulity.
>
> I would now like to draw attention to the materialistic side of these tales, in which the intervention of providence never makes itself felt. It would seem, indeed, that Poe rejects the possibility of that intervention and would fain explain all in terms of physical laws (which he is not loath to invent). One does not feel in him any of the faith that he should get from his incessant contemplation of the supernatural . . . This wretched man is yet another apostle of materialism; but I imagine that it is not so much the fault of his temperament as the influence of the purely practical and industrial society of the United States; he wrote, thought and dreamed as an American, as a positivist. Having realized this, we may still admire his works.
>
> Poe's tales allow us to judge the extent to which he lived in a state of incessant over-excitement. Unfortunately, he could not accept himself for what he was, and his excesses infected him with what he so rightly called 'the horrible disease of alcohol' which eventually killed him.

From this, it is clear what Verne got from Poe: novelty of situations; discussion of little-known facts; choice of themes; and so on. But his heroes are never 'unhealthy and nervous' – quite the opposite, in fact. However, it is interesting to note that the very reproach that he levels at Poe – that he makes little or no appeal to divine intervention – has been levelled at him as well. It seems to me that the grievance, if one may call it that, is in both cases misplaced. No one would dream of criticizing a scientist for not involving God in his experiments. (In any case, a scientist's positivism does not in any way exclude the possibility of his having religious convictions.) Why, then, should anyone carp at a writer's excluding God from his fictions? It would be a very boring novel that called in God at every crisis; and a divinity so used would become equally boring in the long run. Verne knew this, of course, and though deistic to the core, thanks to his upbringing, he limited divine intervention in his stories to the moments when human strength, will and ingenuity could go no further. In the main, however, Verne's fiction is a glorification of human energy.

By contrast, it is apparent from Poe's stories that their author was haunted by the idea of death. Anguished as he was, he believed in God as a necessity rather than as an article of faith; and he tried to justify that belief by resorting to considerations drawn from esoteric experience. More than one of his tales involves spiritualism or trance. *The Facts in the Case of M. Valdemar* is about hypnotically-induced catalepsy. In *Mesmeric Revelation*, Poe goes further still by having the mesmerized Mr Vankirk say: 'You know that the beginning is God . . . He is not spirit, for he exists. Nor is he matter, *as you understand it.*'

Verne seems unjustified in asserting in his essay that Poe is a materialist and a positivist. In point of fact, Poe appears to have had a marked penchant for mystery: his stories are composed of one 'miraculous' event after another. And his use of what Verne calls 'physical laws' is highly unscientific, to say the least.

Verne went in the opposite direction from Poe. His heroes are very much alive and the world they live in is real. Whatever mysteries are involved in his stories are always explained. His world is not the world of spirits but the world of the living. Rarely does he venture outside that world: in fact, there are only three works in the entire canon that can be regarded as notable excursions from the credible: *Voyage au Centre de la Terre* (1864; *Journey to the Centre of the Earth*: 1872); *Le Chancelor* (1875; *Survivors of the Chancelor*: 1875); and his continuation of the 'unfinished' Pym narrative, *Le Sphinx des Glaces* (1897; *An Antarctic Mystery*: 1898). Elsewhere, he mainly sticks to hypothetical developments of facts; and if the results are strange, they are not incredible.

At the same time, he had a slight interest in psychical phenomena. In 1850, at the age of twenty, he had met the hypnotist Alexis, who had told him certain things about his sister Marie and his brother, Paul, including the name and location of the ship that Paul was serving on. 'See!' he wrote to his father on 28 June. 'It's a blessed miracle!' He kept things in perspective, however, and remained sceptical about so-called phenomena that had no basis in scientific fact.

Though essentially quite different, Verne and Poe have many things in common; and indeed at times one feels that Verne had to make a deliberate effort not to follow in the footsteps of the American, on those occasions when his original inspiration was poetic rather than factual. His heroes, in particular, are often just as 'galvanized' as Poe's are. (I am thinking of Hatteras, Zacharius, Lidenbrock — and of course the altogether 'exceptional' Captain Nemo.) In fact, Verne's entire opus owes a certain debt to Poe, even though the influence was never so strong in the later years as it was in the years that followed the publication of the essay.

On 25 April 1864 Verne wrote a long letter to Hetzel that I would like to quote in its entirety, because apart from the light it sheds on the relationship that the author had with his publisher it reveals what his attitude was towards his own work. The discussion concerns the Hatteras novel:

Paris, 25 April 1864

My dear Hetzel,

Knowing me as you do, how could you imagine for a moment that any letter from you would ever be unwelcome here? I shall bear it in mind, I assure you, because all that you say in it is right. I was aware as I wrote that such an extreme pitch of antagonism was puerile, but I am not yet sufficiently in control to do only what I want. Your letter is not that of an editor, but that of a friend in whom I have the utmost confidence. In any case, once again: I agree with you. The duel will have to go — a mere stroke of the pen will take care of that. But I prefer to hold over the reconciliation until later on — and then it will not be the result of a rescue, which would be *trite*. We shall see. Yet don't let us forget that this hatred between an Englishman and an American is very typical and that neither would wish to be the first to back down.

From your letter, I get the feeling that all in all you approve of Hatteras's madness and death. I'm glad: that was what I was most worried about. I could see no other way to end. And it seemed morally right that way, as well. In any case, how could I have brought Hatteras back to England? He would be quite out of place there. It is obvious that a man like him must die at the Pole. My volcano is the only tomb worthy of him.

We can discuss all this when you get back. We'll have a lot to talk about. Have you ever found me troublesome over cuts or rearrangements? Didn't

I follow your advice about *Five Weeks* and leave out the long digression about the adventures of Joe — which in no way pained me?

But let me tell you what I really think, my dear Hetzel. I do not particularly want to be an arranger of facts. Consequently, I will always be willing to change things for the good of all concerned. What I want to become more than anything is a writer, an honest ambition that I think you will endorse. You say some very nice and flattering things about my style improving. You must be referring to the descriptive passages, which I really worked hard at. Nothing could have touched me or pleased me more than such approval coming from you. I admit as much, but in my heart of hearts I wonder whether you didn't intend to sugar the pill slightly for me. I assure you, good and kind editor that you are, that there was no need to do so. I swallow any pill without fuss and without persuasion. I can't help wondering, then, whether you were really as pleased with me as a writer as you claim — and whether you didn't prefer my writing to my novel!

If I told you that to your face, you would hit the roof!

What I am saying is silly, but sincere. All I am trying to say is that I very much want to become a stylist, a serious one. This is my one aim in life. And when you, of all people, write as you do at the start of your letter, I could jump for joy.

The comments of Monsieur Jules Hetzel the younger [then a mere lad] have great weight for me, for in the end I am writing more for him than for his estimable father.

Verne's preoccupation with style comes as a surprise, because he is not generally regarded as a great writer of French. Indeed, several of his critics have taken him severely to task for his disregard for elegance of language. Yet his style is perfectly suited to the events and people that he describes: it is tough, dynamic and serious. Apollinaire for one admired Verne's style, exclaiming in a little parody of it: 'Jules Verne! What a style! Nothing but nouns!'

Verne's unwillingness to be considered an 'arranger of facts' is comprehensible, and indeed for many years he was regarded as just that: a popularizer rather than a *littérateur*. This of course is partly his own fault, firstly for having chosen to deal with facts to begin with, and secondly for spinning such a good yarn. His fictions seem so real that we forget the skill of the storyteller that made them so, a skill based on reader involvement achieved mainly through evocation of place and attention to detail. The M. Lefèvre who wrote to Hetzel in 1863 spoke for thousands of other readers of *Five Weeks in a Balloon*: 'I have been wondering, and would like you to let me know one way or the other, whether Dr Fergusson really did cross Africa in a balloon.' Today, Verne's ability to involve his readers remains undiminished; yet there is a growing awareness that we owe him more than that. He was, after all, the first writer to attempt to abolish the artificial frontier between literature and science.

In 1864, as we have seen, Verne was still working on the second part of the Hatteras novel. His essay on Poe was published in the *Musée des Familles*, as was an enjoyable short story of a very different type, *Le Comte de Chantelaine*, which was probably written two years earlier. (The latter is about an episode in the French Revolution, and may be a notional preparation for a later novel, *Le Chemin de France*.) Also in 1864, he published *Voyage au Centre de la Terre* and began a new novel for publication in 1865, *De la Terre à la Lune*.

The main protagonist of *Voyage au Centre de la Terre* (1864; *Journey to the Centre of the Earth*: 1872) is the young and 'rather irresolute' Axel, the nephew of the eccentric Professor Lidenbrock. Axel is set in his ways. When he unwittingly provides his uncle with the key to a coded document about a mysterious volcano in Iceland, Lidenbrock immediately decides on a voyage of exploration and urges Axel to accompany him; but Axel is reluctant to leave his comfortable home in Hamburg and his fiancée, Graüben, whom he loves 'in a placid and altogether German way'. It is the girl herself, a blonde with blue eyes and 'a rather serious nature', who incites him to undertake the extravagant journey. Nobler of heart than her fiancé, she tells him: 'When you return, you will be a man.'

He leaves. Like Pym, he begins his harrowing of hell on an island strewn with chasms; but whereas Pym's island of Tsalal was purely imaginary Axel's island is very real: the 'supernatural horror' of the Icelandic landscapes is due, Verne tells us, to geological upheavals of igneous rocks. However a meeting with a leper, the face of death, does little to cheer Axel up. Nor does the ascent of Mount Sneffels, the mysterious volcano mentioned in the coded document. The descent into the crater is just as difficult and dangerous; and the silence at the bottom is full of menace. At this point, separated from the professor, Axel has to plunge alone into the bowels of the earth down a narrow passage made by the rush of lava from the most recent eruption; he cannot help thinking that another rush of lava might be due about now. Then come fatigue and the torments of thirst. Axel rebels in a moment of weakness, but pulls himself together when a blow from his pick releases a spring which forms a stream that he has only to follow. 'Now there's no reason why we shouldn't succeed!' he exclaims. From this point on, Axel is strong enough to be a useful member of the expedition.

A further setback awaits him, however. The stream that has been guiding him through the labyrinth disappears. He gets lost. Reconciled to dying a frightful death, plunged into pitch blackness, he is on the verge of the void when a freak acoustic effect guides him back to his companions on the shores of an underground sea. Fortified by his experiences, he is now ready to travel back through the ages and see the lost world of prehistory; he even sees mankind as it was in the era before Adam. After that, 'nothing human seemed impossible; I forgot the past and ignored the future.'

In the course of the struggle back to the surface, his courage fails him and his uncle gives him a final lesson: 'As long as there's a breath of life, I will not allow a creature endowed with will to give way to despair.' And so, having begun his periplus in sombre Iceland, he awakes 'in the heart of one of the most marvellous regions of the earth, beneath the azure sky of Sicily.' Our anguish suddenly dissolves in the apotheosis of the sunlight, which is the apotheosis of the hero also.

At the end of his quest, Axel receives his reward. Like the knight in a courtly romance, he has proved himself worthy of his lady's favours. Graüben says: 'Now you are a hero. You need never leave me again, Axel.' Their marriage will no longer be that of a little bourgeoise from Hamburg and a timid young man, but that of two real people who have known suffering and conquered it: while Axel was enduring the trials of his caverns, Graüben was enduring the trials of separation.

Simone Vierne, in her book *Jules Verne et le Roman initiatique* (1973), has analysed the elements of initiation ritual in this novel. The aim of initiation being to strengthen the initiate's soul by exposing him to a series of trials in order to make him worthy of some object, Axel is served by the strange Lidenbrock who plays the role of the guru. At the end of the journey, Lidenbrock imparts the great teaching of *energy*, as Stromboli crashes into eruption all round them. It is energy that saves us from the impasse, at the point when night falls on all sides and, consciously or not, we call on an unspeaking god to whom we abandon ourselves; and this despairing prayer has the salutary effect of giving us back the courage we need to continue. Providence intervenes ambiguously by giving us the means to save ourselves. Axel is not rescued from the blackness by a mysterious angel, but by the existence of a natural echo: what miracle there is, is the unexpected discovery of the echo.

Journey to the Centre of the Earth is phantasmagoric; but the reader is so caught up in Axel's anguish, sharing his feelings and ideas in the face of his nightmare, that the improbability of the events takes on secondary importance. When we dream, we can never tell real from unreal until we awake — and even then we cannot always be quite sure what was fact and what was imagined. And that is the case with this novel: interior and exterior adventures are so closely interwoven that it is not until Axel has completed his final test that we emerge from the fiction and began to wonder where the truth of the thing was.

The source of the idea for the novel is revealed by Axel, who recalls 'the theory of an English captain who compared the earth to a hollow sphere within which the air stayed luminous on account of the pressure, while two stars, Pluto and Proserpina, revolved in mysterious orbits.' And Dr Clawbonny in the second part of the Hatteras novel names the Englishman as 'Captain Synness, who tried in vain to interest Humphry Davy, Humboldt and Arago in an expedition.' Undoubtedly, Verne was as sceptical as Davy and the others about the scientific value of Captain Synness's theory; but its poetic side must have attracted him greatly.

It is significant that the Hatteras novel and *Journey to the Centre of the Earth* were planned almost simultaneously. The former is based on geographical facts that are so precise that the novel seems to be a carbon copy of reality. The latter, on the contrary, has its source in fanciful notions that Verne's *raisonneur*, Dr Clawbonny, dismisses out of hand. Yet both novels unfold in an atmosphere of anguish and mystery that testifies to a certain state of mind in the author. One feels that the *Journey* was Verne's escape from the factual exigencies of the Hatteras novels — a journey into the world of dream that he was never to undertake again on this scale. Having paid his tribute to angst, he returned in his next novel to the kind of fiction that he is best known for. Speaking for his generation in *Confession d'un Enfant du Siège*, the novelist Michel Corday defined the effect of Verne's fiction on that generation and many a generation since: 'He led us to escape from our stupid jail . . . He inspired in us a wish to know more about the universe, a taste for science, a dedication to masculine forms of energy.'

Corday also expresses astonishment that 'this impeccable writer, this powerful poet, this magical educator, this precursor' was never recognized as a great man of letters in his own day. Yet his reputation among other writers was quite high. Marcel Moré has shown that Villiers de l'Isle-Adam, Léon Bloy and J. K. Huysmans knew Verne's work, and that Villiers had the *Journey* very much in mind when revising his story *Claire Lenoir* for inclusion in the volume entitled *Tribulat Bonhommet* (1887). It would seem, however, that George Sand's story *Laura* (1864), which Simone Vierne has shown to have some points in common with the *Journey*, was in fact independent of Verne's novel.

Both were written in 1863 and were at the printers in 1864. If there is a common source of inspiration, it probably came from Hetzel, who was an intimate friend of Sand and already a fairly close friend of Verne. (The two men saw each other daily.) Hetzel had every reason to enable his protégé to take advantage of the intellectual resources available from his circle of friends; and one of those friends, who was involved in the *Magasin d'Education*, was the scholar Sainte-Claire-Deville, who may well have mentioned in conversation the theories of Davy and Captain Synness. This detail may have fired the imaginations of Sand and Verne; but in any case the question of influence does not arise.

Definite influence was claimed ten years later by a writer named de Ponjest (alias Delmas). Ponjest accused Verne of having plagiarized in *Journey to the Centre of the Earth* a short story of his entitled *La Tête de Minerve*. He demanded ten thousand francs in damages. 'Why not ten million, while he's at it?' Verne exclaimed. The hero of *La Tête de Minerve* discovers a head in a coffin at the top of a mountain. Verne to Hetzel:

> The only point of resemblance . . . is that the position of the coffin is indicated by the shadow cast by a stick in the moonlight; whereas in mine, it is the shadow of a mountain peak in the sunlight that indicates the opening in the ground that leads inside the earth. And that's all! M. de Ponjest's story ends about where mine begins.

Verne gave Hetzel his word of honour that he had not read *La Tête de Minerve* when he wrote the *Journey*. As the claim moved into the courts, Verne wrote:

> It is very important to note that his reason for moving his claim from the jurisdiction of the Writers Guild is that the Guild have just found him guilty of plagiarism himself.

The lawsuit took place in 1875. M. de Ponjest lost and had to pay the costs.

It is not surprising to learn from the short novel *Les Forceurs de Blocus* (*Musée*, 1865; *The Blockade Runners*: 1876) that Verne was following the American War of Secession with close interest. The liberals grouped around Hetzel were naturally on the side of the North, whose anti-slavery views coincided with their own. Lee surrendered to Grant at Appomattox on 9 April 1865; but the subsequent banning of slavery did nothing to dampen Hetzel's ardour on this issue: years later, he was still trying to get Verne to make Captain Nemo a sworn enemy of the slave trade.

Verne's interest in the civil war was broader and more informed, as we can see from his novel *Nord contre Sud* published over ten years later. While the war was still in progress, he was particularly struck by the huge technical advances that both sides made in their use of artillery. As a congenital pacifist, he could not fail to be horrified by the news of the destruction wreaked by the artillery; nor could he help wondering what would happen to the guns and the men once peace came. What could be done with them to keep them out of trouble?

He came up with an answer of sorts in his lively satire *De la Terre à la Lune* (1865; *From the Earth to the Moon*: 1873), which is appropriately unkind to the inventors of these weapons of destruction, which, he says, are 'not nearly as useful as sewing machines'. The answer comes out in the form of a farce not unlike his work in the theatre. Since the guns and the men have to do something, since they are there, why not use them to bombard the moon? The idea was suitably crazy. But in Verne's book it had to be feasible. Drawing on his accumulation of knowledge in physics and mathematics, he set to work to prop up his fancy with science. His calculations showed that at a pinch the project was ballistically feasible. But why not use a shell instead of a cannonball? A shell is hollow; and Verne seemed to hear his friend Nadar muttering that you could get a man in there. But what man would dare to undertake such a crazy adventure? Of course: Nadar himself. Nadar was ready for anything, the crazier the better. So Nadar, rechristened anagramatically Ardan, would be the world's first astronaut.

With his usual scruple for accuracy, Verne got his cousin Henri Garcet to check his calculations. The cosmographer and mathematician established the correct trajectories for the shot at the moon; but many problems remained to be solved: exessive initial velocity, overheating due to friction in the atmosphere, and so on. At the time, these problems were unsolvable, owing to the lack of suitable fuels: even the braking rockets fitted to Verne's missile had to be powered by gunpowder. Verne does not ignore the problems. He admits that they existed but were overcome thanks to (unspecified) scientific ingenuity. As for the rest, his accuracy is remarkable: the parameters followed by his space vessel are correct; the vessel is made of the right kind of metal, aluminium; its height and weight are correct in relation to the proposed trajectories; and there is even a system of air regeneration on board. Finally, the sixteen-foot telescope erected in the Rocky Mountains, able to decompose the Cancer Nebula, is strangely similar in power and location to the giant telescope installed much later on Mount Palomar.

From the Earth to the Moon was published in the *Journal des Débats* in September 1865. From a letter to Hetzel dated 6 September, we find Verne was working 'with enthusiasm and as much pleasure' on a quite different book: 'Robert Grant is becoming a very daring and quite heroic lad.' His next letter informs us that he intended to give *Les Enfants du Capitaine Grant* 'a little rest' in order to think over 'a magnificent Robinson Crusoe story' for which he was getting 'superb ideas'. And he thought that, once completed, it would stand comparison 'in a modest way' with *Swiss Family Robinson*. He was not wrong: *L'Ile mystérieuse*, which was not completed until nearly ten years later, is a masterpiece of adventure fiction.

Verne's relationship with Hetzel is the perfect example of close collaboration between an author and his publisher. As early as 1863, Verne tried to help Hetzel out financially, as we have seen. In 1868, he would have liked his father to buy a share in the firm. On other occasions, we find him postponing payment of Hetzel's notes in order to tide him over a difficult period. In short, he was Hetzel's partner in an enterprise that they both had at heart. Sharing the same aims, they shared the same preoccupations. When Hetzel was away from his office through illness, Verne took his place.

At the same time, Verne depended on Hetzel for his livelihood. Their first contract, made in 1863, guaranteed the author 1,925 francs per volume. The author was to deliver three volumes per year, which meant that his guaranteed income was 5,775 francs per year. These terms were improved under a contract dated 11 December 1865: Verne was to receive 3,000 francs per volume, in consideration of which the publisher would have exclusive rights on each volume for a period of ten years from the date of publication, whatever form that publication might take. Illustrated editions remained the publisher's outright property without limitation. 'In a word, absolute and unlimited ownership in the works is granted to the publisher for sale in illustrated editions.' However, the author was to receive an indemnity of 5,500 francs to cover the five volumes already published. This second contract was for the period 1 January 1866 to 31 December 1871. On 25 September 1871, a new agreement was drawn up stipulating that the author would deliver two, instead of three, volumes per year. The publisher would pay him 6,000 francs per volume, in consideration of which the author granted him an extension of three years on the rights to the non-illustrated editions of all past and future works.

Hetzel continually improved on these terms, which met with the author's satisfaction. Verne would not tolerate any criticism of his publisher. It was the general practise in those days for publishers to buy books outright. Yet Hetzel wrote several articles in defence of the author's rights and may on this account be considered to have been an early pioneer in this field. (In 1875, when Verne was riding the crest, Hetzel persuaded him to abandon his flat-fee policy in favour of a system of royalties that he was working out.) Victor Hugo was the only author on his list with whom Hetzel appears to have had disagreements over money; but then Hugo was notoriously mindful of his affairs. Lamartine, Balzac and Sand, to name only the most famous of the rest, were entirely trusting towards him, as well they might be: he supported Balzac and Sand at their débuts when they were actually losing him money.

On the basis of the five contracts preserved in the Hetzel files at the Bibliothèque Nationale, Charles-Noël Martin has attempted to show, in his biography of Verne, that the publisher exploited his author unscrupulously, from 1866 to 1875, notably by encouraging him to accept what was tantamount to a monthly salary in exchange for all rights in his works. According to Martin, Hetzel earned something like 5 million francs net from Verne's work, as against Verne's million; and in Martin's eyes this puts Hetzel in the vulture category. (Nadar saw Hetzel that way, too, interestingly enough: his sketch of Hetzel for his *Pantheon* portrays Hetzel as a beaked, beady-eyed, clutching bird of prey.) All I can say is that Verne always declared himself satisfied with the financial arrangements between him and his publisher. One might add that he was more *au courant* with the realities of the publishing world, and with Hetzel's activities in particular, than Martin suggests; that his outlays in 1874 (for instance) were far in excess of the annual 'salary' provided for under the terms of the contract then in force (and cannot be explained merely as an extension of a legacy from his father, since large settlements had already been made on Pierre's three daughters at the time of their marriage, with an explicit waiver of inheritance rights by Jules); and, finally, that it would seem that extrapolation from the remains of the Hetzel archives, in the absence of Verne's personal papers, destroyed in 1898, and without reference to the Hetzel papers transferred to Hachette in 1914, is inevitably hypothetical and incomplete.

Of course Hetzel's importance in the life of Verne goes much deeper than their business relationship. Behind the publisher stood the writer and critic; it was hard to separate the publisher Hetzel from the writer Stahl. His standing as a writer enabled Hetzel to intervene in his authors' works without their taking umbrage: the Hetzel exhibition at the Bibliothèque Nationale in 1966 showed an entire page of Balzac crossed out and redone by Hetzel, while George Sand blindly followed his every injunction to revise. Verne, too, gained much from Hetzel's advice tendered as from one writer to another. He received much help also from Hetzel's vast circle of mainly left-wing friends, some of whom became his friends as well: Jean Macé, of course, the editor of the *Magasin*, and several more besides; and he met Sainte-Claire-Deville, Bertrand, Ernest Legouvé and probably George Sand. Etienne Arago, the brother of Jacques (who died in 1865), was also among Hetzel's friends.

It is only partly true to say that Hetzel, Verne's spiritual father, usurped the influence of his natural father. In fact, there was no usurpation, there was a succession. From 1863 to 1870, Piere's influence dwindled as he grew old, whereas the influence of Hetzel grew under the effects of friendship and collaboration. When Pierre died in 1871, Hetzel stepped into his shoes as Verne's adviser and friend. In addition to their personal esteem and affection, the two writers had the highest consideration for each other's work. Hetzel's writing was the reflection of his personality: it comprised grace, elegance of style and a lively sensibility. This romanticist admired Verne's gifts as a story-teller, his knowledge and his skills as a creator of characters – in a word, his prodigious imaginative powers serving his scientific mind – but deplored the fact that he did not appeal very frequently to sentiment.

When Verne got an idea for a story, he always began by discussing it with Hetzel. In the next stage of his work, he made a pencil draft which was subsequently corrected and inked over and then sent to Hetzel. However, his handwriting, though well formed, was so small that it was hard to read; consequently, the book was set up in proof almost immediately. Several sets of galleys and page proofs then went back and forth between Verne and Hetzel, each round of proof bringing new corrections. There were often as many as eight or nine revises. For instance, the first part of the Hatteras novel, which began life under the working title *Voyage au Pôle Nord*, was submitted to Hetzel at the beginning of July, 1863. On 4 September while working on the second part, Verne was eager to see the first part in print and get Hetzel's opinion on the ending. Six days later, he was writing again to secure Hetzel's opinion on the title. On 16 September he agrees with Hetzel that Hatteras must be 'daring and rather unlucky' but refuses to bring a Frenchman into the crew, wishing them all to be English. From proof to proof, *The English at the North Pole* developed considerably through this interchange of ideas until it was finally published in March, 1864. The second part of the Hatteras novel went through a similar process.

In the course of the debate about the Grant novel published in 1867–8, Verne sent Hetzel an important letter that underlines the difference between their respective literary temperaments. After mentioning that he has tidied up in page proof some slipshod writing evidently referred to in previous correspondence, he says:

> I am now coming to the most serious thing. I am very clumsy at expressing sentiments of love. Putting the word 'love' down on paper frightens me. I am perfectly aware of my awkwardness and sit there squirming without getting anywhere. So, in order to get round the difficulty, I mean to be very strait-laced. You ask me to throw in *a few words of feeling* from time to time. Yet, those words of feeling just won't come! If they would, they would already be in.

Hetzel was, if anything, hypersensitive to 'words of feeling', both in his writing and in his reading, and Verne sometimes teased him gently for what he considered to be excessive *sensiblerie*. Today, Hetzel would be called a highly emotive extrovert. Verne, on the other hand, filtered his emotions through his mind. Resisting first impressions, he wrote from the head and not from the heart. This is not to say that he lacked feeling, far from it; but he meant to dominate his feelings. This reticence in matters of the heart led him to repress his feelings, which were never so deep as when he kept them to himself. It was on this account that Mallarmé called him 'curious' and Pierre Véron, 'secretive'.

At this time in their lives, Verne was as vigorous as Hetzel was delicate and, further, was at the height of his powers. Thus, the difference in their mental outlook was reflected in their physical temperament — which no doubt conditioned their outlook, at least partly, in the first place. Both were hard-working and enthusiastic; but the one, weakened by illness, grief and incipient old age, sought consolation in the promptings of his heart, whereas the other, solid, more down to earth, more monolithic, could not and would not invent fictional characters that were not reluctant to dwell on their emotional problems. Verne told Marie A. Belloc (Mrs Belloc Lowndes) in the interview he gave her for *The Strand Magazine* (1895):

> Love is an all-absorbing passion, and leaves room for little else in the human breast; my heroes need all their wits about them, and the presence of a charming young lady might now and again sadly interfere with what they have to do.

Verne knew, despite Hetzel's exhortations, that the psychology of love was not his forte, and that if he tried to foist emotional reactions on to his characters he might merely diminish them. Women are not, of course, excluded from his stories; they are present insofar as they can be. There can be no denying, however, that his best books have no women in them at all.

What women he does depict are always gentle and brave. Frequently, their role is to inspire; sometimes, to be won. Lady Glanarvan initiates her husband's quest for the lost Captain Grant. The indomitable Mrs Weldon is rescued by the boy captain. And so on. But where is love? The insipid idyll between Mary Grant and John Mangles would not convince a schoolgirl. And yet it is Axel's love for Graüben that sends him to the centre of the earth; it is his love for Nadia that enables Michael Strogoff to win through; it is love, again, that drives Sangarre to share the fate of the traitor Ogareff, and that sends Mrs Branican off on the perilous quest for her husband. Mrs Monroe, in *La Maison à Vapeur*, precipitates the dramatic climax in this tale of vengeance.

When they have a direct role to play in the adventures, which are always the main element in the stories, Verne's women are invariably intelligent and dynamic. Many of them show themselves to be capable of withstanding hardship in a way that was not common in those days. Yet, for all that, they are not devoid of feelings: on the contrary, they are all warm and loving. Even that dragon Pauline Barnett in *Le Pays des Fourrures* is recognizably feminine: she remains outwardly strong only through an effort of the will, so that when she succumbs to tears she immediately repents of this shameful weakness. Verne's women have brains and hearts; sometimes, they are moving. The author has much esteem for them: witness the fact that it is often a clever little woman who cleans up the mess made by her husband – Mrs Joliffe, for instance.

Of course, they are not the kind of heroines that we are used to meeting in novels these days: there is no room in their hearts for conflict or intrigue. They do not seem human, since for them the sexual problem does not exist. Verne's novels are not love stories: their main subject is the confrontation of man and nature; hence, the only role for love in them is a secondary one. Verne may have regretted this, for he exclaimed one day: 'If only I could slip in a few adulteries, how much easier it would be! If I had my freedom the way Dumas has, twenty books would give me less trouble than four of mine.'

Verne's wife, Honorine, had shown no interest in his 'balloon story': she could see no reason why anyone should want to spend five weeks exploring Africa. It seems likely that her husband was upset by her attitude, and invented Graüben in *Journey to the Centre of the Earth* as a kind of compensation. Graüben's encouragements to Axel take a form of words that Verne would doubtless have liked to hear his wife use to him; almost certainly, he felt rather misunderstood by Honorine who, pretty and witty as she was, had better things to worry about than the making of a book.

The Blockade Runners, published in 1865, was written some years earlier than that, at a time when Verne still hoped to find inspiration and moral support in a woman. Captain James Playfair runs the Yankee blockade during the civil war. Originally, his plan involved trading weapons for cotton; but under the influence of Jenny

Halliburtt, with whom he falls in love, his main aim is to spring Jenny's father from his Confederate prison in Charleston. Not content with this, Jenny sets out to convince the young Playfair of the rightness of the anti-slavery cause to which she subscribes, demolishing his arguments with fierce logic yet with the sweetest of smiles. Playfair is soon won to her: 'This brave girl is mistress of my ship. If Jenny asked me to throw our entire cargo of contraband overboard, I would do it for love of her.' Finally, he does not hesitate to risk his life and the lives of his crew to implement her plan. And the story ends with a marriage.

Obviously, Verne enjoyed portraying the slender Jenny who, beneath her apparent softness and vulnerability, has the energy to back her lover in his dangerous venture. All his women characters are built on these lines; and there is probably a good reason for his fondness for this type of women. Neither Caroline nor Honorine was that type; in fact, it is piquant to note that when they eventually met they got along extremely well.

In 1865 Verne's marriage had passed the seven-year mark. This is generally considered to be the time when passion moderates to affection; and it is also the time when couples tend to evaluate their union in terms of success or failure. It would seem that for Verne and Honorine this point in their marriage was the consecration of their difference: while he was plunging into the bowels of the earth or setting off for the moon, she was absorbed by the running of her house, her visits to the dressmakers, and the dinners and receptions that she would have liked to hold on a bigger scale than they could afford. To Honorine, who was incapable of following Verne into his imaginary world, the streets of Paris seemed sufficient scope for exploration, and their enticing stores held more exciting prospects of discovery than any dream of her husband's.

Since women, or rather the woman that he knew, took no part in his intellectual adventure, Verne tended to forget them when reproducing that adventure in his fictions. Possibly, their absence saddened him. This sadness seems to come through in *Journey to the Centre of the Earth*, where the inspiring Graüben, though not absent, is very remote. And it may be that Lady Helena in the Grant novel is the antidote to that absence, an antidote created by the workings of his unconscious.

Les Enfants du Capitaine Grant (1867–8; *A Voyage round the World*: 1876–7) is a three-volume odyssey undertaken by Lord Glenarvan to search for Captain Grant, whose ship was wrecked somewhere on the thirty-seventh parallel. During the trials of Glenarvan's yacht, the *Duncan*, off the island of Arran, the crew catch a shark with a champagne bottle in its stomach. The bottle contains a message written in English, French and German. Many of the words are illegible, but by combining the three texts Glenarvan manages to come up with a fragmentary document in French establishing that the message was sent from the *Britannia*, a three-master under the command of Captain Grant. This intrepid seaman is known to be attempting to found a Scottish colony in the Pacific. The rest of the message suggests that Grant and two of his crew are being held by cruel Indians in Patagonia, their ship having foundered.

Edward and Helena Glenarvan have only been married for three months. They have been planning a pleasure cruise in Edward's new yacht. But all is changed by the news of Grant's predicament. Helena urges Edward to sail in search of Grant, whose children, Mary and Robert, she has taken into her care. The *Duncan* duly sets sail for the southern hemisphere under the command of Captain John Mangles, carrying the Glenarvans, the Grants and Major McNabbs, Edward's cousin. It soon turns out that there is another person on board as well: the distinguished scholar Paganel, the notoriously absent-minded secretary of the Geographical Society, who mistakenly boarded the *Duncan* thinking she was the *Scotia* bound for India.

After many miles and many thrills in South America, Australia and New Zealand, the *Duncan* turns homeward having failed to locate Grant. Off Maria-Theresa Island, where Glenarvan intends to dump the traitor Ayrton, Mary and Robert Grant hear a voice in the night shouting for help. Unhesitatingly, they recognize the voice as their father's. Everyone thinks it is a hallucination, except Paganel to whom such explanations are 'unscientific'. The children are not wrong: the following morning, the *Duncan* takes on board Captain Grant and his two men, the sole survivors of the *Britannia*. It only remains for Mary Grant to marry John Mangles and Paganel to wed a cousin of Major McNabbs.

It has been observed that this voyage round the world is a long quest in search of a father, who is found after a series of ordeals that turn the youth Robert Grant into an energetic young man. Significantly, Robert discovers his father through a cry of despair that rings through the darkness and is heard by the children but no one else: their long period of suffering and waiting has prepared them for this vital response. The quest began on the flimsiest of evidence thanks to the insistence of Lady Helena; it was helped along by the others, who backed up her intuition with a rather shaky basis of facts. But all along Robert and Mary had nothing to hold on to but their faith.

Mary is a remarkable girl, and well deserves the love of Captain Mangles. But the real hero of the novel is Robert. He is still a lad when the *Duncan* sets off from the Clyde. He makes his mark when he cries: 'We'll do without it', learning that the document from the bottle does not reveal the longitude of the shipwreck. But he does not really enter the action until he joins Glenarvan, Paganel and McNabbs on their trek across South America. Then he conducts himself so well that Glenarvan tells him that he will be a man at an age when others are still mere children. Glenarvan admires the lad's pluck; he cannot help becoming attached to him, particularly since he feels responsible for allowing him to take part in the ascent of the Andes which is beyond his strength. Hence, when Robert disappears after a terrifying earthquake, Glenarvan is plunged into despair and refuses to abandon the search for him even though all hope seems lost. When he finds him again, miraculously preserved from the talons of a condor, he gives 'the most terrible shout of joy that ever passed human lips'. Robert's first words on regaining consciousness reveal that nature of the relationship that has sprung up between them: 'Oh, it's you, my lord . . . my father!'

Robert is at an age when he still needs a father to protect him and teach him. Fate has willed that he be separated while still very young from the father he is seeking. Instinctively, he falls back on the man who gives him the sense of security that he has been deprived of, just as he falls back on his sister to replace the mother he never knew. No conflict is possible in this surrogate relationship, because his intentions are the same as Glenarvan's. True, problems might arise after the discovery of Grant, if the two fathers entered into competition; fortunately, this does not happen, with the result that the two father images are allowed to blend without mishap. For his part, Glenarvan, the spiritual father, helps Robert to discover his real father without once thinking that he may lose his son by returning him to Grant. All of this is conveniently forgotten by those commentators who have busily tried to show that Robert's problem was Verne's problem also: Robert *has* no problem; the image of a spiritual father can quite well be superimposed on that of an absent natural father.

Even though there are providential events in this novel, the instrument of providence is men themselves. Paganel promised as much to Lady Helena, hearing her exclaim: 'May God help us!' 'He will, my lady,' the scholar replied, 'for I assure you we shall help ourselves.' This remark underlines what is surely the latent theme of the novel: fulfilment through force of character.

Paganel is the prototype of the absent-minded professor. Having devoted his life to experimental science, he brings his vast intelligence to bear on the reality that he perceives. The trouble is that the reality that he perceives is not the world around him. Thinking he is boarding the *Scotia*, he finds himself on board the *Duncan*. Intending to go to India, he sails for America. He takes his telescope for a walking-stick, learns Spanish from a book in Portuguese, writes New Zealand when he means Australia, and forgets that he knows that Maria-Theresa Island has a different name in French. His interest in the search for Grant is not so much the search itself as the problem of interpreting the document that will enable him to be found. He brings his sagacity to bear on this experimental object, intent on solving the problem rather than on finding Grant. If he is brave, it is because he is indifferent to mere events. Always cheerful, he sees nothing in the worst catastrophes but their value as scientific curiosities. Never at a loss for a maxim, he professes that 'the less you have, the less you need; and the less you need, the happier you are'. (This opinion was Verne's own; it marks the first appearance of a theme to which he returns constantly in his later works: the wrongness of what he calls 'gold fever'.) Undoubtedly, Paganel is one of Verne's most successful creations. He remained in the popular imagination, as the typical absent-minded professor, for over fifty years.

Verne's admiration for the Scots is apparent throughout this long story. Equally apparent is his dislike of the English. In truth, he was less averse to the English, whose energy he admired, than he was to England and above all the Empire, that colonial blood bath; but it is not easy to make the subtle distinction between a country and its inhabitants, even though some of those inhabitants may belong to a protesting minority.

At any rate, Hetzel could be happy: in this novel, at least, he got his 'few words of feeling'.

On 26 December 1878, the trials and tribulations of the unfathered

Grants were ushered onto the stage of the Porte Saint-Martin theatre
in Paris. The adaptation by Verne and d'Ennery, an old hand at the
game, is a travesty. Hollywood could hardly do worse. There are not
two children, but three: a second son shares the father's solitude on his
desert island — which is renamed Balker. Paganel slays a whale. The
whale has been dragging an old harpoon on which is engraved, believe
it or not: 'Captain Grant, 1877, Balker Island.' And where should that
island be, but the Antarctic! Of course: Grant was attempting to discover the South Pole. And so on. I have never been able to fathom why
Verne let them do it — or why he did it, which is worse.

1865-1871

LOOKING FOR A HOLIDAY HOME for his family, Verne naturally thought of the Somme estuary, about forty miles downstream from Amiens. In 1865, perhaps for the second year running, he spent the summer at Le Crotoy, a little fishing port on a flat and rather un-lovely coast that becomes impressive only twice a year, when the spring and autumn tides come crashing in with nothing to stop them.

Verne liked the place, and Honorine did not dislike it. Suzanne and Valentine and little Michel could play on the sands; and Michel, in par-ticular, could work off some of his surplus energy. At four, Michel Verne was already a difficult child. (He soon became known as the Terror of Le Crotoy.) His tantrums frequently disturbed his father's work. One day, Verne came striding out of his study with a face like thunder to ask what all the row was about. Honorine, undaunted, replied that Michel wanted the clock. 'Give him the clock, then,' Verne exclaimed, 'if that will shut him up!' The child encountered no resistance. His every caprice was tolerated if not encouraged. His father had no time for him and more often than not his mother was amused by him. On another occasion, he was out walking with Honorine and deliberately dropped his little walking stick down the first coal hole he saw. Tantrums to get it back. Honorine rang the bell and asked the people in the house to have it fetched. Repossessed of his toy, and asked to behave himself, he did exactly the same thing at the very next coal hole. Instead of spanking him as he deserved, Honorine burst into laughter. How could she stand up to such a charming little monster, who was wont to kneel and gaze at her, saying: 'How lovely you are, mummy!'

Despite his decreasing interest in finance, Verne continued to make an occasional appearance at the Bourse and the Eggly office on the Rue de Provence, travelling in from his rented apartment in Auteuil. But in

March 1866, he decided to move his home to Le Crotoy. Michel and Honorine were installed in a little rented house near the harbour, while Valentine and Suzanne (twelve and ten) remained at boarding school and Verne himself divided his time between the capital and the coast. In March 1869, the Vernes' move to the seaside became permanent: their lease on the Auteuil apartment was not renewed and their furniture was removed to Le Crotoy on 20 March. Verne explained the reasons for the move in a letter to Hetzel written in August 1869:

> Though I have settled at Le Crotoy, I have not abandoned Paris. Yet, in the situation that I was going to find myself in, needing a bigger apartment and all my expenses increasing, I would have been unavoidably hard-up because my income was insufficient. Here, we can get by easily and still live well. Since my family seem to like it, why hesitate? Remember that I have three children, and though the future holds no fears for me, the present can be hard.

In the calm of Le Crotoy, he could work as he pleased. Down at the harbour, he could relax and chat with the fishermen. Before long, he could afford to buy a boat. Fitting it out gave him great pleasure, and it was to become his pride and joy. The *Saint-Michel*, as he called it, in honour of his son, who christened it, was a fishing boat, strong enough to stand up to long hours at sea in all weathers. It soon became his normal means of transport. Rounding Cotentin and Finistère, he followed the coast down to Bordeaux, where Paul was doing business, and sailed back to Nantes along with his brother. After spending twelve days in Bordeaux, he had a magnificent trip back, 'blustering high winds threatening to dash us against the coast – in short, a real gale.'

Meanwhile Verne himself was bound to admit that his son was in turn charming and odious. Eventually, however, he was forced to realize that the boy's changing humours were merely childish strategies for getting his own way. Systematic schooling was needed. Michel had spent some time at school in Le Crotoy; but in February 1869, it was decided to entrust him as a boarder to the strict discipline of the priests of Abbeville College. (Abbeville, half-way between Le Crotoy and Amiens on the line to Paris, was easily accessible by train for them.) Things were complicated by the fact that Michel was of delicate health. 'We have Michel down with a high fever again, and I've just been to see him in Abbeville,' Verne wrote from Le Crotoy in 1869. And again:

'The child's health is giving us a hard time.' And again: 'He has been badly brought up, I agree, but how can one punish or be inflexible with a lad who has a fever every day?' The problem is a common one. At Le Crotoy, Verne worked extremely hard. While still writing the third part of the Grant novel, he was drafting out a story with the working title of *Un Voyage sous les Eaux* and labouring at a further task foisted upon him by Hetzel: 'I'm in for a spell of hard labour,' he told his father on 19 January 1866: 'Can you believe it, I'm writing a dictionary! Yes, a real one, an illustrated geographical dictionary of France selling in parts at ten centimes a throw, a department at a time – in other words, a pot-boiler. Théophile Lavallée was supposed to be doing it, but the poor chap's on his deathbed and I've agreed to take over.'

All that summer, he slaved over the dictionary and completed the Grant novel, asking Hetzel to do the revise himself on the latter since he was 'a geographer for the moment, not a novelist.' By August, he was exhausted. He had delivered forty parts of the dictionary and yet had still found time to do some reading for Hetzel: 'Your *Great Discovery* is a Poe without Poe's genius. All in all, I don't think much of it.' At the end of September, he had completed fifty-five parts of the dictionary, of which thirty-three had already appeared. Yet he still had forty-five parts to do. 'You can't know what it's like,' he told Hetzel. 'However, the more I go on, the more care I take.' And he signed his letter with a pun: *'Votre bête de Somme!'* whose layers of meaning include 'Your fool on the Somme' and 'your beast of burden'. In December, he was worrying about his novel due in 1867: 'Even if I croak, as they say, all I ask is that the Grants get together in time.' Hetzel, who had read the proofs of the second volume, was querying the earthquake in the Andes: 'That's the way it happens, exactly the way. It has my guarantee.'

We may wonder why he ever agreed to take on such a thankless and finicking task in the first place. His father wondered the same thing. 'It's a deal that can earn me fifteen to twenty thousand francs, and that puts me fifteen months up on my contract, which I was wrong to make so long.' (12 December 1867.) As we have seen, his contract at this time provided for three volumes per year; intent on meeting his com-mitments to the letter, he was beginning to realize how heavy those commitments were.

Revising two parts of the dictionary a week, he was so determined not to skimp the job that he finally became interested in it. It had to be 'as modern as possible', he told Hetzel, and include all the latest facts; he would be satisfied if it had fewer faults than its predecessors – and it *would* have! 'Yet, it's diabolically long, my divine master. Three million characters in all, that's to say the equivalent of seven and a half octavo volumes.' It was a great relief when he was at last able to write to his father: 'Next week, I'll have finished my geography, at least as far as the text is concerned. All thanks to Honorine. Poor thing, I have been making her write eight hundred lines per day... Whew! What a year! By way of a rest, I'm going to start in on the *Voyage sous les Eaux*. It will be a real pleasure.'

However, from mid-March to mid-April 1867, he had the opportunity of sailing to America with his brother on the gigantic passenger liner, the *Great Eastern*. The crossing was very rough, and took fourteen days instead of the ten it was supposed to take. All the same, Verne managed to visit the Niagara Falls – twenty hours by train from New York – while the ship was being turned round for the return voyage.

In his article for *The Youth's Companion*, Verne told his young American readers:

> I'm ashamed to admit that I spent only one week in your country. But it couldn't be helped: my round-trip ticket did not allow a longer stay. All the same, I can say that I have seen New York. I stayed at the Fifth Avenue Hotel, travelled up the Hudson to Albany, visited Buffalo and Lake Erie, marvelled at the Niagara Falls from the top of Terrapin Tower with a lunar rainbow showing in the spray of the falls, and crossed the Suspension Bridge into Canada. And then I came home! It is one of my deepest regrets to think that I shall never see your country again. I love America; and every Frenchman can love her as a sister of France.

Evidently, the intention of writing up the voyage was in his mind right from the start. In a letter to Hetzel written 'within sight of the American coast' he says that his book on the *Great Eastern* would be more varied than he would have wished, because 'incidents and, unfortunately, accidents' had occurred in plenty. His brother had never seen such terrible seas. 'The *Great Eastern*, in spite of its size, was tossed like a cork, its bow was swept clean away – it was terrifying.' He had had enough emotion to last him the rest of his life, but he was apparently delighted with the experience: 'Ah, the sea! What an admirable element it is!' From his copious notes he extracted a novel, *Une Ville flottante*, which was not published until 1871.

In the meantime, he had still to write his *Voyage sous les Eaux*, which had been growing in his mind since 1865. By January 1866 the synopsis was ready; but his work on the dictionary and the final volume of the Grant novel held him up. That he was impatient to begin is apparent from several letters written in 1866, including one to Hetzel in which he says: 'If I were to botch this book, I would never get over it. I've never had my hands on a finer subject.' But it was not until the spring of 1867, after what he called 'fifteen months of abstinence', that he was able to start the first draft of what was to be *Vingt Mille Lieues sous les Mers* (1870; *Twenty Thousand Leagues under the Sea*: 1873).

During its long gestation, this novel underwent a considerable change. To begin with, Verne had intended to write a kind of hymn to the sea and his own love for it. This was the time (1866) when he was fitting out the *Saint-Michel*: 'I'm in love with this assembly of nails and planks, the way one is in love with a mistress when one is twenty. And I shall be more faithful to my boat. Ah, what a beautiful thing the sea is, even at Le Crotoy where we only see it twice a day.' But true love goes deeper than outer appearances: the waves are merely the face of Amphitrite; to know that goddess entirely, one would need to plunge beneath them and sound the splendours of the hidden depths. An 'underwater journey' was what was needed. The means existed: submarines had come a long way since Fulton's *Nautilus* in 1797. The Americans had already used them in combat during the War of Secession. And Verne was certainly familiar also with the experiments of a Frenchman from Nantes, Villeroi, whose submersible was among those used during the war in America. Thus, from his knowledge of these precedents and from long discussions with his brother, Verne was able to imagine a *Nautilus* of his own, a vastly improved version of these primitive machines. His *Nautilus* is so sophisticated, indeed, and so vividly described, that it has tended to overshadow the rest of the novel. To Verne's mind, however, the submarine was merely one facet of his novel; for him, as the story developed still further, the imaginative dynamic of the novel was his exploration of its hero, a kind of *genius marum* in modern dress, the unforgettable Captain Nemo.

Nemo loves the sea passionately. He says:

> The sea is all. Its breath is pure and healthy. The vehicle of a supernatural and prodigious existence, it is pure movement and love. The sea is beyond the pale of despots. On its surface, they can yet exercise their iniquitous

rights, fight there, destroy there, import there all the horrors of life on land. But thirty feet down, they have no sway. Beneath the sea, that's the only place for independence! There I acknowledge no master! There I am free!

This is the creed of a poet and philosopher. But Nemo does not stop there. He acts against the despots, revealing himself to be 'a terrible executioner, a veritable archangel of hatred' as he watches the end of the warship that he has caused to founder.

Such violence horrified the gentle Hetzel, who pleaded with Verne to soften the rougher edges of the implacable Nemo, suggesting that the *Nautilus* should be *forced* to sink the cruiser in order to escape from being trapped in shallow waters. Verne rejected this suggestion: if the *Nautilus* had got itself trapped in shallow waters, it was no longer the 'incomparably superior ship, faster and stronger than any other' that it was supposed to be. And how could a cruiser be sunk in shallow waters?

Read on, my dear Hetzel, and as you do so remember that the provocation comes from the other ship; that it is the other ship that has attempted to destroy the *Nautilus*; and that the other ship belongs to a nation that Nemo detests, intent as he is on avenging the deaths of his family and friends. Supposing the situation were *as I intended it to be*, and as my readers will *feel* it to be; supposing Nemo were a *Pole*, and the sunk ship a *Russian* ship, could anyone raise the shadow of an objection? No! A hundred times, no! Read on, then, my dear Hetzel, and when you have done so send me back the manuscript so that I can do what must be done; but do not forget what I have been saying and what the original, true, logical and watertight idea for the book was all about: a Pole versus Russia. Since we cannot make it explicit, which is in some ways unfortunate, let us leave people to suppose that this may be the case. (*1867*)

Undoubtedly, Hetzel shared Verne's views on the Czar's brutal repression of the Poles after their insurrection against the Russian dictatorship in 1863. Every thinking person in France was appalled by the bloodshed – the Republicans, in particular, who saw the oppression in Poland as a dramatic heightening of their own situation under the autocratic rule of Napoleon III. However, Hetzel had experience of public affairs. He knew something of the difficulties that the French government was facing: if Prussia pressed its claims against France as it had already done against Denmark and Austria, Russia would be an invaluable ally. A solitary Pole fighting Russia, and winning, would be construed as a provocation; in the current state of French diplomacy, the book would just be banned. Therefore, Hetzel tried to persuade Verne to make Nemo a champion of the cause against slavery. Verne was furious:

> If I can't explain his hatred, I won't. I'll say nothing about the reasons for his hatred, about his former life, his nationality and so on, and if necessary I'll change the ending. But to suppose for a moment that Nemo is living as he does out of hatred for slavery and to rid the seas of slave ships which no longer exist would be wrong-headed, in my opinion. You say that what he does is a moral infamy. I refute that. Again, remember what the original idea for the book was all about: a Polish aristocrat whose daughters have been raped, whose wife has been hacked to death, whose father has been tortured and murdered, whose friends have died in Siberia and whose nationality is due to vanish from Europe under the tyranny of the Russians. If that man has not the right to sink Russian frigates wherever he finds them, vengeance is just an empty word. In his situation, I would sink them without remorse. Anyone who does not feel as I do on this issue can never have known what it is to hate. But let us forget all about the Pole and the Russian. The reader will suppose what he likes depending on his temperament; I shall not mention the knout, nor Siberia, because that would be too direct. It is not my intention to be political; it does not suit me, and politics has nothing to do with it. The ending – Aronnax and his companions drawing closer and closer to the Maelstrom without realizing it, then being sucked down into the whirlpool along with their boat – will be superb. Yes, superb! Then, a shroud of mystery forever over the *Nautilus* and its master! Why, I grow warm as I write . . .

It is hard to know what to think of this violent letter. However, one thing is certain: there is less passion in the book. Long digressions cut across the flow of the narrative, like dams set up to contain the author's enthusiasm or to lessen the impact of the rushes of turbulence. Even so, it is surprising to find this book being published in a series for children and, presumably, being read by children with their parents' consent. Nemo says things that no good conservative in 1870 could ever agree with. Hetzel realized this, and saw no point in adding insult to injury in the form of the Polish question, on which opinions were no doubt equally divided. Eventually, Verne gave in. A letter dating most likely from 1868 sums up his feelings on the matter:

> The best thing would have been to have Nemo fighting society as a whole. That would have been fine, but hard to make believable, because there is

no motive for that kind of fight. Less good, would have been the fight of an exile pitted against the power of banishment, a Pole versus Russia. That was a clear issue. We rejected it on purely commercial grounds. Now all that we have left is Nemo versus an unreal adversary who is as mysterious as Nemo himself – a duel between two individuals. That makes the whole thing seem singularly petty. No: as you say, we'll just have to stay vague.

It is precisely the lack of particularity that makes Nemo such a great figure, a symbol of revolt against tyranny from any source. In spite of his violence, which sometimes goes as far as cruelty, the enigmatic master of the *Nautilus* is infinitely charitable: it is only because he loves the oppressed too much that he hates the oppressors. This view of Nemo, which may seem surprising, is not gratuitous. Indeed, it seems to have been Verne's own view of his hero, judging from the following letter (1869):

I can see that you are dreaming of a very different kind of chap from mine. This worries me a great deal, because I am quite incapable of writing something that I do not feel. And it is obvious that I do not see Captain Nemo the way you do.

We are in agreement on two main points: *primo*, modify the author's horrified comments on the Captain after the great execution, in the interests of the characters themselves; *secundo*, speed up the action after the sinking of the battleship.

This I will do, but for the rest it will suffice if I justify the Captain's terrible act in terms of the provocation that he receives. Nemo does not chase the ship to sink it. He does not attack, he counter-attacks. But nowhere, whatever your letter says, will I allow a man to kill for the sake of killing. He is at heart a kind man whose feelings are shaped by the milieu in which he lives. His hatred for mankind is sufficiently explained by the suffering inflicted on himself and his family; no reader can expect more than that, because *anyway* that is not the point of the book.

You tell me the abolition of slavery is the greatest economic event of our times. I agree. But I cannot see what that has to do here. The John Brown incident pleased me because it was concise, but to my mind it diminishes the Captain. We have to stay vague as regards both his nationality and his former life and the reasons for his living as he does. Furthermore, the Alabama (or pseudo-Alabama) incident is unacceptable and inexplicable: if Nemo wanted revenge on the slavers, all he had to do was join Grant's army and that was it.

I now come to the part of your letter that tells me that the second volume is very different from the first, in that the Captain becomes more violent.

That proves that you do not remember the first volume well enough, because I am sure that I followed a very natural crescendo. There are kind sentiments *especially* in the second volume, and it is only the turn of events that makes our hero become a sombre executioner.

...It is the final pages that have given you pause. You are right about the effect on Aronnax, and I'll change it. But it's a different matter as regards Captain Nemo. By giving him a different explanation, you change him for me and I can't recognize him.

You will readily understand that if I had to redo the fellow completely — which would be quite impossible, considering that I have lived with him for two years and can't see him any other way — I would have needed a month in Paris, not one day.

Diplomatic finesse among trouble-making governments can sometimes be useful. Thanks to what our papers would call a 'tense international atmosphere' Verne was led to create one of the world's great fictional characters, a man for all seasons in whom everyone can recognize part of himself. His stand for individual liberty seems particularly timely today, when our personal freedom is subject to so many controls. An anarchist he undoubtedly is, but only in the sense that he will accept no curbs on his autonomy but those dictated by a high sense of morality. He is by no means entirely admirable or even consistent with himself, since like many revolutionaries he imposes violence of his own making, as he wavers between love and hate, pity and revenge. He does not cry, like Blanqui, 'No God, no master!' because he sees himself as God's instrument in a holy quest for purity, and because he is both a slave to his principles and prejudices and a master to his crew. His impotent revolt leads him to despise human institutions and even men themselves; and he ends up in what Verne, who thought his thoughts and lived his life, called 'the absolute situation': the impasse of solitude. As Nemo says in *L'Ile mystérieuse*:

'Solitude, isolation: those are sad things, beyond human strength . . . I am dying from having believed that one might live alone.'

Verne was never averse to breaking off his work on one book if he got a good idea for another. While writing the long Hatteras novel, as we have seen, he was suddenly struck by the possibilities of a hypothesis advanced by Dr Clawbonny, whereupon he promptly abandoned Hatteras in the Arctic Circle and dashed off *Voyage to the Centre of the Earth*. Meanwhile, the end of the War of Secession prompted him to write *From the Earth to the Moon*. Having got these two stories out of his system, he then returned to the Hatteras novel and completed it with the same gusto as before, his heroes having received a new lease of life from their sojourn in limbo.

A similar thing happened while he was writing *A Voyage round the World*. He took off momentarily to explore the possibilities of 'superb ideas' that he was getting for a 'Robinsonnade'. He then returned to the Grants, drafting a synopsis of *Twenty Thousand Leagues* at about the same time. Work on the latter was held up by the geographical dictionary, which overlapped with the completion of the final volume of the Grant novel. With the dictionary out of the way, he was free to begin writing *Twenty Thousand Leagues*; but halfway through this novel he veered off again to write a continuation of *From the Earth to the Moon*. No wonder he was complaining of headaches and dizziness! Yet he always managed to keep each work distinct in his effervescent imagination, and his chopping and changing never led to confusion.

From the Earth to the Moon ends on a note from the director of the Cambridge observatory announcing that the projectile has fallen short of its target and has been swept into an elliptical orbit around the Moon. Either it will eventually be attracted to the surface of the Moon by lunar gravity, or it will remain in orbit for ever. However, the introduction to the continuation volume, *Autour de la Lune* (1870), informs us that the astronomer was overhasty in his assumptions and that there is a third possibility.

The idea of sending the projectile into orbit existed from the start, since the manuscript of the earlier volume, which was published simply as *De la Terre à la Lune*, is entitled *De la Terre à la Lune et autour de la Lune*. However, the second part of the story stayed in abeyance for some time. Verne does not seem to have begun actually writing it until 1868. He was certainly working on it at the end of December 1868, and had finished it by February of the following year – by which time also he had half rewritten the second volume of *Twenty Thousand Leagues*.

The interim between the two parts of the moon trip gave Verne time to think about the problems involved in such an exploit. These problems were in fact insoluble, and Verne had been obliged to admit as much in the earlier volume while masking the difficulties as best he could with a few touches of humour. He realized that if his heroes landed on the Moon they would be stuck there. There was no way that a rocket, let alone their shell, could carry enough fuel to ensure decelera-

tion during the descent and sufficient thrust to escape from lunar gravity on the return. The American landings were achieved through use of
the Lem, which required less fuel than its parent module. With no Lem
at his disposal, Verne had to rely on his auxiliary rockets to steer Barbicane and his companions back to within the gravitational pull of the
Earth.

He sent in the manuscript from Le Crotoy in July 1869. Hetzel had
arranged for it to run as a serial in the *Journal des Débats*, which had
published the earlier volume of 'the *Moon*'. Verne was not too happy
about this:

> It may be regarded as a *tour de force*, but I don't really see it as a serial. As
> far as I'm concerned, I'd be quite happy to do without the kudos of the
> *Débats* if *you* can do without the money.

Indeed, it would seem that there was some haste involved in this or
another deal:

> The minute I got your letter, I dropped everything and set to work on the
> *Moon*. But it will take at least three or four days to go over the whole
> volume and redo the first chapter in the way it is needed.

Nonetheless, he insisted on having his cousin Henri Garcet check the
calculations prior to publication, and repeatedly stressed to Hetzel that
he must have time for this to be done:

> I do hope the *Débats* won't hurry me along too much. I have to get it
> checked by my cousin, the mathematician who works with M. Bertrand. I
> won't take the risk otherwise. There are some very tough problems in it.

This Bertrand was the permanent secretary of the Académie des
Sciences. When Verne told him of his plan to write a continuation of
the *Moon*, Bertrand said airily: 'Quite an easy little book, I should
think'. Nonetheless, he condescended to look over the 'very scientific,
very algebraic bits' and give them his seal of approval. 'If he had given
the matter a week's thought,' said Verne, 'he would have changed his
mind about it being easy.'

In a remarkable Preface (1967) to this novel, Charles-Noël Martin
writes:

> He, and he alone, had the daring and the extraordinary intuition to im-
> agine the possibility of sending a shell to the Moon, as well as the even
> more astonishing fact of satellization (noted by Newton in his *Principia* in
> 1687) which recurs several times in his work.

This remark is all the more pertinent when one knows that Verne had not read Newton: 'Why didn't Bertrand tell us, when we talked about our story, that Newton had had the idea of a projectile to the Moon?'

Verne's eminently *scientific* fiction never received a finer consecration than the mission of Apollo 9, one hundred years later. 'It cannot be a mere matter of coincidence,' Frank Borman, the astronaut, wrote to me in 1969. 'Our space vehicle was launched from Florida, like Barbicane's; it had the same weight and the same height, and it splashed down in the Pacific a mere two and half miles from the point mentioned in the novel.' Frank Borman told me also, which is proof enough of the power of Verne's fictions as such, that his wife, having read Part One of the *Moon*, was terrified lest he might never come back. He suggested she read Part Two.

Finally, to the ever-anxious Hetzel, who had already had several protests from diocesan headquarters that his list was not sufficiently religious, and who was worried about the reactions of the Church authorities to a novel based solely on science, Verne wrote: 'I seem to remember that Barbicane, who is a religious man, says somewhere: "A God is watching over us".'

Twenty Thousand Leagues under the Sea and the second part of *From the Earth to the Moon* were published in serial form at the end of 1869 in the *Magasin* and the *Débats* respectively. Both were very successful. However, Verne was upset to find that *Twenty Thousand Leagues* had been clumsily cut for magazine publication, and looked forward to its publication in book form at the end of 1870.

In the meantime, he had rented a pied-à-terre in Amiens, Honorine's home town, which was conveniently close to Le Crotoy and which gave easy access to Paris. Honorine disliked Le Crotoy in winter, while Verne made fairly frequent trips to Paris; and since the *Saint-Michel* was in any case laid up in dry dock for most of the winter season, and Honorine's family were glad to see more of her and the children than in the past, the place that Verne rented on the Boulevard Guyencourt was a good solution for all concerned. Nonetheless, Le Crotoy remained his official residence and his main home until he moved to Amiens permanently several years later.

At the beginning of 1870, Verne was hard at work on a further compilation effort, an *Histoire des Grands Voyages et Grands Voyageurs* that was intended to form the final three or four volumes of Hetzel's

Bibliothèque d'Education series. At the same time, he was drafting out his 'Robinson' novel: 'I'm inventing things that will astonish. I've thrown myself into it and can think of nothing else. Apart from Paris, that is! I always get there *furens amore* and return in the same state.' (How should we translate *furens amore* in the context of Verne's life? Probably as 'full of ardour' or some such phrase in the Horatian manner.)

The social and political climate in Paris at this time was more than ordinarily tense. In January 1870, Victor Noir, a radical journalist, had been shot by a certain Pierre Bonaparte. In the ensuing scandal, a schismatic confrontation emerged between the partisans of the Emperor on the one hand and the republicans and social radicals on the other. Demonstrations and street fighting occurred in Paris. In order to strengthen the régime against these outbreaks of manifest opposition, Emile Ollivier, the prime minister, submitted a number of reforms and the continuation of the imperial régime to a plebiscite, which was held on 10 May 1870. The result of the plebiscite was overwhelming support for the régime – the very régime that was to fall only four months later. A letter written just after the plebiscite makes clear which side Verne was on: 'At Le Crotoy there were 285 ayes, ten noes and five abstentions. They have all been misled into voting against the Republic. What a nation!'

In addition, there was a definite feel of war in the air. Verne urged the ailing Hetzel to go to Switzerland for treatment. (In fact, Hetzel spent the war in Monte Carlo.) 'Here people seem to think that there is going to be a war with Prussia,' Verne told him: 'I can't believe it, I don't believe a word of it. What do you think?' The possibility of war was to him unthinkable, because any kind of armed conflict struck him as being absurd. To a bellicose correspondent from Nantes, he replied: 'I have never been particularly tempted to thrash the Prussians and I'm even less tempted to be thrashed by them, which may well turn out to be the case, I'm afraid.' This realistic view of the situation was far from being shared by most Frenchmen at the time.

That spring, he returned to Le Crotoy intending to spend all summer there: 'Here all is well. Ah! my dear friend: oilskins and boots, sea air, the boat, Le Crotoy! That's the life for me! What made me ill in Paris makes me healthy here.' An unexpected postscript to the same letter asks Hetzel to write back saying that he is needed in Paris at the end of the month for the proofs of *Une Ville flottante*. One begins to wonder what he was up to. But it turns out that his intentions were quite innocent: 'You tell me that you would like to come to Le Crotoy on your way back from Brussels. I'm very glad to hear it. But don't forget that around the twenty-fifth [of July?] I'm off on a big trip to Paris with the *Saint-Michel*. In fact, I asked you in my last letter to fix things for me by writing that I was urgently needed in Paris for the illustrations to *Ville flottante*. So hurry me along.'

Honorine thought the whole idea was ludicrous, as she made plain to Aunt Amélie in Provins (and doubtless to her husband also): 'The minute he is back, Jules is leaving me again. He has the notion of going to Paris with the *Saint-Michel*. What with the drought and all, he'll end up on a sandbank. Serve him right if he does! That will teach him to go rushing off all the time.' In fact, the voyage was a fairly easy one. The *Saint-Michel* moored at the Pont des Arts for ten days and attracted much attention. The return was somewhat livelier: a day later and the boat might not have made it back, because the Seine was almost dry.

Verne was home by 13 August, only days before the Prussian invasion of France. A 'pleasant surprise' was waiting for him on his return: he had just been awarded the Légion d'Honneur. He wrote to Hetzel:

> Your letter says that you were happy to be able to do something for me in this respect. Rest assured that you did everything, absolutely everything, and that I owe it to you and you alone . . . I am certain that at this moment my father and mother are very happy and very proud. You are sufficiently broadminded to accept in others the little weaknesses that you do not share . . . Your office must be disorganized at present owing to the conscription . . . Has Jules been called up? . . . How serious it all is. In all the towns I visited, the feeling against Napoleon was very great. This must be the end of the dynasty, but we are likely to pay a high price for it.

It is said that the decree granting Verne his Légion d'Honneur was the last decree to be signed by the Empress-Regent. In this case, the ardent republican Verne would ironically enough owe his decoration to the régime that he detested. Hetzel tried to minimize this in his reply to Verne's letter of thanks: 'You deserved it, whatever the political circumstances in which you received it . . . I'm glad that you have it and that I was partly responsible. But do drop a note to Weiss [the influential critic, and friend of Hetzel], who was perfect about it. The distinction came from one scholar to another.'

Honorine herself wrote to thank Hetzel for his efforts on behalf of her husband; but her letter of thanks soon rambled off into something else:

This morning your kind letter came and made us all very happy and maybe it will bring some joy back into the house because as you know Jules has been sad and out of sorts for several months now. Does his work tire him? Or does it come less easily to him than it did? Anyway he seems discouraged, and I'm the one to suffer from all the worry brought on by it. I can see that he has trouble in settling down to work; as soon as he sits down he's up again, he complains about this state of affairs and I'm the one he complains to. What can I do? What can I say? I just weep and feel disheartened. When the house annoys him and overtires him, he takes his boat and goes away, most of the time I don't know where he is. When *you* are doing all you can to make him into a distinguished writer, do you think *I* should give up the idea of making him into an acceptable husband? Do forgive me for being so personal; when I started my letter I only wanted to thank you but big events like this make you feel like talking. Maybe you can find a way to get us out of this strained and unhappy situation.

I don't know whether Jules has ever talked to you about all this. So please keep it strictly to yourself; if you feel like writing either to console me or give me some of your advice send it to Le Crotoy poste restante, I'll go along on Thursday morning to see. Did Jules write to you about going away? Did you get a letter from him last Tuesday? Please let me know, he was very sad, perhaps he told you what was on his mind.

In my opinion, the worst thing my husband ever did was to leave Paris. He is too much on his own here, he is always by himself. Goodbye, dear friend, forgive me and pity me, my husband is slipping away from me, help me to hold on to him.

Did Verne have a lady friend towards the end of his life – and, if so, who was she? The question was asked by Mme de la Fuye, but not answered. Her existence came to light, by chance, just after her death around 1885. Let there be no mistake, however: she was very different from what our malicious imagination might suggest, stimulated by the coy hints of Verne's romantic biographer. She was a lady, and an intellectual with whom he could talk seriously about the things that interested him; and her home gave him the opportunity to work undisturbed. I remember that she lived in Asnières, which in those days was a tranquil suburb. And her name – as anyone with the curiosity to examine the archives will discover, because I was unwise enough to cite it in a letter to Mme de la Fuye, who left my letter among her papers – was Duchesne. My letter adds that the name was supplied by my brother, because I had forgotten it.

Therefore, I am doubtful about my facts here; I have tried to discover who the lady might be, without success — except that there are families in Nantes by the name of Duchesne. It may be, then, that the lady in question was an old acquaintance of Verne's with whom he re-established contact and I think now that she may have been his young love Herminie (Mme Terrien de la Haye). Whoever she was, there can be no doubt that she and Verne were very close, in a relationship of mutual regard and affection. I am aware that in a relationship between a man and a woman affection is called love; let us use the word, then, remembering that love has many nuances and that the love of Laura and Petrarch gave rise to nothing more than words. It is significant that Honorine, learning of this lady's existence, twenty years on, merely laughed; yet Honorine was far from obtuse, as her letter to Hetzel shows. No, this friendship, however loving it may have been, remained a friendship, and as such is much more interesting than if it had been something else.

As the Prussian advance continued, rumours reached Le Crotoy that barricades were going up in Paris. Verne was worried about the situation in the capital, but remained optimistic about the outcome of the war in the belief that the Prussians would be stopped on the plains of Champagne. When news came from Nantes that his father's health had taken a turn for the worse, he did not hesitate to travel down from Le Crotoy via Paris. (This was his first visit to Chantenay since Christmas 1868.) He found his father greatly aged, but still alert. The house that had been so cheerful in his youth seemed sad, and several members of the family had already fallen in battle. He encountered considerable bad feeling towards the Emperor in Nantes; it was plain that whether the war was won or lost the Emperor would never be able to return to Paris. 'Our conscripted men are great quarrellers and officer-punchers, and are very undisciplined. Yet it would really seem that the news is better. If any Prussians get to besiege Paris, there will not be many of them and I do not think you have much to fear. The main advance seems to have been halted.'

Verne's optimism was ill-founded. Sedan fell on 2 September, the Empire fell two days later, and the Prussians marched on Paris. 'What can the Republic do? The new government is very popular, here and everywhere else. But there is one huge and over-riding question: have we any weapons? All hangs on that one question, and unfortunately it seems that we have no arms at all.' He left Nantes to return to Le Crotoy, but was obliged to take a roundabout route in order to avoid Paris. He doubted whether his letter of 21 September would ever reach Hetzel, since the Le Mans railroad was on the point of being cut off. He wanted Hetzel's son to know that whatever happened, they would always be together. But the situation could not last. The Prussians could not hold out through the winter; and in any case the forts around Paris were regarded as impregnable. Paris would never fall, unless it was betrayed from within. 'The provinces would dearly defend themselves, if only we had arms. In Le Crotoy, we have nothing. In Nantes, there were only fifteen muskets for 400 men.' Nonetheless, he joined the home guard and managed to find a small cannon for the *Saint-Michel*, with which he patrolled the estuary of the Somme. Honorine and the children were sent to the relative safety of Amiens, where he was able to visit them despite the Prussian occupation. Honorine had four Prussian soldiers billeted on her house. 'They like it there, I can tell you,' he wrote to his father, on 17 September. 'They don't get fed like that at home. Honorine gives them a lot of rice to make them as constipated as possible, it's less messy. They are quiet, nice fellows from the 65th Infantry. As usual, Honorine has everything perfectly under control.' Three days later, he was back in Le Crotoy, his legal domicile, to which, in common with everyone else, he was confined for the duration of the war.

On 3 January 1871 he succeeded in sending a letter, unsealed, to Hetzel. A decree had just been passed by the national defence government extending conscription to every able-bodied male between twenty and forty. In expectation of the age limit being raised to forty-five, Verne had packed his bag and bought a musket. At the same time, he was not convinced of the legality of the decree, since the government that issued it was not an elected government. He would have preferred to have taken his orders from a constituent assembly, which in his opinion should have been formed the minute the Empire fell.

Peace was not far away, he believed. 'After that', he wrote to his father, 'we shall have a civil war, but it will be little compared with this. I sincerely hope that the conscripts will be kept on in Paris for a while and that they will shoot the socialists like dogs. The republic can survive only if this is done, and it is the only government that has a right to be pitiless towards the socialists, because it is the only government that is just and legitimate.'

His attitude towards the socialists must be seen in context. The popular uprising that had taken place in Paris on 31 October 1870 during the Prussian siege had appeared to him and many like him to be a crime against France and the Republic, the 'betrayal from within' that he had feared all along. By making political capital out of an essentially patriotic rebellion, the socialists – a term that in Verne's vocabulary signified communists and anarchists – had endangered the country when it was already under threat, particularly during the peace negotiations after 26 February 1871. The French wanted peace and would brook no interference with the process of the peacemaking. Consequently, they went to war against their countrymen in Paris: the civil war lasted for two months and achieved a horrible tally of arrests and summary executions. At least 17,000 people died and at least 50,000 were arrested. Verne cannot have imagined that the reprisals would assume such murderous proportions. The anger in his letter is that of an ardent republican who sees the institutions that he cherishes being threatened arbitrarily and unfairly: 'Paris was a lost cause . . .' he wrote to Hetzel on 15 February 1871. 'But you don't know the provinces, especially when they are under the invader . . . After Sedan, you would have got a clear Republican majority. Now, after all our efforts, only half the seats will be ours.' Finally, it is worth noting in this connection that Hetzel gave his backing to Proudhon and communists such as Grousset and Reclus, and that Verne himself worked with Grousset and admired Reclus.

Having joined his family in Amiens, Verne managed to visit Paris three times during the Commune or shortly afterwards. He objected strongly to the wording of the laissez-passer issued by the police, which began: 'We, the delegates of the people . . .' He regarded the Commune as 'a horrible, grotesque farce'. 'But it is only the beginning of the International. We have beaten it this time, but eventually it will devour us.' On another occasion, later on, he gave himself 'a devilish jolt' by attending an execution. It was an experience that he wished never to repeat. To recover, he took a few days off work to take his son out sailing.

At the beginning of the summer, he accompanied Honorine and the children to Nantes with the intention of going up to Paris again as soon as the army moved in. In fact, he got there barely a week after the ratification of the peace treaty on 21 May 1871. He discovered that Henri Garcet had died during the siege, and that a friend from the Club

des Onze-sans-femme, Charles de Becchenec, had gone mad. With his
brother, he visited 'those lamentable ruins' and informed Hetzel, still in
Monte Carlo, that the Rue Jacob had escaped with a few scratches,
whereas the Rue de Lille next to it was severely damaged. Worried
about the future, he began to prowl around the Bourse, wondering
whether it was safe to put one's trust in literature at a time like that.

During the months of the war, Verne had continued to work as usual.
On 15 February 1871 he brought his 'very dear Hetzel' up to date on his
activities:

> Yes, I have been doing a lot of work. That much I was capable of. I was
> alone here, anyway. When I see you, I will have two volumes ready for the
> printers. Not the Robinson, however, because I need to discuss that one
> with you again . . .
>   One of the volumes that I will bring you is *terrifyingly realistic*. It is
> entitled *Les Naufragés du Chancelor*. I believe it outdoes the *Medusa* for
> sheer horror, but above all I think it will ring true if I am not mistaken.
>   The other volume has no title, but might be described as the adventures
> of six scientists in South Africa. It's about an Anglo-Russian commission
> sent to measure a meridian; it's scientific, but not too scientific. I got the
> idea from the writings of Arago.
>   Finally, I am just starting a new book, *Le Pays des Fourrures*.

The horrific *Chancelor* was not published until 1875, after much
rewriting, and *Le Pays des Fourrures* did not appear until 1873.
However, the 'volume with no title' came out in 1872, immediately
after *Une Ville flottante* which had been written in 1869.

Une Ville flottante (1871; *A Floating City*: 1876) is an unpretentious
fictionalized account of the trip that Verne had made on the *Great
Eastern* in 1867. For once, the story is a love story; but the romance is a
strange one. Ellen loves Fabian, whom she hopes to marry, but is forced
to marry instead the horrid Harry Drake and as a result goes mad. A
stroke of chance brings the three together aboard the *Great Eastern*.
Fabian wanders forlorn round the ship trying to forget his sorrow;
Ellen is locked in her cabin to avoid scandal but manages to slip out at
night and haunt the deck like a ghost; and her brute of a husband makes
a nuisance of himself. Fabian and Drake fall out over a trifling incident
and fight a duel during a storm at sea. Suddenly noticing the mad night-
wanderer whom he recognizes to be his beloved, Fabian throws down
his sword; at the same moment, Harry Drake is struck dead by light-

Jules Verne at the age of 40

An illustration from the original edition, by J. Férat, of one of Verne's most
famous creations – the *Nautilus* submarine, which appears in both *20,000
Leagues Under the Sea* and *The Mysterious Island*

Four scenes (by A. de Neuville) from perhaps Verne's most famous novel, *20,000 Leagues Under the Sea*. Captain Nemo is at the wheel: 'The sea is all. Its breath is pure and healthy ... Beneath the sea, that's the only place for independence! There I acknowledge no master! There I am free!'

Jules Verne in the role of Professor Aronnax from *20,000 Leagues Under the Sea*, as seen by Riou

Two illustrations, also by E. Riou, from *Five Weeks in a Balloon*, Jules Verne's first novel, published by Hetzel in 1863. The hero, Dr Fergusson, was an Englishman, and the first in a long line of Vernian eccentrics. The book was an immediate bestseller, in both the adult and the children's markets, and was heralded as a new kind of fiction

From the posthumously published *L'Etonnante Aventure de la Mission Barsac* (drawing by G. Roux)

Rivalling the eagles: a scene (by Roux) from *Master of the World*

The 'Albatross' reappears, this time above Paris in *Master of the World*

The 'Albatross', from *The Clipper of the Clouds* (drawing by L. Benett). This 'serious fantasy' about heavier-than-air flight was expected to arouse protests from the partisans of the balloon. It was published in 1885 and set in 1895

ning. When the ship docks in New York, Ellen is transported to a villa near Niagara Falls and recovers from her madness. We feel that everything will work out, although the novelist does not say so explicitly. Verne tends to harp on this theme of thwarted love and forced marriage, as though he were subconsciously expressing rancour and regrets of his own. When a passenger gazes at a young couple and says: 'How lovely to be young!' Verne, as it were, replies: 'Yes, when there are two of you.'

In the next book, *Aventures de Trois Russes et de Trois Anglais* (1872; *Meridiana*: 1873), there are no women at all — just six bachelors: three English and three Russian geographers who move around a rather undramatic and uninspiring plot set in South Africa, which they are trying to measure along a meridian. Given its lack of emotional interest, the book is suprisingly easy to read. This is due entirely to Verne's skill as a narrator: he keeps the story moving along rapidly by the use of a simple and direct style and holds the reader's interest by having recourse to many secondary incidents. Also, he makes the most of the rivalry between the Russians and the English and their nationalistic prejudices. Split by the hostilities in the Black Sea between their two countries, the six men of science only join forces when they are in danger from rampaging tribesmen. Common sense triumphs in the words of Colonel Everest: 'Here there are no Russians or Englishmen, only Europeans united in mutual defence!' The book may well have been written for that sentence alone.

1871-1876

THE WAR had seriously undermined Verne's confidence in his future as a writer. He had four volumes ready, but it was very uncertain when they could be published. In a letter to his father he wrote:

> Furthermore, Hetzel owes me quite a lot of money and the situation is beginning to become worrying. I'm greatly afraid that M. Thiers will not have the energy required to build a government on the ruins of the Commune. What is more, the Versailles Assembly seems to lack all sense of policy and argues about trifles like a parish pump parliament. Yet the Republic alone can save France.

To Hetzel, who was still convalescing on the Côte d'Azur, he wrote:

> You say that it must tire me to produce three volumes per year. That is very true and I'm the first to feel it. You suggest that I revise our contract in order to reduce the number of volumes due annually to two without any loss of earnings for myself. I can see your kindness at work again.

Unfortunately, an annual return of some nine to ten thousand francs was no longer sufficient, given the inflation, to meet his ever-rising expenses: 'hardship is just around the corner.' Should he not try to find another way of earning his living – perhaps even go back to the Bourse despite his earlier failure in finance? Hetzel managed to reassure him, and their contract was revised on 25 September 1871: twelve thousand per year for two volumes.

He was hard at work on a third volume to *Le Pays des Fourrures* and drafting out a *féerie dramatique* (spectacular musical play) based on the Hatteras novel, when news came from Nantes at the beginning of November that his father was dying. He arrived just in time to be with him at the end, on 3 November. To Hetzel, he wrote simply: 'He was truly a saint.' He was buried in Nantes, where Sophie Verne remained until her death fifteen years later: her world — family, friends, habits — was there and nowhere else. And she was soon to have the doubtful pleasure of the company of Michel.

The idea of extending *Le Pays des Fourrures* was Hetzel's. Verne had originally completed the novel in Nantes at the beginning of the summer. Agreeing to extend it, he nonetheless turned down Hetzel's notions as to how it could be done. 'Your suggestion is in flat contradiction with the facts of the story.'

Le Pays des Fourrures (1873; *The Fur Country:* 1873) is about an expedition sent out by the Hudson's Bay Company to establish a trading post on Cape Bathurst at seventy degrees north latitude. The expedition, which is led by Lieutenant Hobson, is joined by a courageous lady explorer, Mrs Paulina Barnett, and an astronomer called Thomas Black who has been sent along to observe the eclipse of the sun due on 18 July 1860. Mrs Barnett's motto is, 'See everything, or try to see everything.' She has been a widow for fifteen years, and is very tall and manly-looking: she exudes more determination than gracefulness. She is travelling with her companion, Madje, who is 'devoted and brave, Scottish in the old mould, a woman fit to marry a Caleb and please him.' The astronomer is a nonentity: though intelligent and quite practical, he lives in his telescope. It is he, however, who determines the expedition's position and who eventually saves all their lives.

Young Hobson duly founds Fort Esperance at the very tip of Cape Bathurst on a peninsula joined to the mainland by a narrow isthmus. Friendly Eskimos frown at his choice of site but say nothing. An earthquake occurs during the polar night; the relief ship is late; there appear to be no tides; the eclipse is partial instead of total; their latitude appears to be three degrees further north than it should be: Hobson is forced to conclude that he founded his fort of hope, not on rock, but on an iceberg that has broken loose after being joined to the mainland for centuries. Meanwhile, back on terra firma, the Eskimos nod their heads knowingly: the old legend has come true.

On the floating fort, there is no despair. Kalumah, a clever and pretty little Eskimo girl, paddles up in her kayak during a terrible storm and is promptly taken under the wing of Paulina Barnett. But the iceberg is melting! By the time it has drifted into the Bering Sea, it has shrunk from its original one hundred and fifty square miles to the size of a raft. At this point, Thomas Black emerges from his splendid isolation and contrives a makeshift compressor to freeze the rim of the raft. After covering a distance of eighteen hundred miles, the castaways finally manage to land on the northermost of the Aleutian Islands.

All his life, Verne was fascinated by the polar regions: from *A Winter amid the Ice* (1855) to *The Lighthouse at the End of the World* (1905), he returns time and again to 'these lands of night' as Hobson calls them in *The Fur Country*. The appeal that they had for him could undoubtedly be explained in psychological terms. But we should not forget that they also provided him with the ideal setting for his favourite drama: the struggle of man against nature. As Hobson says: 'I have reason to believe that they will hold out against the explorers for longer than any other part of the world. In the Arctic or Antarctic regions, it is not the inhabitants that halt the expeditions but nature itself.'

In 1872, Verne moved finally to Amiens, his wife's home town, an unlovely industrial city in the heart of one of France's gloomiest provinces, Picardy – two hours from Paris by train, about the same from Le Crotoy and an hour from Abbeville, where the fathers of religion were still attempting to instill a fear of God into Michel. Why Amiens, of all places? Verne wrote to Charles Wallut:

> At my wife's behest, I am fixing my home in Amiens – a quiet town, well-governed and level-headed; its inhabitants are cordial and literate. It's near to Paris – near enough to feel a reflection of Paris but without its insufferable noise and sterile agitation. And when all is said and done my *Saint-Michel* will continue to be berthed at Le Crotoy.

However, long after he was forced to give up sailing, Verne remained in Amiens; and it was there that he was to die.

To begin with, he and his family lived at the little place they had rented on the Boulevard Guyencourt. In March Verne was elected to the local learned society, the Académie d'Amiens. Five months later, he was present at the mother of academies, the Académie Française in Paris, to hear the proclamation of his prize for literature – greeted with thunderous applause, with Verne blushing behind a pillar.

In celebration, possibly, Honorine's daughters were married off. Suzanne, aged twenty, married Georges Lefèvre and spent all her life in Amiens; Valentine, aged twenty-one, married Captain Henri de la Rue de Francy and lived in regimental married quarters. A compact, rather severe-looking, but quite fine and spacious house was rented at 44 Boulevard Longueville.

Meanwhile there was trouble with Michel. The fathers at Abbeville confessed to failure. Verne tacked to psychology. The famous French psychologist Dr Blanche was called in. (His speciality was the treatment of juvenile insanity.) Blanche prescribed a stay at a mental institution, whither Michel was despatched late in 1873. In 1874 he was declared to be 'slightly improved'. Unfortunately the improvement did not last. A M. Blanchard was called in, the director of the Colonie de Mettray, a home for juvenile delinquents. After eight months at Mettray, Michel's condition had worsened to the point where it was feared he might go mad or resort to suicide. Force had failed again. However, M. Blanchard wisely advised that the child be allowed to live at home in order to come under the influence of his family, and the advice was rather dubiously accepted.

At a time when travelling had become so much easier and quicker, thanks to the steamship and the railroad, it no longer took much time to go all round our little planet. Exactly *how* long would it take? As René Escaich has pointed out in his book *Voyage au Monde de Jules Verne,* Verne was not the first to ask the question, nor to provide the answer: an article published in *Le Magasin pittoresque* in 1870 suggested that in the age of steam the trip would take eighty days.

Verne must have read this article; but he saw immediately that the date line made the proposed solution a relative one: eighty days for the man writing the article, but seventy-nine or eighty-one for the traveller, depending on whether he went east or west. The same ambiguity had already been used in Poe's humorous tale, *Three Sundays in a Week,* about which Verne had written in the *Musée des Familles* in 1864; and this 'cosmographic oddity' enabled him to finish his novel on a splendid coup de théâtre. (Strangely enough, it would seem that Hetzel tried to persuade him to change this last scene. 'When Fogg comes home, he finds that his clock has stopped,' Verne wrote. 'It *has* to have stopped, because it has a date hand; if it hadn't stopped, he would realize that he had gained a day and he musn't. As for Jules's idea about sending for Fogg at his house, it destroys my ending entirely. Fogg has to appear on the fatal day at the club; everyone has to be waiting for him at the club . . . But no one must suspect that he is back . . . The sting is really effective when he turns up unexpectedly at the club.')

Le Tour du Monde en quatre-vingts Jours (1873; *Around the World in Eighty Days:* 1874) gave him much enjoyment.

> I have dreams about it! I hope our readers enjoy it as much as I. You know, I must be a bit crazy: I fall for all the extravagant things my heroes get up to. There's only one thing I regret: not to be able to get up to those things with them.

Writing it, he said, taught him how different a novel was from a play. He would have it ready by the beginning of October (1872) and would be glad if it could be published in *Le Temps*. (It was, and it made a fortune for the newspaper, which more than tripled its circulation during the serialization, according to Martin.)

Around the World was by far Verne's biggest success in fiction during his lifetime. In its popular edition it sold 108,000 copies at three francs, and in its illustrated edition over three times that number at an average of around seven francs. Verne appears to have drawn no direct royalties on its sale until 1882; but serial rights, translation rights and, above all, the stage version of the novel earned him even before 1882 quite a considerable sum. (Hetzel undoubtedly did just as well out of it, if not better.) It was this novel, more than any other, that made Verne world-famous, but not until several years later, after news of the unprecedentedly extravagant stage play had made headlines in all the illustrated magazines.

At the start of the novel the members of a London club are discussing the theft of a large sum of money from the Bank of England and arguing about the robber's chances of getting away with it. Phileas Fogg is led to wager that it is possible to go around the world in eighty days, basing his assertion on an article in the *Morning Chronicle*. To prove the *Chronicle* right and win his wager, he sets out immediately with his new manservant, Passepartout. However, Inspector Fix of the Metropolitan Police is convinced that Fogg is the man who robbed the Bank of England and goes after him to arrest him. After a headlong chase around the globe, Fogg returns to London twenty-four hours late, on Sunday instead of Saturday, a ruined man. However, there is some consolation for him: Aouda, the beautiful widow whom he saved from death in India, proposes to him, and his stiff upper lip trembles as he avows his secret love for her. The marriage is fixed for the morrow. The final chapter takes us back to the club, where the members are waiting for Fogg, but not expecting him to show up on time at 8.45. At the very last second, he enters and surprises everyone, including the reader: it turns out that he was wrong in thinking he got back on a Sunday; by travelling east all around the world he had gained twenty-four hours.

As always, Verne discussed his ideas for his novel with Hetzel, who thought that the subject was a good one and suggested that it would make a better play than the Hatteras novel. In the meantime, the impresario Larochelle had agreed to stage a comedy that Verne had written twelve years earlier in collaboration with Charles Wallut: *Un Neveu d'Amérique*, which opened at the Cluny Theatre on 17 April 1873. Verne mentioned Hetzel's suggestion concerning *Around the World* to Larochelle, who immediately expressed interest. At the instigation of Larochelle's wife, Verne took as his collaborator on the new play a writer named Cadol, who was apparently hard-pressed for money.

Victor Edouard Cadol, three years younger than Verne, had his first play produced in 1864, after working for the railways and writing the farming column in *Le Temps*. From his childhood he had been a protégé of George Sand's — indeed, he formed for many years part of her odd ménage at Nohant. He was not a good writer. Of his plays, only one, *Les Inutiles* (1868), was anything like a success; and most of his short stories and his innumerable novels are puerile. Already, Mme Larochelle had contrived to get Cadol involved in the rewrite of Verne's play *Un Neveu d'Amérique*. Now he prepared a version of *Around the World*, duly registered with the Société des Auteurs, which not even Mme Larochelle's influence could pass off as anything but bad. Larochelle suggested that Verne should try again, and put him in touch with an established and successful playwright, Adolphe d'Ennery, who had accumulated over two hundred titles and novels, a collection of oriental art now in the Musée Dennery in Paris, and a sumptuous villa on the French Riviera. Théophile Gautier once said of him: 'D'Ennery is a thief with good taste.'

In January 1874, while Verne was working with d'Ennery at his villa 'Les Chênes Verts' at Golfe Juan (now the Boulevard du Cap at Antibes), Cadol wrote to *Le Figaro* claiming that the novel of *Around the World*, which had just been published, contained episodes and dialogues that he, Cadol, had written for the play that had been turned down. Verne was incensed, and wrote to the newspaper to point out that Cadol had given him carte blanche to do what he liked with the play and that in any case all the incidents, characters and situations were his and not Cadol's. Only a few snatches of dialogue were the same, barely ten sentences in the whole book.

> It's preposterous! Believe me, my dear Hetzel, I have no wish to enter into polemics about all this, and I hate to attract the attention of the public in such circumstances. But I could not have it said in a newspaper that Cadol provided the plot, incidents, characters and situations, since it is not true.

However, Cadol did not give in. He sent Larochelle 'a beastly letter insulting everyone: d'Ennery, Mme Larochelle and myself. Larochelle sent it back . . . Apparently, Cadol wants to submit the dispute to arbitration. What dispute? . . . No one has ever disputed that he collaborated on the play, and he has been paid. I don't understand.' As he always did when he was in trouble, Verne went running to Hetzel: 'I will not enter into any agreement without consulting you first. As you well know, I tell you everything, and even this deal on *Around the World* was done on advice from you.' Honorine joined her husband in Antibes and the two of them went to see Hetzel in Monaco before the publisher himself became d'Ennery's guest in Antibes. Eventually, Verne settled with Cadol for half of his share in the second version of the play, refusing to clutter his mind further with 'a mere matter of money'. Hetzel was indignant, because the settlement meant that Verne would only get a quarter of the profits from the play. 'Don't scoff!' Verne replied. 'That quarter share is still worth having.'

One may wonder what Phileas Fogg would have thought of a deal like that, he who risked forty thousand pounds to get to the end of the novel. But what, in fact, did Fogg's wager win for him? 'Nothing, unless you count the charming lady who, strange as it may seem, made him the happiest of men. In truth, would not any of us go around the world for much less?'

During the siege of Paris in 1870–71, Verne's friend Nadar had organized an emergency postal service using balloons. Sold off at the end of the war, many of the balloons toured France as fairground attractions offering ascents to those daring enough to accept them. One such balloon, the *Meteor*, came to Amiens in September 1873. Together with a friend, Albert Deberly, Verne made an ascent in the balloon, along with its balloonist. Their ascent started from the Place Longueville, near Verne's house, and ended twenty-four minutes later

at Longueau, a nearby village. To judge from an article that he wrote
for the local paper, Verne was impressed.

He had given up his financial activities on his move to Amiens.
Wishing to have some interest outside his writing, he entertained
himself with the Académie d'Amiens. It would seem that he took this
learned body quite seriously; he attended its meetings fairly regularly. In
June 1873, he read a few chapters from his forthcoming novel *Around the
World*. In May the following year, he read his play *Monna Lisa*. And so
on: the Académie was a distraction for him, and its members were useful
guinea-pigs. (At the end of 1874, he was elected its chairman.)

In 1874 Hetzel reprinted *Un Voyage en Ballon* (1856) as *Un Drame
dans les Airs* and reissued it in the same volume as *Une Fantaisie du
Docteur Ox*, which had originally been published in *Le Musée des
Familles* in 1872. *Une Fantaisie du Docteur Ox* (*Dr Ox's Experiment*:
1874) is set in a little town in Flanders called Quiquendone, a fictitious
and punning name for a place that might well be Amiens or some
similarly sleepy provincial borough. Nothing ever happens in
Quiquendone. Its inhabitants are calm, moderate, cold, phlegmatic
Flemings who take life much as it comes. The town council has only
one aim, which is to avoid making any decisions. All the same, they
have agreed to let Dr Ox install street lighting, at his own expense,
using a method that he has invented himself. In fact, Dr Ox's experiment has nothing to do with street lighting, which is merely a pretext.
Instead, he secretly pumps pure oxygen down the mains. His first
target is the theatre. The fourth act of *The Huguenots*, which began so
lento that its composer would have turned grey had he heard it, speeds
up into a *prestissimo*. The singers barely have a chance to sing, because
the audience rises to its feet, applauds, encores, shouts and acclaims in
a fever of excitement. The conductor breaks his baton on the
prompter's desk, the violinists saw through their strings, the tympanist
splits his skins, the clarinetist swallows his reed. 'This fourth act,
which in Quiquendone normally took six hours to perform, that night
lasted for eighteen minutes.' The epidemic of excitement spreads as Dr
Ox saturates the whole town with oxygen. The inhabitants, the
animals and even the plants take on a new lease of life. Quarrels and
altercations become frequent. Finally, as the Quiquendonians reach
their peak of exasperation and muster an army to attack the

neighbouring village under the pretext of righting a wrong done to them nine hundred years before, the oxygen works explode and the inhabitants rapidly sink back into their former lethargy.

This was Verne's last farce. Nothing that he wrote subsequently captured the note of extreme gaiety apparent in his vaudevilles and in novels such as *From the Earth to the Moon*. However, Verne did not lose his sense of fun until much later. In 1877 he declared that he was only half-satisfied with Philippe Gille's and Offenbach's comic opera *Dr Ox*, adapted from his novella, because it was not lively enough.

After the fantasy *Dr Ox's Experiment*, a lighweight amusement for the author and his readers, Hetzel published an adventure story that fitted in well with the educational aims of the *Magasin:* the three-volume novel *L'Ile mystérieuse* (1874–5; *The Mysterious Island:* 1875). An engineer, a journalist, a seaman, a Negro and a child, who represent the successive stages in the evolution of mankind, are involved in a balloon accident. With great difficulty they manage to reach a desert island, where their only chance of survival lies in their own ingenuity. However, they have plenty of energy and a keen sense of kinship; in this respect, and in the sense that they are at grips with the most basic wants, their little society is cast away in the Stone Age. Fortunately, Cyrus Smith, the engineer among them, is a walking repository of the sum of knowledge that mankind has acquired over thousands of years. First he obtains fire by making a lens out of two watch glasses. Then he maps the island, which he calls Lincoln Island, makes bows and arrows for hunting, and discovers clay, coal and various ores which enable him to make first an oven, then a forge with which he manufactures iron and steel for their first implements. With some difficulty, he next manages to obtain various chemical substances which include nitroglycerine. This powerful explosive is used to open up a way to a lake on a granite plateau. Cyrus Smith then discovers a huge cave with a vertical shaft through which the waters of the lake used to overflow and pour down to the sea. Here the hardworking castaways make a comfortable home for themselves, complete with a rudimentary elevator for reaching the shore via the shaft. They plant crops and build stables for the animals that they have domesticated; and the farm is linked to the house in the cave with an electric telegraph. This lesson in applied science might well have been boring, had it not been for Verne's skill as a narrator. 'The reader does not ask to be taught, but to be amused', Verne wrote in 1880. 'If you want to teach him something, do so without seeming to. The teaching has to be slipped into the action or it misses its aim.'

Strange things start to happen: Cyrus Smith is inexplicably saved from drowning and is found unconscious on the shore with dry clothes; a sachet of quinine turns up at the bedside of the dying journalist; a message in a bottle informs them that there is a castaway on the nearby Tabor Island — it is none other than Ayrton from the Grant novel, struck dumb by ten years of solitude; a pirate ship that attacks Lincoln Island is blown up by a mine in a stretch of sea where no mine should be; and six bandits are found with neat little holes through their foreheads. Pencroff, the simple sailor, says it is spirits. His companions point to providence. But Cyrus Smith infers that somewhere there is a mystery man. At this juncture, rumblings announce the coming of a volcanic eruption. Down the telegraph comes an electric message telling Cyrus and his companions to follow the wire, which they do without delay, and discover that a second wire has been secretly joined to theirs: it leads them to a crypt opening on to the sea. A boat is waiting for them at the end of the wire. They row into the crypt, which suddenly opens up into an immense underground lake, on the surface of which lies a submarine. Going inside it, they discover a dying man: Captain Nemo.

The master of the *Nautilus* reveals that he is an Indian prince. His entire family having been massacred by the English during the colonial wars, he has vowed eternal hatred and revenge on the British Empire. He tries to justify himself: 'Everywhere I have done what good I could and what evil I had to. Not all justice lies in pardon.' Cyrus Smith answers sagely: 'Where you were wrong was in believing that you could resuscitate the past. And you have fought against human progress. Some admire such errors, others condemn them, but God alone is judge.'

Nemo's last wishes are for the settlers to scuttle the *Nautilus* so as to send it bearing his body to the bottom of the ocean. Before he dies, however, he informs them that the island is about to explode, because the thin wall of rock separating the crypt from the volcano will burst under the force of the eruption and send the water rushing into the white hot lava. That is what happens. Lincoln Island is destroyed, all but a barren lump of rock upon which the settlers huddle in utter desolation, right back where they started. All their efforts have been in vain; the forces of nature have conquered their ingenuity and their energy; the knowledge of the engineer was of no use to them. The parable is clear: however great man's achievements may seem, they are necessarily ephemeral in a world whose very surface is only apparently stable. Only Ayrton, the traitor, has the strength to hope. Scanning the horizon, he suddenly notices a ship. Cyrus Smith exclaims: 'Almighty God, thou hast willed that we be saved!' Thus, it is the repenting sinner who receives the sign, and it is the scientist who defers to the universal power. The pessimistic, if orthodox, note of this novel might have affected the faith of Hetzel's readers, who *needed* hope in order to act; their susceptibilities had to be spared. Therefore, the *Duncan* sails up on her way to retrieve Aytron from his ten years of expiation, rescues the settlers, and sets off to deposit them in America to start afresh.

Charles-Noël Martin has drawn attention to the differences that exist between the four men of science depicted in the three novels that come together in *The Mysterious Island*. Nemo, as much a man of letters as a man of science, observes natural phenomena directly. His active involvement in his discoveries sets him in direct contrast with the academic Professor Aronnax. Paganel is a patient, if absent-minded, proponent of successive hypotheses. Cyrus Smith, on the other hand, is essentially a technician. Together, these four characters symbolize the various facets of the role that science plays in the human endeavour.

As we have seen, the writing of *Captain Grant's Children* and *Twenty Thousand Leagues under the Sea* overlapped with an early draft of *The Mysterious Island*. This draft was entitled *L'Oncle Robinson*, and was in fact a copy of an earlier manuscript with the same title. The first *L'Oncle Robinson* appears to date from the period when Verne was the secretary of the Théâtre Lyrique: the writing is so small that it is almost illegible. However, the later copy is very clearly written out, partly in what appears to be Honorine's hand: it probably dates from around 1866. It may have been this copy that Hetzel saw in 1870 and did not like. The story is different from that of *The Mysterious Island* and more like *L'Ecole des Robinsons*, *Seconde Patrie* and *Deux Ans de Vacances,* Verne's later 'Robinsonnades'. (His persistence in this vein modelled on Wyss's *Swiss Ramily Robinson* was almost obsessive.) Among the castaways in *L'Oncle Robinson,* the victims of a mutiny, is a woman whose husband, an engineer, is miraculously found when presumed lost, their three children, and a seaman. The engineer is an early version of Cyrus Smith and the sailor has some of the characteristics of Pencroff. Hence, the principle is the same: the castaways are forced to rely on their ingenuity, and their efforts enable them to become fairly prosperous. However, the narrative of *L'Oncle Robinson,* which Verne seems to have returned to in the summer of 1868 and 'entirely rewritten' before submitting it to Hetzel in 1870, is flat and tedious. Hetzel must have impressed upon him that it was well below the standard of his best work.

As a result of Hetzel's criticisms, Verne reworked his 'Robinsonnade' yet again:

> I am spending all my time on the *Robinson,* or rather on *The Mysterious Island.* It has been going very well, but I am seeing a lot of chemistry professors and chemical works, getting my clothes covered with stains that I shall have to charge you for, because *The Mysterious Island* is going to involve chemistry. I am taking very great care to build up the suspense due to the unknown presence of Captain Nemo, so as to have a successful crescendo – like caressing a lovely woman that one is intent on leading you know where. That, then, is how I stand on 2 February [1873].

The potent charisma of Nemo transformed Verne's early conception of the novel completely. The scene in which he dies, as anonymous and symbolic as ever in spite of his tardy Indianization (a sop to the reader's curiosity, merely), is one of the best that Verne wrote. The manuscript itself is heavily corrected at this point; and many further corrections to this scene were made during successive readings of the proofs.

The third volume of *The Mysterious Island* appeared in the first half of 1875. To finish the year, as he put it, or in other words to provide Hetzel with the second volume required for that year under the terms of their new contract, he revised the 'terrifying realistic' novel that he had written during the winter of the war: *Le Chancelor* (1875; *The Survivors of the Chancelor:* 1875).

The *Chancelor,* a three-masted merchantman, sets out from Charleston on 27 September 1869 with a cargo of cotton and eight passengers: J. R. Kazallon, the narrator; M. Letourneur and his invalid son André; an American couple called Kear, and Mrs Kear's companion, a twenty-year-old English girl called Miss Herbey; Falsten, an engineer from Manchester; and Ruby, a vulgar wholesaler. Unexpectedly, the ship sails due south, the cargo catches fire; as the crew hose down the decks to prevent the fire from spreading, we discover that the captain has gone mad; and a storm dashes the ship on to an uncharted reef. The fire is extinguished by the sea water that gushes into the hold through a hole in the hull. As the mate, Kurtis, tries to refloat the vessel, an idyllic love affair springs up between the ill-treated Miss Herbey and the invalid André. For both, it is their first, but fleeting, taste of happiness.

Kurtis manages to get the ship off the rocks; but his makeshift repair to the hull does not hold, and the ship begins to sink. Kear, the nouveau-riche American, bribes mad Captain Huntley and three sailors and takes off in the only lifeboat, abandoning his wife, who dies of exhaustion. The others hastily make a raft out of a few planks and abandon the ship just as it founders. Two sailors and a cadet, losing their heads, jump overboard and are drowned. The only victuals on the raft are a barrel of dried meat and two barrels of water. Before long, the eighteen survivors are tormented by thirst and hunger. Horrible scenes occur in which several men meet their deaths. Unable to bear the suffering any longer, the eleven people left are forced to decide that one of them must be sacrificed to feed the rest. They draw lots, and the loser is André Letourneur. However, his father manages to substitute his own name; he suggests that instead of killing him they merely cut off both his arms and keep the rest for the next days. This is about to be done, when Kurtis and Kazallon attempt to prevent it. In the ensuing struggle, Kazallon is shoved overboard. To his great astonishment, he realizes that he is swimming in fresh water. This can only mean one thing: the raft has drifted close to the mouth of the Amazon, whose discharge pushes the ocean back over twenty miles. Soon the raft reaches land. The survivors are repatriated and André marries Miss Herbey.

From the correspondence it is clear that Verne watered down the earlier version of this dramatic tale. Judging from what is left, it is not surprising that the even meatier original version made the delicate Hetzel blench. In the event, *The Chancelor* was overshadowed by its predecessor, *The Mysterious Island,* and went by virtually unnoticed. I am bound to admit, for my part, that the dramatic aspects of the *Chancelor* story once led me to attempt to put it on the stage. It was rightly objected to me that the only stage appropriate to such a series of horrors was that of the Grand Guignol, whose regular conventions of blood, gore and melodrama could alone cope with it.

Ever since the days of Peter the Great, successive czars of Russia had attempted to reinforce the frontier with Asia by conquering the steppes above the deserts surrounding the Aral Sea. Since 1865, Russian penetration into western Turkistan had become a veritable colonial war, the apogee of which was marked by the taking of Khiva in 1873.

These events struck Verne's imagination at the time he was completing *The Mysterious Island*. It was not unreasonable to suppose that the Uzbeks of Khiva might have attempted to forestall the Russian invasion by launching a previous invasion of Siberia. For his next novel, he decided to depict the adventures of a courier of the Czar sent with an important message for the governors of Irkutsk.

Once again, Hetzel took fright. Was it wise policy, he asked, to write about Russian affairs at a time when the diplomats were attempting to bring about a Franco-Russian rapprochement? Evidently, Verne thought it was. Hertzel then objected that his rebel heroine, Nadia, was not sufficiently convincing. He suggested that Verne should transform her into a kind of gipsy Gavroche — the Paris brat immortalized by Victor Hugo — with a dog trained to guide the hero in his blindness. Verne found this idea absurd and kept Nadia as she was. Her devotion to Michael Strogoff emerges gradually and is explained by the incidents that occur during their journey. The bond between them is a communion of intent before it becomes a communion of souls, and it could not be otherwise without detracting from the action and diminishing the stature of the heroes.

Fortunately, Verne kept faith in his book and once again became totally immersed in the fiction that he was writing. 'I can think of nothing else, it's so exciting — a wonderful subject', he wrote to his publisher. And again: 'I'm rushing through Siberia at such a rate that I think I'll never be able to stop.' In the same letter, he tries to calm Hetzel's fears by claiming that the novel is 'not so much Russian as Tartar and Siberian' and by suggesting that it should be vetted by the Russian novelist Turgenev, who was living in Paris at the time. In the event, Turgenev made only one objection: the Tartar invasion of Russia imagined by Verne was improbable. 'I suppose the invasion of 1870 was probable, then!' Verne retorted, putting his finger on what was undoubtedly the reason behind Turgenev's objection: his patriotism could not allow him to approve of a Czarist defeat, particularly in a region that had brought so many setbacks to Peter the Great and Nicholas I. But Hetzel had continued to have qualms; he had proposed that a preliminary note should clearly say that the work that followed was a work of fiction. Verne exploded: 'The Tartar invasion is my right as a novelist. To regard an invasion of Nizhni Novgorod as more probable than an invasion of Irkutsk is to forget the Ural mountains, it's absurd. And did I warn the readers of *Hatteras* and *Twenty Thousand Leagues* that it wasn't true?' However, to avoid what he called 'caviardages' (censorship), he agreed to Hetzel's cutting anything that might be taken to refer to the present Czar or his father. 'I wish people would read more closely before criticizing', he continues, answering quibbles about the accuracy of his facts. 'Turgenev, who knows Russia just as well as they do, saw nothing to complain about. I did *not* consult "outdated works"; I read Russel Killaugh, whose travels took place in 1860.' Just to make sure, however, the novel was submitted to the Russian ambassador, Prince Orloff, for his comments. He had none to make. Nonetheless, Hetzel seems to have insisted that Verne should water down his text still further, since when the story appeared for the first time in serial form in the *Magasin* in 1875, Verne was still complaining that they should have published it as it stood and run the risk of its being messed up later in Russia.

The original title of the novel was *Le Courrier du Tzar*, and that was the title used for magazine publication in 1875. For the book itself, however, Hetzel got Verne to agree to a change of title in line with his wish to avoid controversy, and it came out the following year as *Michel Strogoff* (1876). Less susceptible than Hetzel, or less fearful of censorship, Verne's English publishers, Sampson Low and Marston, plumped for an unambiguous combination title: *Michael Strogoff, the Courier of the Czar* (1876–7). The novel's success in France in the illustrated editions particularly was stupendous. (It is still the best selling of Verne's titles in the Hachette list.) Duquesnel, the impresario, offered Verne twelve per cent of the gross and six per cent of the net receipts for a stage adaptation to be produced at the Odéon in March 1878, the year of the Paris Exhibition. 'If I take a collaborator, I get ten per cent of the gross.' In the event, however, the play did not open until 17 November 1880 at the Châtelet. Verne wrote it in collaboration with d'Ennery. The staging was so lavish that it became the custom to describe anything fine as being *beau comme Strogoff*. Astrakhan and fur trimmings became the fashion, turning success into a smash hit. Several impresarios made their fortunes with this play, which continued at the Châtelet, alternating every two years with *Around the*

World in Eighty Days, for fifty years without a break. My father used to worry that the plays would become worn out through sheer repetition, but the huge auditorium of the Châtelet was full until the end. In September 1928 the theatre manager, M. Rolla, was still getting full houses for *Michael Strogoff.* 'The work has the same powerful effect on our audiences as it ever had', he wrote to us. However, the clever M. Lehman, wishing to free his theatre for more modern shows, persuaded my brother and myself, as executors of the estate (and very poor ones we were), to allow him to transfer the two Verne plays to the Porte Saint-Martin, where *Around the World* had originally opened in 1874. Unfortunately, the public had grown accustomed to meeting Fogg and Strogoff at the Châtelet, whose immense stage enabled the plays to be produced on an enormous scale. The transfer to the much smaller Porte Saint-Martin killed them dead.

1876-1886

I N 1876, after the success of *The Mysterious Island* and the novels and plays of *Around the World* and *Michael Strogoff,* Verne's situation was happier and more prosperous than ever before. His new contract with Hetzel signed on 17 May 1875 (which was to remain in force until his death) had brought order into the rather confused situation that had existed previously, as contract succeeded contract resulting in overlapping expiry dates. Henceforth, he would get a royalty of fifty centimes (sixteen per cent) per copy on ordinary editions (unillustrated) and ten per cent on the illustrated editions (five per cent on the first twenty thousand). In addition, he would get half of all serial and translation rights.

The percentage on the illustrated editions replaced the rather unbalanced flat fee system that had obtained previously. Since 1867, in fact, Hetzel had been publishing in November, for the gift season, a handsome uniform edition (with the famous illustrations) of the works that Verne had previously published in the *Magasin* and in the ordinary edition. For this illustrated edition, Verne had received no payment, having sold his rights to Hetzel in exchange for an annuity. The new system of royalty payments was much fairer to Verne, considering that the illustrated editions, which sold for five to twelve francs, depending on their length and binding, apparently ran to twice or three times as many copies as the ordinary editions.

As a result of this change in policy, Verne's income increased significantly. Another factor that helped his finances was a sudden spurt of translated editions abroad, from which he gathered in a share of the price paid for the rights. In 1876 no fewer than seventeen Verne titles were published in England, as the British public discovered the backlog of the author of *Around the World*; and a similar phenomenon occurred in America at about the same time. (After 1876 the flood

118

diminished. From an anarchical and farcical situation where three different English publishers – Sampson Low, Ward Lock and Routledge – were producing three competing editions of the same title in different translations, Sampson Low emerged as the publishers of what they called their 'Author's Edition' or 'Low's Authorized and Illustrated Edition'. Low published all but two of Verne's non-posthumous novels – the two exceptions were never translated – and held exclusive British rights on Verne's works from 1880. In America, Verne's publishers were diverse.

With a similar scramble for his books occurring in Russia, Italy, Germany, Poland and Portugal, Verne could afford to feel contented. Celebration seemed to be called for; and his first thought was for the sea.

Since 1865 he had spent a very great deal of his time at sea on the *Saint-Michel*, living and working on board in an existence that was quite separate from his life in Amiens and Paris. Though small, the boat could sleep, in addition to himself, the two-man crew, one of whom was 'the best skipper on the bay', and at least one guest. It seems that Hetzel never allowed himself to be inveigled into joining his friend on one of his trips around the Channel ports: the publisher preferred the blue skies of the Côte d'Azur to the gales that Verne thrived on. ('Much shaken around on the way back to le Crotoy, *very* much. But that's the whole charm of it.') On at least one occasion, Honorine accompanied him on an outing; she was not afraid, but she seems not to have cared too much for sailing. In any case, when he went off to work (or just to get away), as he did whenever he could, she doubtless preferred to stay with the children and her family. Verne did much of his writing on board. The first volume of *Twenty Thousand Leagues* was completed off Gravesend in the course of a trip to London; and this book in particular seems to have benefited from the inspiring virtues of life at sea: 'What a book it will be if I pull it off! What wonderful ideas I have had while sailing on the *Saint-Michel*!' There can be no doubt that the thoughts of his mariner heroes were his own, and that Nemo especially was a man in his own image. Hence, the importance of the *Saint-Michel* in his life and works cannot be overstated. Even though he visited few of the faraway places frequented by his heroes, he was a sailor, well-versed in sailing and broken to the dangers of the treacherous seas between Boulogne and Bordeaux.

The first *Saint-Michel*, the re-rigged fishing boat that took off like a seagull with a good breeze behind her, was the real boat for Verne. However, by 1876 she was getting rather old, and he replaced her in that year of success with an elegant new boat, more like a yacht, which he called the *Saint-Michel II*. Built by Normand in Le Havre, the new boat was 43 feet long with a beam of 12 feet. Verne's guests must have found it more attractive than the old *Saint-Michel I,* but I doubt whether it ever gave Verne the same pleasure as the converted fishing-boat. To begin with, he was enthusiastic. 'I have been absorbed in the *Saint-Michel,* which has been launched and is a marvellous boat. One could go to America with a boat like her.' He tried vainly to persuade Hetzel to come on board, telling him how charming the new *Saint-Michel* was. All the same, he kept it for barely more than a year, for in the summer of 1877, while he was in Nantes with the *Saint-Michel II,* a friend (Captain Ollive?) suggested that he should buy a steam yacht, the *Saint-Joseph,* which had just been built for the Marquis de Préaulx but was for sale. Verne was unwise enough to go and inspect it with his brother, Paul, who as a former naval officer of much experience was his most respected adviser in matters of sailing. Paul was greatly impressed by the boat, which seemed to be a materialization of their childhood dreams. This was not a boat for tacking around the Channel in; it was built for cruises to faraway places, which the brothers would at last be able to visit together. Verne was tempted. On 1 September 1877 he wrote to Hetzel: 'I've finally concluded a big deal for a new *Saint-Michel.*' In fact, the negotiations were still in progress, for on 14 October he wrote to Nantes insisting that he could not afford the asking price of 55,000 francs and would not go above 40,000 subject to trials. Yet his resistance was a pure formality since he had already conducted sailing trials off Quiberon in September; at the end of October, he was in Nantes for the sale:

> What madness! 55,000 francs! I'm paying half cash down and the rest in a year's time! But what a boat, too, and what trips in store! The Mediterranean, the Baltic, the northern seas, Constantinople, St Petersburg, Norway, Iceland, and more besides! And what a reservoir of impressions and ideas for my books! I'm sure that I will get back every penny – and in any case the boat will still be worth what I'm paying two years from now: she cost over 100,000 francs to build. I'm bound to say that your present (for that's what your payments for the continuation of the *Grands Voyageurs* amounted to) was partly responsible for my embarking on this extravagance. But then again I *need* this excitement, and I can foresee a

few more good books ahead. My brother is delighted with my purchase and was very eager for me to make it.

The 'present' referred to in this letter to Hetzel was presumably an advance payment made to Verne in respect of three further volumes of *L'Histoire des Grands Voyages et Grands Voyageurs*, the first part of which had been published in 1870 and had done very well. Hetzel was anxious to cash in on this success. However, Verne's imagination had meanwhile taken other paths and the project had remained in abeyance until October 1877, when it was decided that a research assistant at the Bibliothèque Nationale, Gabriel Marcel, would be employed to do the spade work on the continuation volumes in return for fifteen per cent of the copyright fee of 5,000 francs per volume, whereas Verne would 'edit and rewrite' Marcel's text and 'make it his own'.

This scheme had the merit of freeing Verne for more important tasks while ensuring that Hetzel & Co. (i.e. Hetzel and his son, also called Jules) reaped an ample harvest from the grain sown seven years earlier. At all events, Verne was delighted with the deal, because together with the royalties that were rolling in from the play of *Around the World* it enabled him to make the down payment on the *Saint-Michel III*. *L'Histoire des Grands Voyages et Grands Voyageurs* was published in 1878–80 (*Celebrated Travels and Travellers*: 1879–81). A similar rewrite job planned in October 1880, a four-volume history of science and industry, proved abortive.

The *Saint-Michel III* was 92 feet long, 12 feet wide and nine feet deep. Built by Jollet et Babin, later known as Chantiers de la Loire, she was powered by sail and by a Normand 25 h.p./300 bar steam engine developing over one hundred horsepower. The machine room stood amidships. Aft, the mahogany drawing-room with two divans that could be transformed into bunks gave on to the light oak bedroom with two normal beds. Forward, a quarter-turn companionway culminated between the captain's quarters, with a single bunk, and the pantry. Next to the pantry was the dining-room, with two couchettes. There was a bunk in the galley for the cook. Together with the four bunks in the crew's quarters, that made a total of twelve, or if we are to believe Paul Verne's article *De Rotterdam à Copenhague*, which mentions *six* bunks in the crew's quarters, fourteen.

In 1878, after a trial run to Brest, Verne took the *Saint-Michel III* on a long cruise to North Africa. Starting from Nantes accompanied by his brother, Paul's son Maurice, his friend from Nantes Raoul Duval (the Bonapartist politician, at that time out of office), and Jules Hetzel *fils*, he put in at Vigo, Lisbon, Cadiz, Tangiers, Gibraltar, Malaga, Tétouan, Oran and Algiers. They had a few days of bad weather in which the boat behaved admirably. Her master, Captain Ollive, was thoroughly trustworthy: he had been a skipper for twenty-five years; he was a good seaman and took no risks.

In 1879 Verne took Michel and a friend on a trip to Edinburgh and the British east coast ports. Later the same year, the *Saint-Michel* was almost lost when a three-master collided with her in a gale while she was at anchor off Saint-Nazaire. The bowsprit and the bow were smashed, but the ship did not sink. Hastily putting out lights, the crew were obliged to tack around among the sixty-odd ships at moorings in the bay to avoid further collisions, since both anchors had been cut by the previous accident. 'What a night that was!' Verne wrote to Hetzel's son, on 17 September. 'If it had been a full-on collision, we would have been sunk, and your father would have had to finish *La Maison à Vapeur* himself!' Michel, Paul and Paul's three sons were on board. Everyone had had to run up on deck in their nightshirts. Fortunately, however, the damage was not serious.

Two years later, Verne, Paul, Paul's eldest son, Gaston, and Robert Godefroy, a lawyer in Amiens, planned a voyage to St Petersburg via Christiana, Copenhagen and Stockholm. However, the itinerary had to be changed. From Le Tréport the *Saint-Michel* crossed to Deal and Yarmouth, and was then held up by bad weather in Rotterdam. Impatient to continue, they decided to make their way along the canals linking the Maas to the Schelde as far as Antwerp. They had got to Zierikzee, when the barometer started to rise and they went back to their original plan. Off Flushing they picked up a stiff but tricky breeze, rounded the entrance to the Zuider Zee and put in at Wilhelmshaven, where they were well received by the port authorities. The Baltic now seemed out of their reach; they were resigning themselves to making do with Hamburg, when the harbourmaster's staff pointed out to them that they could easily reach the Baltic, without having to go round Jutland, by taking the Kiel Canal. They let themselves be persuaded. Unfortunately, the locks on the canal were too short for the *Saint-Michel*. Loath to be defeated by such a simple obstacle, Verne 'had the ship's nose cut off': the bowsprit was dismantled, with some difficulty, and the boat got into the locks with a foot to spare. They spent a mere twenty-four hours in Kiel, where Verne saw again the enormous Prussian cannon that had rightly worried him at the Paris Exhibition in 1867, and then made for Copenhagen. At nightfall on 18 June, Verne reported a comet above the North Star; this was a surprise, because no comet was supposed to be visible in the northern hemisphere at this time. This was Tebbut's comet, first sighted at Windsor on 22 May 1881. (I am grateful to Robert Sagot, librarian of the *Société astronomique de France* for this and other information, which enable us to date this cruise definitely for the first time.) The stay in Copenhagen lasted for a week. Paul and Godefroy climbed the spire of Freisers church in Amager where Professor Lidenbrock had given Axel a head for heights in *Journey to the Centre of the Earth*. Leaving Godefroy behind to continue to North Cape, the *Saint-Michel* returned to Le Tréport via the Kiel Canal and Deal and was sent into dry dock at Nantes. An account of this cruise, *De Rotterdam à Copenhague* by Paul Verne, was published in the Nantes paper *L'Union Bretonne*, later the same year.

The voyage to Ireland, Scotland and Norway with Hetzel *fils* and Raoul Duval referred to by Mme de la Fuye and situated by her in 1880 has left no trace in the correspondence, which mentions only the trip to Scotland with Michel and a friend in 1879. However, since Verne undeniably got in as much sailing as he could, he may well have undertaken a voyage such as Mme de la Fuye suggests.

The last cruise of the *Saint-Michel III* took place in 1884. The ship left Nantes on 15 May and put in at Vigo, whence Verne wrote to Hetzel on 6 June: 'I've let all the happy band, Duval, Jules and my brother go off on a ten-hour carriage ride in ferocious heat – too hot for me.' Honorine had gone ahead to wait for them in Oran, where her sister lived. Godefroy and Michel were with her. Verne and his companions joined them there on 27 June, after a short stop in Gibraltar, where they valiantly withstood the treacherously strong punches served to them by the officers of the British garrison, for whom Verne's arrival was a bit of excitement in their otherwise tedious existence. In Oran the local geographical society held a meeting in his honour. The *Saint-Michel* then went on with them all to Algiers, where Honorine was able to spend some time with her daughter Valentine, whose husband, Captain de Francy, was serving there. Verne was a little surprised to find crowds gathering on the quay to catch a glimpse of him; but he was delighted to be able to welcome on board his cousins

Georges and Maurice Allotte de la Fuye. The former was an officer in a
Spahi regiment and had been in Verne's mind when he was writing
Hector Servadac, whereas the other was a subaltern in the Engineers
and a budding archaeologist for whom Verne had much esteem and
liking. Consequently, he was in excellent spirits.

On 10 June, the yacht moored at Bône, en route for Tunis. The
weather was so bad that Honorine took fright, remembering the recent
loss of a transatlantic liner in this area. At her insistence, Verne agreed
to go on to Tunis overland, leaving Captain Ollive to follow with the
Saint-Michel. The French agent in Bône, a M. Duportal, placed
himself at the party's disposal for the travelling arrangements. Unfortunately, Duportal was not aware of the fact that the railroad remained
uncompleted and came to a sudden stop in Saqqara. Verne's party were
obliged to spend the night at an inn that was so badly kept that there
was general annoyance. There were bugs everywhere and the evening
meal made everyone ill. Verne did not miss the chance to rant against
'this vile terra firma' on to which he had strayed through the fault of his
wife, who in addition to the discomfort had to put up with a row. Next
morning, they managed to find an ancient carriage that drove them the
sixty bumpy miles to Garnadaou, where the railroad began again. They
must have been in a sorry state when they arrived at the train station;
but to their surprise and joy they discovered that the Bey of Tunis had
sent his private train to meet them. Later, he gave them a sumptuous
banquet.

From La Goulette, the *Saint-Michel* next headed for Malta, but
heavy seas soon forced her to seek shelter on Cape Bon. The calm
waters of Sidi-Yussuf bay, which is surrounded by high dunes, looked
temptingly cool. The beach was deserted and gave its unexpected
guests the chance to feel free. Casting off the trammels of civilization,
they played at being castaways. Verne the famous writer was changed
back into the 'king of the playground' for a few magical minutes, and
went whooping and dancing around an imaginary totem pole. Seeing
this, Michel, who had remained on board, became very excited and
fired a shot into the air, whereupon the apparently deserted dunes
suddenly swarmed with angry Arabs shooting back in the belief that
they were under attack. The bathing party beat a hasty retreat to the
Saint-Michel, which sailed the next day for Malta. Off Valetta, the ship
encountered a violent storm and was in danger of being dashed on to the
rocks. Captain Ollive hoisted the pilot flag, not daring to enter the

Valetta straits in such weather without a pilot. But no pilot came out, and they were forced to weather the storm all that night. Life on board was not of the gayest: according to Godefroy, Verne even went so far as to invoke St Michel-of-peril-at-sea, the patron saint of Mont St Michel. At dawn, the situation became desperate; but the saint must have been moved, since a pilot managed at last to reach them and steer them into the military harbour at Valetta.

Honorine declared that it was time to head back to Paris. Verne, who had undertaken this voyage with the intention of writing it up into a novel recounting a complete circuit of the Mediterranean, was reluctant to turn back without having visited the Adriatic. But Honorine insisted, and Verne gave in. The sixty-odd miles between Malta and Sicily were crossed without incident. After climbing Etna, they left Catania and had a bumpy crossing to Naples, whence they went on to Civitavecchia.

Here, Honorine resolutely refused to continue the journey by sea. Having got her feet back on dry land, she intended to keep them there. It was decided that the ship would return to Nantes with the crew while the rest of the party visited Italy. All in all, Verne was quite happy with this arrangement, because he had always wanted to tour Italy; in addition, the new itinerary met with the support of the young Jules Hetzel. So they trundled ingloriously up to Rome in the train. Verne was soon obliged to abandon the incognito he had adopted for the visit. There was a grand reception given by the city of Rome, at which Verne told the Prefect things about the topography of the city that the Roman himself did not know. And on 7 July, he had a private audience with the Pope, who told him that in addition to the scientific parts of his work he appreciated its purity and its moral and spiritual value; he bestowed his blessing on Verne's books and encouraged him to continue writing. Verne must have been deeply moved. Without being malicious, however, one may suppose that Hetzel was no less satisfied with the audience, because it gave him an answer to the criticisms levelled at his list by the Bishop of Paris.

In Florence, Verne's presence escaped unnoticed. Not so in Venice, in spite of his having registered at the Hôtel Oriental under the name of Prudent Allotte. Was he betrayed by Honorine, who enjoyed the flummery that he despised? Mme de la Fuye thinks he was. However that may be, the Venetians made a great fuss of him, putting out lanterns and bunting and banners saying *Eviva Giulio Verne,* and shooting off fireworks. Mme de la Fuye's account of the festivities is correct, judging from the stories I heard as a child. I remember that Verne was supposed to have been given a crown of laurels at some reception or other. Soon afterwards, he disappeared and the party returned to the hotel in the early hours to find him sleeping peacefully, far from the fuss, with the crown tossed nonchalantly on to his chamber-pot (known as a *jules*). Similarly, he was supposed to have agreed to attend a review given in his honour on condition that he could appear in his shirt sleeves. The family thought that his behaviour on these occasions was reprehensible. Personally, I think that he must have got much more pleasure from the visit of the Austrian Archduke, Louis Salvador of Tuscany, who was a man of letters, and an artist and scientist into the bargain. From his base in the Balearics, Louis Salvador pursued oceanographic surveys from his yacht, the *Nixe*. He presented Verne with his works. Subsequently, a friendly correspondence grew up between them.

Finally, it was time to leave. In Milan, Verne is said to have studied Leonardo da Vinci's notes and sketches on flying machines. This may well have been the case, because he had been interested in Leonardo since his youth and because the plans for the first heavier-than-air machine could not fail to attract him.

The *Saint-Michel III* was the only extravagance Verne ever allowed himself for his personal satisfaction. For Honorine, however, he made several, starting with one that was very unlike him. To the incredulous Hetzel he announced on a Sunday in 1877: 'On Easter Monday, we are giving a fancy-dress ball in Amiens. Seven hundred invitations sent out, three hundred and fifty accepted. The town is humming.'

Unfortunately, Honorine fell ill. 'My wife is still laid up', Verne wrote to Hetzel. 'I'm terribly embarrassed. Her ball is due in a week, but will she be able to attend? Everything depends on her being there.' But a few days later (21 March) her presence seemed highly unlikely:

> My wife is still in bed, unable to stop the haemorrhage. She is gradually getting her strength back, but the problem is this fancy-dress ball that we're giving on 2 April, which is costing our guests an estimated 100,000 francs and which can neither be cancelled nor postponed. I'm in a funk that my wife won't be able to attend. That, my dear friend, is the extent of the mess that I have got myself into. But, I repeat, I'm not so much worried as embarrassed.

Poor, disappointed Honorine did not make it to her ball. While the
flounces and frills swirled around the Salons St Denis, hired for the occasion, Honorine remained laid up in bed. Verne received the guests
with his step-daughter, putting a brave face on things. The costumes
were original, and they included the three cosmonauts from *The Earth
to the Moon,* with Nadar playing himself.

Hetzel, who disapproved of the ball, was not there. Verne described
it to him:

> All the money spent in Amiens and Paris cannot have been a bad thing. . .
> You know why I am here. Life in Paris with a wife like mine was un-
> thinkable But if you can't beat them, join them, and I'm not sorry that I
> did. Out of the three hundred and fifty who turned up, two hundred were
> in fancy-dress. Most of the costumes made by Baron or Babin. The rooms
> were magnificent. It would have been perfect, if only my wife had been
> able to come. It was quite impossible to cancel it, because people were
> coming from outside Amiens and from Paris.
>
> My wife is very ill and very weak. It's the same illness as last year, but
> more serious. It may take her weeks to get better. I can assure you that it's
> a terrible business for all of us, her especially; but the doctors do not think
> there is any reason to be anxious.

As if shocked by his own extravagance, Verne repeatedly tries to justify
it to Hetzel:

> To return to the ball. I had absolutely nothing to do with the pictures and
> reports in the newspapers. I'm sorry that it ever got beyond Amiens. I gave
> the ball so that my wife and her children might have the position in the
> town that they should have but did not have. You know what I mean. But
> now I shall no longer be invited out alone, as sometimes happened. Per-
> sonally, I would have preferred to spend the 4,000 francs that it cost me on
> a trip somewhere!

As late as August, he was still harking back to it:

> When you live with provincials, you have to go along with provincials:
> hence the ball, which was magnificent. I knew it would give immense
> pleasure to my wife, yet my wife was unable to attend! I alone in Amiens
> could have given that kind of ball. My name, which is neutral, got together
> a brilliant assembly that no name in politics or industry could ever have
> rallied.

Things almost ended in tragedy. On 15 April, Georges Lefèvre,
Suzanne's husband, sent Hetzel an alarming note: 'Mme Verne is very

ill . . . completely anaemic . . . on the danger list.' Verne confirmed
this a few days later:

> The haemorrhage was stopped ten days ago, but she is declining rapidly.
> She received the last rites four or five days ago, when we thought it was all
> over with her. There is no suffering, she is just drifting away . . . She is
> aware of her condition, and is fighting back. But it's all too much to bear.

At long last she appeared to be getting better and the doctors were less
anxious, although all visits were forbidden. Then there was a definite
improvement. Very slowly she recovered, was allowed to get up, but
was confined to her room. Verne's first thought was for his own
favourite remedy: 'What she needs is the sea and fine weather.' The
convalescence was a long one. She remained very weak: it would seem
that there was more involved than a mere haemorrhage, more like
'decomposition of the blood' − presumably pleurisy. But Verne's optimism returned, and he wrote that a change of air would doubtless
complete the admirable work of the doctors. He asked Hetzel to advise
her to go to Nantes, where the milder climate would be better for her. It
was agreed that she should travel to Nantes alone by train, although she
was still unwell, while Verne sailed round to join her from Le Tréport
with the *Saint-Michel II*. The crossing was 'very tempestuous, but
very relaxing'. Honorine stood up well to the train journey, and on 1
December 1877 we find her and Verne living at 1, Rue Suffren in
Nantes. 'My wife is much better . . . She may accompany us to Brest
by sea. She'll be ill, but no matter, it will only take us twenty-four
hours.' Honorine did not take part in this trial run of the *Saint-Michel
III*, and it was undoubtedly better that she did not.

The purchase of the *Saint-Michel III* only partly masked a dimension
of worry that was gradually moving into the foreground of Verne's life.
Much of this worry was centered around his son, whose sixteenth
birthday on 3 August 1877 set the seal on a difficult childhood and
opened a new period of obnoxious hobbledehoydom.

In 1877 Michel was attending the lycée in Nantes, where Verne
rented an apartment at 1, Rue Suffren from 1874 to 1878. 'There is
nothing serious about Michel's conduct', his father wrote in
September, 'aside from his extravagance and his unawareness of the
value of money, which is hardly to be believed. But in other respects,
the family here have noticed some improvement.' Nonetheless, he

mixed with undesirables and got into debt, incapable of making proper use of the freedom that he demanded for himself; and whenever his family tried to intervene he became insolent and rebellious.

This kind of adolescent is only too well known. Impervious to any logic that is not his own, he skilfully surrounds his actions with facile justifications. This crisis of juvenile eccentricity with its attendant intransigence and impulsiveness is a veritable neurosis with which adults have great difficulty in coping; yet it is not serious in the long run, and may be explained in terms of the son's struggle to assert himself vis-à-vis his father. Of course, this struggle is all the more dramatic when the father in question is particularly distinguished.

Such is the opinion that we can have today, but for parents living in 1877 this interpretation would have been incomprehensible. Hetzel wrote to Michel in an attempt to bring him to his senses. Here is Verne's report on the effect it had:

Your admirable letter moved me deeply. But Michel will not understand. His vanity will brook no criticism. His absolute lack of respect for everything respectable makes him deaf to all entreaties. But with my family behind me to a man I shall act with all the energy at my disposal. And if he will not submit, he will be sent to sea for several years. He does not know that that is what he is heading for, but he will find out if he has to. With the family – uncles, cousins, everyone – working on him in this way, he may well finally understand that he must climb down. I have no delusions, however, and no false hopes, because there is a streak of precocious perversity in the boy, who behaves as if he were twenty-four when he is only fourteen. [He was seventeen.] I shall have done my duty to the end.

In the last resort, the parents panicked. Verne went to see the chairman of the county court and obtained an order committing Michel to prison until such time as it was possible to send him to sea. (Incarceration by way of *correction paternelle* and by order of the chairman of the *tribunal d'instance* was replaced in 1935 by committal to a reform school. Nowadays, the father's powers are restricted to requesting the chairman of the juvenile court for a measure of 'educative assistance'.) Michel was taken off to the town jail (according to a letter of 16 January 1878) while his father came to an agreement with the captain of a ship that was bound for India. When Michel was informed of his imminent departure, he appeared delighted. He accepted the punishment with enthusiasm. All he asked was that his father's new books be sent to him while he was away.

Verne was certainly unhappier than his son was. He did not have the courage to accompany him to Bordeaux and see him off. This job was done by Uncle Paul. Michel sailed on 4 February 1878. 'What will become of him?' his father wondered. 'I cannot tell. But the doctors here are agreed that in his present state of crisis the boy is nowise responsible for his actions. Will the sea bring him to his senses?'

In truth, the punishment was not especially harsh. Michel had been signed on as an apprentice pilot and dined at the captain's table; the voyage was more like a cruise. On 26 April the ship reached Mauritius. The news quickly spread that the son of the famous writer was on board; and that same evening one of the local planters, who could not have done him a greater disservice, held a dinner for two hundred people in his honour. Mme de la Fuye gives an account of this dinner based on information obtained from a M. de Rauville, who was present. All I can say is that my father remembered enjoying himself immensely in Mauritius. Finally, the three-master reached India. To the great amazement of the natives, Michel disembarked wearing a frock coat and a top hat. He was still joking about it forty years later.

In the time-honoured way, he pretended to his parents that the voyage was unpleasant. Unable to resist the temptation to appear hard done by and to vex his father, he sent him the following letter, which Charles-Noël Martin discovered among the then-uncatalogued Hetzel papers in the Bibliothèque Nationale. It affords a useful insight into the relationship that existed between father and son:

Assumption, Calcutta, 28 November 1878

Just a few lines today. I had begun a letter like my others, but unfortunate changes in our itinerary have forced me to tear it up and write these few words instead.

As I told you in my previous letters, the ship was supposed to be bound for Le Havre and Bordeaux. But at dinner last night the captain told us that the plan had fallen through and that we should not count on it any more. The disappointment was all the keener since our hopes had been raised previously by a more official announcement. It is very sad to be dragged willy-nilly far from one's country, one's family and all one loves. Of course, it's my own fault, I should not complain. But is it not a damnable tyranny of thought and feeling, of the mind and the heart, of all that is sacred in a thinking being? I have to put up with that tyranny without a murmur, since I deserved it. [Here, 'I no longer deserve it' has been crossed out.] But if I could break free of it I would prove through the use that I would make of my material freedom that I am worthy of moral freedom.

Let me just ask you this, in all truth: what can I do for my mind here? Instruct it? Form it? Nothing! Elevate it, then, through the contemplation of higher things? That particular phrase has always struck me as being one of the bits of balderdash that writers mix in with the fine things that they write. To my mind, it is the equivalent of the huckster's big drum: a lot of noise, but little sense. I have never believed in the emotion that one experiences in taking to the sea, the 'horror of the depths' and the 'unquieting deep'. Now I see that I was right! It's a lot of claptrap. As you know, I've always been extreme – too extreme – in my ideas about this, and a beautiful landscape leaves me superlatively unmoved. In that, I'm wrong, I admit; but I am in no wise an artist. Nonetheless, I can understand that lovely countryside, wild rocks, high mountains do something to us; but without experiencing the shadow of an emotion, we find them beautiful and that's all. In all the ten months that I've been sailing, it has never occurred to me to find the sea beautiful. When it's quiet, it bores me, because we don't get anywhere; when it's angry, it frightens me. But whatever the weather, water, water and more water just strikes me as being monotonous. The objection against this will be that great poets have found their best inspiration in the sea. Certainly not: the contemplation of what is called the beautiful strikes our eyes without reaching our hearts, and it is from the heart that poetry stems! Did Musset find the anguish of his poems and tales in some wild valley? I think not. It was in his own heart that he found the tones and the anguish that he depicts in others. When he describes, in the *Confessions*, his walks in the woods with Mme Pierson, do you not think that whether true or false it would have been just as well described if it had taken place in the narrowest backstreet of Paris? The beautiful, the beautiful: it's easy to say. But what is beautiful, what is ugly? If I choose to find something detestable that someone else finds magnificent, who can refute me? It is based merely on an opinion that is widespread, but not universal; it is general, but not absolute. But I might go too far; let us return to our muttons. My mind has no need to be elevated, nor improved; it is already over-developed for someone of seventeen. What it needs is to be instructed, and I ask you in all conscience whether that is what it will get here.

As regards my feelings, they needed this experience, but only in one sense. My heart is open to all kinds of impressions, but I needed to form my imagination a little, because it sometimes countered my affection for you. That result has been obtained. But do you really think that it was obtained through pulling levers or scrubbing decks? I've had time to think, and ten months have gone by: that's the heart of the matter!

Let it be clearly understood that there is no recrimination in all this. This voyage has been useful in the way I have just mentioned, it has let time go by without any kind of disturbance. That was all that was required. I won't even ask you to bring me home, even though I can hardly see the need to continue with a remedy once the patient has been cured. I won't ask you, because I know that it would upset you and because I know you would refuse. After all, I may be wrong, and the disease may continue for ever more; maybe the madman yet has need of hellebore! What I'm afraid of is that I will become *intransigent*. Nothing like that has happened up to now, and I don't expect it will. But who can foretell the future? Let's just hope that it won't happen. In any case, please believe in my affection for you.

Michel-Jules Verne

Much love to mother. How are you all? A mail boat leaves Brindisi every Sunday. Use it. You only need to mail a letter every Monday marked 'via Brindisi and Bombay' and that way I'll hear from you.

My regards to my sisters, brothers-in-law, Nantes, Amiens, everybody.

Many thanks to the captain on my behalf.

Love and kisses to you both.

Is this the letter that Verne sent on to Hetzel with the comment: 'I have received the most horrible letter that any father could receive'? Charles-Noël Martin thinks that it probably is. If so, Verne's reaction seems excessive. In any case, the attack on writers, and himself in particular, cannot have hurt him as a father. Michel's outburst, intended to wound, can only have made him smile; it was certainly not 'horrible'. There must therefore have been some other reason for his indignation. To my mind, that reason is found at the end of the long third paragraph, where Michel writes that his mind is already over-developed for someone of seventeen, and that what it needs is to be instructed. On the first point, Verne would not have disagreed, since he had already made a similar observation to Hetzel. On the second, however, he must have felt vulnerable. Michel's letter was 'horrible' because it brought home to him the fact that he had failed his son. He had been too aloof. His work had kept him glued to his desk, absorbed and remote, at a time when his son needed to feel an active fatherly interest in his education. Verne's only concern had been for Michel's health; and he had quite failed to realize that the boy's delinquency was a claim for concern of a different kind. It would seem that Verne was deeply hurt by the realization of the wrong he had done his son by using force to counter what was in effect an appeal for his love. Later on, much later on, when he began talking to Michel, he discovered how close he and Michel actually were.

At the end of this letter, Honorine has added:

Here is a letter from Michel. [Verne was presumably in Paris for the play of *Captain Grant's Children*.] The poor child is very disappointed, his return has been cancelled. Write and cheer him up, or I'm afraid he may slip back into his old ways. I'm still getting better, but hope that the play won't go on until after Christmas. Goodbye for now. A kiss with my love.

And she signs: H. Verne.

As we have seen, Verne tended to overreact to Michel's eccentricities; he panicked, showing how emotional he could be in irrational situations. The only antidote that he knew against sickness and worry was isolation: his boat and his work. Yet this escape was more metaphysical in its motives than material. For his next novel, *Hector Servadac* (1877), he posited an hypothesis whose implications were, literally, cosmic: what would happen if a cataclysm carried off a few acres of our petty planet into space? His thoughts turned to his cousin Georges Allotte de la Fuye, whose attempts at escape had led him to drag out as deadly an existence in his Algerian backwater as if he had remained in France. In his imagination, the silhouette of this captain stationed in Algeria blended with the idea of an escape into space.

A few strokes transformed Cousin Georges into Hector Servadac, who is swept into the cosmos along with several square miles of Mostaganem and a bit of the Mediterranean. The new asteroid carries with it some Russians, some Spaniards, an Italian girl and, inevitably, a few English soldiers from Gibraltar. They all get along well together, apart from the English, who stand aloof from the rest of the inhabitants and cling to the few remaining fragments of the rock of Gibraltar awaiting further instructions from the Admiralty. A dying scientist reveals to Servadac that the star they are riding on is in fact a comet, which brushed the surface of the Earth and took part of it with it.

The English leader is arrogant and scornful towards anything that is not English. As a result, he is blinkered; and the officers from Gibraltar make no allowance for their precarious situation. Their wilful isolation from the rest of the population leads to their downfall: the comet splits into two, and the little English colony is swept into outer space. Palmyrin Rosette, the astronomer, is full of pride: the comet that he has discovered is *his*. He foresaw its collision with the Earth, and the fact that he was right has made him exultant about the exactness and infallibility of science. Servadac saves him by a miracle, but he remains just as unbearably smug. However, his eccentricity and single-mindedness make him likeable.

A third character, a Jewish moneylender, is as much a type as the other two, a descendant of Shylock. The High Rabbi of Paris found him sufficiently overwritten to complain to Hetzel that Verne was encouraging anti-semitism, and I must say I got the same feeling when I read the book for the first time. Yet I do not think that Verne was anti-Jewish, despite the odious Samuel and Sarah's grasping old Jewess of a duenna in *Martin Paz*. Silas Torenthal in *Mathias Sandorf* is a vile Catholic; the abominable financier in an early play, *Les Heureux du Jour*, is not a Jew; the miserly and unscrupulous Patterson in *Les Naufragés du Jonathan* is an Irish peasant, despite Verne's liking for the Irish; and the Jewish diamond merchant in *L'Etoile du Sud* is a man of the highest morality.

Hector Servadac was first published in 1877 (translated 1878). Verne regarded it as being 'more fantastic than *From the Earth to the Moon*'. He told Hetzel that it was 'a lot of fantasy mixed with a great deal of serious science'. He enjoyed writing it; but it is not one of his best novels: the basic hypothesis is so unlikely that the reader suspects from the outset that it will all turn out to be somebody's dream, as it does.

The same year, Verne's readers were plunged into the dark reality of the mines of Scotland. After enjoying the amourette of Nina and Pablo on the golden-tailed comet, they shuddered with pity at the dramatic amours of Nell and Harry in the underground hell of Aberfoyle. *Les Indes noires* (1877; *Child of the Cavern*: 1877) was written quickly during 1877 and published towards the end of the year, after Verne had lengthened it; Hetzel was apparently in some haste to satisfy the editor of *Le Temps*, who had contracted to carry it as a serial.

The former 'overman' of Aberfoyle mine, Simon Ford, has settled in the abandoned mine workings with his family, not wishing to desert 'his old nurse'. He has been there for ten years when he discovers traces of fire-damp in the lane leading to the last-worked coal face. No fire-

damp without coal: Simon concludes that there are deposits un-
discovered, and calls in the engineer, James Starr. Together with Simon
and his family, Starr blasts his way into an immense cavern opening off
a natural avenue, like the Mammoth Cave in Kentucky. Rich veins of
coal run between the layers of sandstone and shale. However, an unknown, hostile and ghostly presence in the mine seems determined to
prevent its being reopened: the discoverers of the cavern are almost
killed on their way back to the surface, and once the workings are
started up again there are many incidents.

Harry Ford, Simon's son, is determined to find out who, or what, is
responsible for these incidents. After fighting off a monstrous owl
called a hartang, he stumbled across an underground lair in which a girl
is being held prisoner by her grandfather, Silfax, a former miner whose
job it was to set fire to the small pockets of fire-damp, before the invention of the Davy lamp, and who has gone mad after many years at this
dangerous occupation. The charming little Nell, his granddaughter, has
never seen the light of day, because Silfax has set himself up as the
guardian of the mysteries of the abandoned mine. However, Harry
Ford undertakes to accustom her to life up top; the two become in-
separable, and at the sight of her first dawn – a fine if rather purple one
– they confess their love for one another. Whereupon, catastrophe
strikes: the waters of Loch Katrine burst into the cavern through a hole
in the roof. Nell and Harry go ahead with their wedding in spite of warning notes signed Silfax; in the middle of the ceremony, a rock falls
away at the edge of the underground lake and Silfax appears standing
in a boat and holding a Davy lamp, shouting: 'Fire-damp! A curse on
you all!' Failing to light the gas that has accumulated under the cavern
roof, the madman leaps from his boat and is drowned.

Of course, this dramatic story is partly a pretext for teaching the
workings of a mine. Verne made sure of his facts by visiting the colliery
at Anzin, near Amiens, in November 1876. However, his initial plan
was more ambitious. A trace of it is found at the end of Chapter Nine:
'Although unsuited for crop production, this cavern could have served
to house an entire population. Who knows, one day in the constant
temperatures of the collieries of Aberfoyle, Newcastle, Alloa and Car-
diff, once their deposits have been exhausted, the working classes of
England may find their refuge.' This was the theme that Verne
originally wanted to write about, as he states in his letter of 21 March;
but Hetzel demolished it, maintaining no doubt that an underground

England was inconceivable. Verne had to make do with a cavern, but it is interesting to note that in *The Time Machine*, twenty years later, H. G. Wells used a similar idea to great effect. The sudden appearance of Silfax from behind the rock was apparently an idea of Hetzel's. Amusingly enough, Hetzel always used to tease Verne about his melodramatic endings!

Marcel Moré suggests that *Child of the Cavern* is a projection of Verne's nightmare reaction to the wedding of his childhood love, Caroline. (As we know now, the dramatic dream was in relation to Herminie.) It may well be, as Moré says, that the marriage of Harry and Nell is a fantasy equivalent of a marriage between the boy Verne and his sweetheart; but it is far from certain that in his mind this event was linked with thoughts of death. Harry and Nell appear at their wedding in mourning clothes. True; but they do so because Silfax, the only obstacle to their happiness, has disappeared. And their troth was plighted at dawn, which is the symbol of birth. No, it seems more significant to me that this love drama is set in the darkness of an underground labyrinth, the image of Verne's unconscious. Nell, a 'strange and chàrming creature' comparable to a 'rather supernatural elf', is indeed straight out of a dream. But is she Caroline? Surely the gentle Nell has nothing in common with the sparkling and mischievous girl from Nantes. Other images must have blended with his memory of Caroline to form this dream of 'a girl who seemed only to half-belong to the human race'. Are we to conclude that the love that we dream of is to be found in the darkness? 'Darkness has beauty, too', says Nell. 'If you only knew all that can be seen in darkness by eyes accustomed to its depths.' That is doubtless what Jules Verne thought, shrouding himself in the gloom of his retreat in Picardy. Did he ever encounter there the 'rather supernatural elf'? Perhaps, if *Le Château des Carpathes* (1892) is a veiled confession.

Child of the Cavern uses some of the material from Verne's unpublished account of his trip to Scotland in 1859. James Starr, the engineer called in by Harry Ford, travels from Edinburgh to Crombie Point on the *Prince of Wales*, the name of the steamboat used by Verne and Hignard in 1859, when the crossing was equally as rough as Starr's. Nell's first excursion up top is to Edinburgh, and her enlightening dawn is perceived from Arthur's Seat, with 'the panorama of Edinburgh, the New Town and the rest', spread at her feet. The phrase comes straight from the *Journey to Scotland*. The young trippers from *Child of the Cavern* stay in the same hotel, Lambret's, as the two tourists from Paris, before leaving on their tour of the lochs, which takes the same route as that recommended to Verne and Hignard by Miss Amelia, the daughter of their hosts in Edinburgh. In fact, it may well be that Verne's memory of the charming girl who inspired the tour in 1859 was the moving force in the writing of the novel of sweet, gentle Nell.

Verne took pleasure in allowing Michel to accompany him on the *Saint-Michel*. These comradely voyages led the novelist to ask himself what might become of a youth at grips with the sea, alone and dependent on his own resources. In *Le Capitaine de Quinze Ans* (1878; *Dick Sands, the Boy Captain*: 1879) his imagination set to work and came up with the silhouette of a 'fifteen-year-old hero' who joins a whaler, the *Pilgrim*, as an apprentice pilot. En route to San Francisco out of Auckland in New Zealand, the *Pilgrim* encounters a crippled vessel whose crew has disappeared. The only people on board the ghost ship are five Negroes, who are dying of thirst; there is also a dog. Hetzel, kept informed of Verne's plans as always, wanted these Negroes to be slaves, and the ship a slave ship, like the ones he had wanted Nemo to crusade against. Hetzel had an obsession about the slave trade; but Verne considered that it was outmoded both in fact and in fiction: he preferred to make his Negroes free men who had been passengers on the ship at the time of its being attacked on the high seas. However, he promised Hetzel that he would have them fall into the hands of slavers later on. In any case, he objected, the Negroes would not have starved to death in irons, as Hetzel would have liked, because they would have eaten the dog. And the dog had an important role to play in the novel.

As for the fifteen-year-old hero, Verne thought it best to warn his publisher that he would probably not be the kind of lad that Hetzel was imagining. Hetzel had a predilection for little boys of the Gavroche type; he had already asked Verne to write a Gavroche into *Michael Strogoff*, and now he would have liked Dick Sands, the boy captain, to be of that ilk. 'I'll never be able to see this little American as an urchin of Paris', Verne objected. 'I prefer to keep Dick Sands the way he is.' The boy had to be a hero. Which he is, the minute he is left on board by Captain Hull, in temporary command, while the skipper goes off in a whale boat with his crew in pursuit of a large white whale. The whale hunt ends in tragedy: the boat is smashed by the maddened whale and skipper Hull and his men are drowned. Only one sailor is left on board the *Pilgrim:* Dick Sands, who has the awful responsibility of repatriating the shipowner's wife and son, their old nurse, and the five Negroes. Not to mention Dingo, the dog, and the cook, Negoro, a very shady character. Negoro is the enemy against whom the boy captain is obliged to assert his authority. By contrast, he can count on the support of the five Negroes and Dingo, who happens to detest Negoro.

Dick sails east, towards South America. He proves himself to be an excellent seaman by bringing the *Pilgrim* safely through a hurricane. Unfortunately, Negoro rigs his compass, with the result that he rounds Cape Horn instead of reaching Valparaiso, crosses the Atlantic and ends up on the coast of Africa instead of South America. Africa: slaves and slavers! Hetzel must have rubbed his hands with glee. Yet Verne warned him: 'I'd better let you know that they are going to drop like flies in Africa.' The contingent from the *Pilgrim* are led into the Angolan interior by an accomplice of Negoro, one Harris, who maintains that they are in Bolivia. Finally, they are made captive and are forced to join a caravan of slaves belonging to an Arab slaver.

The second volume is for the most part devoted to the slave trade and its attendant horrors, which Verne described in such accurate detail that the squeamish Hetzel protested. 'I agree, it's too revolting', Verne wrote back. 'I'll water it down.' After many misadventures, our heroes are saved: Dick kills Harris and Dingo kills Negoro. Only poor Nan, the nurse, who dies of exhaustion, never makes it back to her beloved America.

Dick Sands, the Boy Captain is a classic children's novel, with a strong plot and plenty of action. Some of its descriptive passages are excellent, and many of them are instructive. The bits relating to equatorial Africa and the slave trade are scrupulously (and dreadfully) accurate, as Verne makes sure to indicate by giving his sources and by quoting an extract from an account of the travels of Cameron.

The author's position on colonization seems unambiguous. He approved of it, insofar as it tended to put an end to revolting cruelty. But he hated it when it was pursued by force, in a spirit of callous disdain for the native peoples and with the sole aim of exploiting their territory. Hence his dislike of the British Empire, towards which he remained nonetheless fairminded – he considered its civilizing influence admirable. Not that he admired western civilization exclusively, however advanced it appeared to him. 'Are those you call savages any worse than the others?' Nemo asks. And Paganel goes so far as to consider the cannibalism of the Maoris 'entirely logical', after pointing to the bravery and independence of these ferocious warriors. One cannot be more objective and fairminded than that.

While cruising in the Mediterranean in 1878, Verne amused himself with a draft of 'a fantasy in the same style as *Dr Ox*'. It was to be about a man who had himself murdered, and it was to be set in America. On reflection, he found that the idea of suicide by proxy was unlikely to occur to an American; the man he needed had to be inactive and tired of living, neither of which attributes was particularly American. A Confucian philosopher seemed more appropriate to give such a lesson, and an overly rich Chinaman more apt to receive it. He changed his setting to China, more exotic than America, and had only to write the book, with a score of reference volumes at his elbow. *Les Tribulations d'un Chinois en Chine* (*The Tribulations of a Chinese Gentleman:* 1880) was first published in *Le Temps* in 1879.

Ten years later, Verne went to Cap d'Antibes to try to turn the story into a play in collaboration with d'Ennery. It proved to be a difficult undertaking. By the end of January, the scenario was ready. 'All I have to do now is write the play', Verne told Hetzel. He did not do so until September 1890. Duquesnel asked to read it, and Rochard wanted it for the opening of the Porte Saint-Martin season in October 1891. But it was a failure, as was an adaptation presented by Claude Farrère at the Sarah Bernhardt around 1925.

In 1878 Hetzel had mentioned to Verne that he was looking for a writer to ghost a manuscript by someone he wanted to help. The manuscript had been recommended to him by a priest, whom Simone Vierne has identified as the Abbé de Manas. At the time, Verne had merely made a few negative noises; but subsequently Hetzel had asked him openly if he would be prepared to take on this job and rewrite the novel. Verne read the manuscript after completing his work on the proofs of *The Boy Captain*. He did not think much of it:

> The novel, if that's what it is, is a complete dud. There is absolutely no action, no struggle, and consequently no interest in it. I've never seen such a hotchpotch; and just as you're about to get interested, nothing happens . . . It's an utter dud. The abbé gets all excited about his new torpedo thing, but I'll be hanged if we ever see it work . . . I've never seen such ignorance of the simplest skills of the novelist . . . It would need rewriting

completely, supposing there's a subject in it somewhere, or at least one that I could deal with.

It turned out that the author of the manuscript, which was called *L'Héritage de Langevol*, was none other than Paschal Grousset. Born in Corsica in 1844, Grousset was a violent radical. During the Paris Commune in 1871, he had become a member of the executive committee; his arrival in power was marked by a purge. At the fall of the Commune, he attempted to escape disguised as a woman, but was caught and sentenced to be deported to New Caledonia. However, he escaped from internment to the United States and thence to England, where he became a schoolmaster. He was now in financial difficulties, and hoped that he would be able to earn something from writing. He was no fool; but as far as writing went he was still a beginner. Later on, he was to do quite well under the pseudonyms of Darryl and of André Laurie; his series of novels on school life did well both in France and abroad, and he was also a successful translator (of *Treasure Island* and General Gordon's *Letters from the Sudan*) and adapter as well. As Tiburce Moray, he wrote a hagiography of the English monarchy. In 1878, however, he was very hard up. Hetzel subsequently gave him much advice and large advances, but he could not envisage publishing such a misbegotten book as *L'Héritage de Langevol*; all he could do was buy the manuscript. It contained two ideas: one, the rivalry existing between a German town devoted to the manufacture of arms and a French town devoted to the easy life; two, the competition between a cannon launching a shell filled with carbonic acid and an aerial torpedo. But it was all very flimsy and theoretical, as Verne pointed out.

However, to help Hetzel and his protégé, Verne agreed to rewrite the novel. On reflection, he quite liked the basic ideas, because he, too, had been horrified by the war of 1870–71 and had been hurt by the French defeat. In addition, he could still remember his shocked reactions to the exhibition at which Krupp had displayed his products, among them an advanced cannon of huge proportions. However, the novel that he extracted from Grousset's manuscript, while voicing the general fears of German might and bellicosity, is not endemically anti-German. Herr Schultze is not reviled, but is presented as a man of great intelligence and good breeding; and Dr Sarrazin, speaking for Verne, regrets that such a man has not seen fit to join his rare intellectual qualities to the qualities of the French in order to pursue a common aim. Verne's novel is not chauvinistic, merely clear-sighted. Stahlstadt is of course Essen, the city of steel and Krupp. France-ville is an idealized garden city in which all is rational, luxurious and hygienic — a flower of culture and civilization.

Les Cinq Cents Millions de la Bégum (*The Begum's Fortune*: 1880) was published in 1879, under Verne's name. As Verne had feared, it turned out to be somewhat short. Consequently, he published it with a short story, *Les Révoltés de la Bounty* (*The Mutineers of the Bounty*).

As we have seen, Verne spent the latter half of 1877 and most of 1878 in Nantes, at the rented apartment on Rue Suffren. The mild climate helped Honorine to convalesce; and the family atmosphere was supposed to contribute to the reform of the wayward Michel. Honorine got better, but Michel got worse. Nonetheless, by September 1878 Verne's tribulations were in a state of abeyance, because Michel was away at sea and hopefully on the road to recovery. Verne went off to Le Tréport to do some sailing. (His new yacht was too big for the little harbour of Le Crotoy.) It was at Le Tréport that he completed *The Begum's Fortune* and began to draft his ideas for his next novel, which was to be about India, whither his son was bound. At the end of the autumn, he returned with Honorine to 44 Boulevard Longueville in Amiens, while the *Saint-Michel* was laid up.

Tipu Sahib, the Sultan of Mysore and a staunch enemy of the English, had died in 1799; but his son, Nana Sahib, had continued the struggle against colonization and had taken the head of the Sepoy revolt in 1857. It was thought that he had died around 1862. These events could provide a colourful backdrop to a pleasure trip through British India. In *La Maison à Vapeur* (1880; *The Steam House*: 1881), Colonel Munro and some friends set out to cross the Raj in a strange machine built by an English engineer for a nawab who has just died: a steam-driven elephant drawing two wheeled pagodas. This contraption is so comfortable that the account of the trip would have been boringly cosy, had not the author introduced a moving chapter about the revolt of the Sepoys, a long succession of murders and massacres countered by bloody reprisals. Verne gives an impartial account of the atrocities committed by both sides, ending with the taking of Gwalior, where Nana Sahib's devoted wife was killed in close combat by Colonel Munro.

In an ambush, Munro is captured by Nana Sahib's men, but his orderly, Gumi, manages to escape. His other companions remain in the steam house, which has broken down. The Colonel is taken to the fort of Ripore, where he comes face to face with Nana Sahib, who has him tied to the mouth of a cannon in preparation for his execution at dawn the following day. That night, the legendary madwoman who roams the region carrying a lighted torch makes one of her strange appearances. The Colonel recognizes her to be his wife, whom he had presumed killed in Cawnpore in 1857. In her trance, she runs her torch over the cannon to which Munro is strapped and appears likely to set the fuse alight, when Gumi suddenly reappears and sets his master free, saving him from a horrible death. The two men make their escape with Lady Munro, but run into Nana Sahib, whom Gumi lays low at the very moment that Munro's friends trundle up in the steam-driven elephant, which they have managed to repair. All ends well, except for Nana Sahib, who is left strapped to the neck of the mechanical pachyderm and is blown to bits when its boiler explodes.

The real subject of the novel is India; and Verne is careful to point out that the mass of the people was not involved in the wars that he describes, which were essentially wars of interest between one imperial power, that of the rajahs, and another, that of the British. The Sepoy revolt itself was not a popular uprising, but a mutiny of native troops encouraged by the usurped local potentates.

Verne reacted strongly to Hetzel's criticisms of his treatment of a minor character, Van Guitt. His reply shows that he was feeling touchy and discouraged:

Speaking generally now, if it is proven that the public is tiring either of me or of my kind of books, I will not be the last to recognize the fact, believe me. I'm already thinking of doing just one book a year, because I am evidently getting tired. Don't think that I'm saying that because I am vexed. You know me better than that! As you know, I am not one to go on about myself and what I do. You are aware of my very decided views on the adventure novel. It has done well, agreed; but it does not always do well, and an author will come along who will do something different and better. I am perfectly aware that that may happen, and I'm expecting it. But I can assure you that the public will be interested in the dramatic events that take place in *The Steam House*. There are plenty of them, and so far as India is concerned, the book was written with such care that things specific to that country are to be found throughout. If I am wrong about that, then I have lost my ability to write a novel.

The emotional tone of this letter, which dates from 1879 or 1880, reflects the deterioration that was taking place in the climate at home. The apprentice pilot's cruise lasted for eighteen months instead of the several years that he had been threatened with. He returned in July 1879. In October the whole family was together in Amiens. Things did not go well (4 October):

> Although his professor has told him that he can take the baccalauréat examinations in April, Michel has already stopped working. It has all started all over again: dissipation, debts beyond all reason, theories that are horrifying to hear coming from a boy of his age, avowed intentions to get money by all possible means, threats and so on — the whole scene as before. The wretched boy is revoltingly cynical. You would not believe how bad it is. Even allowing for what is undeniably a small dose of madness, he is a thorough delinquent. So long as he was working, I put up with everything. But now that he has stopped working entirely, I must act. But how? Show him the door. Of course. Then at seventeen and a half [he was eighteen and a quarter] he will go wandering around Paris on his own. The future is terribly worrying; once he is gone I shall never see him again. Ah, my dear Hetzel, I am very unhappy, it can't go on! What would you do in my place? Throw him out and never see him again. Yes, I will be forced into it eventually. I am unbelievably unhappy.

In December, after increasingly violent scenes, the charming monster was duly thrown out of the house. He did not go far. 'He has taken lodgings in town. The doctors say it is madness and not perversity.' The public attorney, the mayor and the chief of police promised to keep a close watch on him and act if the need arose. The need never did arise, because if Michel flouted the moral conventions he did not defy the law. Verne's second mobilization of the authorities seems greatly unnecessary.

Michel was quite incapable of doing anything dishonest. However, he was compromising his future by committing indiscretions of a different kind. Obviously, if he preferred to stay in Amiens rather than go off to Paris, there was a reason for it: he had fallen for the juvenile lead at the Municipal Theatre. As Verne told Hetzel:

> I had to have an interview with Michel yesterday in the office of the chief of police. He is running up debts again for the local leading lady, and has requested his legal emancipation, I suppose in order to marry her, at any rate with the intention of following her at the end of the season.

The girl was charming, and would have made a charming wife; but in planning to marry her, Michel was forgetting his own lack of stability.

> I merely said that when he had done his military service and was over twenty-one, I would see. By then this folly will surely have been superseded by another. For the moment, however, he is undeniably very smitten and when the girl leaves with the company at the end of the month, he will go with her. The only way I can stop him is by committing him to prison. I have already tried that, and it only made things worse.

At the end of March 1880, Michel ran away with his actress and lived with her in Le Havre, where she was appearing. Verne to Hetzel:

> Now that she is certainly his mistress, I do not think that he will go and get married in England, although he had the church banns published in Amiens. Debts and grievances on all sides, and there is nothing I can do. He is heading straight for the madhouse along the road of poverty and shame.

The terms used are too strong to be taken seriously. In any case, his recriminations had no effect on his son, who stuck to his guns and married the girl, who might otherwise have remained his mistress. Thereafter, Verne's interference incited the contrary Michel to detach himself from his wife and consider his marriage as something that could not last.

Verne's very moral and indignant stand was illogical from the start. While threatening his son with hell and high water, he arranged with Hetzel for him to be sent a monthly allowance of one thousand francs, which in those days was quite a tidy sum. In doing this, he doubtless believed, as many parents in a similar situation do, that his son would be kept out of debt. In point of fact, he was encouraging something that he had disapproved of; and Michel, living in affluence, had no chance to come up against the realities of life. The young couple moved to Nîmes. Probably, Michel did not care for the itinerant life; and he was never easy to get on with. At all events, the marriage began to break down. While his wife was rehearsing, Michel was playing the role of the faithless husband, riding around town on his horse in quest of another victim.

What with his wife's ill-health and his son's extravagance, most of 1879 and 1880 was for Verne a period of joyless and unremitting labour,

which at least kept him sane but which, unalleviated except by the odd
excursion on the *Saint-Michel III*, left him with the impression that
his powers had gone into a decline. Fortunately, the triumphant
success of the stage version of *Michel Strogoff*, which opened on 17
November 1880, restored his morale and his finances at a time when
both were at a low ebb. The next five years were to be relatively
carefree and very prosperous.

In July 1880 he had taken his wife to Le Tréport for the summer. At
Le Tréport, he met up again with the Comte de Paris, whose acquaintance he had made the previous summer. The two were astonished to
find that they had more in common than they would have believed:
Verne, the Saint-Simonian liberal, discovered that the pretender to the
French throne was as broadminded as himself. They took walks
together, accompanied by the Duc de Montpensier and the Comte
d'Eu, whose wife, Isabella la Redentoria, Empress of Brazil, was a
noted opponent of slavery. From Le Tréport, Verne moved to Nantes,
where the heat was such that he asked Paul Verne and Raoul Duval to
accompany him on a long voyage to the north. This was the voyage that
was supposed to take him as far as St Petersburg; in fact, he did not get
beyond Kiel.

In the meantime, he worked on his next novel, *La Jangada* (1881;
The Giant Raft: 1881), in which an entire chapter is devoted to the
geography and history of the Amazon and reaches the conclusion that
the importation of 'civilization' into these vast regions was to the detri-
ment of the native races. However that may be, Joam Garral, a wealthy
Portuguese planter living in Peru, is planning to sail down the Amazon
on a giant raft with all his family and a hundred retainers to marry his
daughter, Minha, in Belem, Brazil. Fragoso, an itinerant barber, is discovered trying to hang himself at the end of a liana; he joins the voyage.
At a stopover, an adventurer and former slaver named Torres inveigles
his way on board, just in time to save Garral's life during an attack by
crocodiles. When Garral thanks him, Torres replies mysteriously that
Garral's life was more precious to him than any other. In the course of a
secret tête-à-tête, Torres accuses Garral of being Dacosta, a fugitive
from justice, adding that he can prove that Garral is innocent and will
produce the real criminal's signed confession if Garral gives him his
daughter in marriage. This attempt at blackmail fails, and Torres informs the police of Garral's identity; Garral-Dacosta is arrested.

Brought before Judge Jarriquez, Joam Dacosta can only protest his innocence. Torres, who alone can prove his affirmations, has disappeared. Unfortunately, Benito, Joam's son, rushes off in anger and kills Torres in a fight. The blackmailer's body falls into the Amazon, carrying the innocence-proving document with it. Benito searches the river bed in a diving-suit, and eventually finds a case on Torres's body which is opened by Judge Jarriquez. It contains a coded document. Luckily, the judge is a subtle man who spends his time solving puzzles, riddles, anagrams, logogriphs and so on − like Verne himself. Examining the code, he finds that it cannot be cracked without some clue to the cipher. Fragoso finds out that the man who wrote the confession was called Ortega. Applying these six letters to the signature, Jarriquez obtains a cipher that enables him to decode the rest of the confession, just in time for him to stop Joam's execution.

The code is the whole point of the novel. Verne was very proud of it, and backed it against Hetzel's perplexed complaints that he did not understand it. 'In *The Gold Bug*', he wrote (23 March 1881) 'which is only thirty pages long, ten pages are given up to figures, and Edgar Poe knew very well that the code was the whole point of the story, and yet a man's life didn't depend on it.' He had not been as clever as he thought, however, because a student at the Ecole Polytechnique managed to crack the code before the publication of the final chapters. (Verne claimed that there had been a leak at the printers.) To please Hetzel, Verne did abridge some of the decoding process; and to make the rest of the story fill two volumes, he planned to tack on an amusing short story. But he never found the time to write it; instead, he asked his publisher to complete the second volume with his brother Paul's account of their voyage *From Rotterdam to Copenhagen*.

While *The Giant Raft* was still at press, he was already working on a fantasy along the same lines as *Dr Ox*, yet another variation on the Robinson Crusoe theme: *L'Ecole des Robinsons* (1882; *Godfrey Morgan:* 1883). An American millionaire called Kolderup has just bought a paradise island in the Pacific, outbidding a rival who is intent on revenge. Kolderup's nephew, Godfrey, has a craze for travelling and is also an avid reader of castaway stories. To cure him of these two manias, Kolderup has arranged for the ship on which he is sailing round the world with his rascally dance teacher, Tartelett, and his fiancée, Phina, Kolderup's ward, to be rigged so as to make them believe they have been shipwrecked. The wreck duly occurs just off Kolderup's newly-acquired island. Godfrey is fooled and begins putting his Crusoe theory into practice. To make things more lively, Uncle Kolderup has arranged for the castaways to come to grips with fake savages, one of whom becomes a fake Friday; there are also a fake bear and a fake tiger. But the presence of a real crocodile, real snakes and real lions gives an unexpected twist to what was supposed to be a practical joke. Kolderup arrives in the nick of time to repatriate his nephew, who marries Phina. It turns out that the wild beasts on the island were imported by Kolderup's aggrieved rival to make it uninhabitable.

The publication of this amusing trifle was followed by that of *Le Rayon vert* (1882; *The Green Ray:* 1883), which is completely unlike anything else that Verne wrote. This *roman anglais*, as he referred to it, is an insignificant love story which has none of his usual vigour. He told Hetzel that the heroine had to be young, but very eccentric and original, without being improper; and the story had to be written with great lightness of hand. He had steeped himself in the misty poetry of the Ossian poem, worrying about his intrusion into a field that was not his own, but more like his friend's. This novel, which Verne himself qualified as 'slight', avoids the charge of mawkishness thanks to the descriptions that it contains of the mainland coast and the Hebrides, borrowed in part from the *Journey to Scotland*. There is a particularly fine description of the inevitable Fingal's Cave.

Godfrey Morgan and *The Green Ray* were written at a time when Verne was temporarily sitting back and enjoying life. He had his yacht, and made full use of it, intent on making up for the two previous years. He moved to a larger house on Rue Charles-Dubois, where his wife could receive her friends in the grand surroundings to which she thought she was entitled. Life was good, expansive, secure. Had it not been for Michel, Verne might have esteemed himself a happy man. As it was, he worked away contentedly at half pressure. D'Ennery tried to infuse a sense of urgency into a plan to write a new play entitled *Un Voyage à travers l'Impossible*: another author was working on a similar project. But Verne could not get the play to work itself out. It was finally completed, however, and opened at the Porte Saint-Martin on 25 November 1882.

In the meantime, Verne had been entertaining himself with a novel with what he called 'a cheery side' to it. He had been nurturing for some time the idea of a novel that would take his readers on a complete tour of the Mediterranean. Dropping this idea for the time being, he decided to write a story with a quite different angle about a tour of the Black

Sea. He began it in January 1882. In December he was still working on the second volume.

Kéraban le Têtu (1883; *Keraban the Inflexible*; 1884–5) is the story of an eccentric who refuses to pay the low toll exacted for the crossing of the Bosphorus and goes all the way round the Black Sea in order to invite a friend, Van Mitten, to dinner in Scutari. It is a picaresque novel of no great pretensions, but it has one or two good *trouvailles*: the Kurdish widow who accuses Van Mitten of attempted rape in order to force him into becoming her fourth husband; or Keraban crossing the Bosphorus in a wheelbarrow pushed by a tightrope walker in his second attempt to get out of paying the toll. On the whole, however, *Keraban* has the same defect as Verne's rejected plan for a Mediterranean novel: it is 'in some respects childish'. Amasia, the fiancée of Keraban's nephew Ahmet, and her servant are well-behaved and puerile. Ahmet himself has trouble in giving himself three dimensions. The attack by wild boars, the encounter with the flame-throwing mud volcanoes on the Taman peninsula, the storm at Attina, the fight in the Nerissa gorges – none of this is enough to give the story some life. What saves it is the dialogue, quick and sparkling like the ripostes in a stage comedy. It is interesting to note that from the very first Verne had the intention of turning this novel into a play; from the book it would seem that in spite of himself he was doing half his work for the stage in advance. Some of the best exchanges concern marriage. The Dutchman Van Mitten confesses to Keraban that he has come on the trip to escape from his wife, after a violent and costly argument that ended in their throwing their collection of tulips at one another. Keraban, the hardened Turkish bachelor, observes that Mahomet knew what he was doing when he allowed his followers to take as many wives as they could. 'Ten wives are easier to handle than just one. However, no wife at all is even easier!' Yet there is no misogyny in *Keraban*. Beneath a mask of charm and gentleness, the 'enchanting sex' is firmly in control of the blustering male.

Keraban the blusterer is, in fact, the real subject of the book. He is not merely central to it, he dominates it in every way. He is the illustration of stubbornness, contrariness and revolt; constantly challenging the rules out of an uncontrollable will to power and using force if necessary to get his own way. Keraban is convinced that he is always right; if events prove him wrong, he flies into a rage. Verne's immediate entourage provided him with many examples of such behaviour, notably in the person of a young man who gave him much cause for concern. Though far from being a fool, he was constantly foolish; a rebel without a cause; never taking no for an answer; persistently rushing down blind alleys; ever arguing from paradoxes for the pleasure of sinning against common sense; never giving in until his wishes were gratified; yet not lacking in generosity and understanding – in short, a person whom Verne found incomprehensible: his son. That he took Michel as a model for Keraban is certainly not the case. But that he thought of depicting a mule because he was at grips with a mule is probable. Keraban's voice gives rise to too many echoes in my memory for me to doubt this fact. At the same time, I do not doubt that the process of transfer was an unconscious one, because the myriad scintillating facets of the charming monster who was my father would have enabled Verne to depict a character far more complex than Keraban.

Keraban was published in 1883. The same year, in fulfilment of his promise to himself, Verne put the novel on the stage. It was not a success. Verne blamed the failure on Larochelle, who cast it with serious actors instead of comedians. 'D'Ennery would never have agreed to a cast like that', he observed sadly. Whatever its cause, the failure came as a keen disappointment to him; he did not write for the stage again.

The novel of *Keraban* seems to have enabled him to write much of his bad humour out of his system. His next book, *L'Etoile du Sud* (1884; *The Vanished Diamond*: 1885), is a lively adventure story about a studious and loyal young man called Méré and a delightful dream of a girl called Miss Watkins. Alice Watkins is a heady combination of the home-loving girl of charm and beauty and the sharp young intellectual. It is she who inspires Gabriel Méré, a research student at the Ecole des Mines, to attempt the manufacture of an artificial diamond, which he hopes will enable him to marry her. This mutual love among the pestles and mortars has been known to raise smiles; but formulae are the sonnets of the world of science, and collaboration between a man and a woman is no base form when love exists between them. This seal that Verne sets on love should not be dismissed lightly; furthermore, Miss Watkins is the most feminine of all his heroines, and the lovers' conversation is not lacking in tenderness.

The Southern Star, the biggest and finest diamond in the world, has been stolen in the South African Republic. There is an immediate and sordid scramble to recover it: deaths, betrayals and quarrels abound. Only the pure, shining hero emerges unscathed, thanks to the devotion and intelligence of two humble 'Kaffirs' and an equally humble Chinese. This hero is Méré; and the robber is an ostrich. Méré opens its crop and finds the precious stone inside, but to his confusion the Southern Star turns out to be genuine and not artificial. Unlike that of his competitors, Méré's interest in the diamond is not governed by greed: he wants the girl, not the money. However, his land surveys proves that the owner of the diamond is an old Jewish lapidary, who has been cheated out of his lands by the father of Miss Watkins. The Jew takes possession of the stone, but noble-heartedly presents it to the young couple, to whom he also wills his fortune. The diamond finally explodes during a storm and is never seen again. The moral is clear: the value that we put on material things is a delusion, because they are essentially ephemeral. Those people who pursue them exclusively are chasing chimeras that lead them to their destruction.

The Vanishing Diamond may have been a rewrite of a further manuscript by Grousset, as Charles-Noël Martin suggests. It seems that in 1880 Grousset was working on a manuscript which Hetzel had bought for two thousand francs but which had to be drastically revised. At the same time, we should note that a letter to Hetzel which can be ascribed to 1867 mentions that Verne was working again at 'the diamonds'. If these diamonds are the same as those in The Vanishing Diamond, the genesis of the novel occurred well before 1880.

Both The Vanishing Diamond and its successor, L'Archipel en Feu (1884; The Archipelago on Fire: 1886), are relatively half-hearted affairs, and seem to indicate that the centre of Verne's interest had shifted from his work to his yacht – and, of course, to his son. Both novels are lively and very professional; but one does not feel about them that Verne is involved in his heroes' adventures, as he does seem to be in his best work. In his own words, The Archipelago on Fire is about 'Albaret and Hadjine; a girl who devotes all of the fortune amassed dishonestly by her father to alleviating the evil that he did; and a boy who is poor and makes himself worthy of her. The story is necessarily linked in the past with the war of Greek independence.' In fact, the passages about the war are the best part of the novel, and one regrets that Verne did not comply with a suggestion of Hetzel's and take the war as his theme instead of using it merely as an historical backdrop. If he had not rejected it as being too vast for his purposes, this terrible war might be better remembered outside Greece than it is. The chapter that he does devote to it is a very telling one.

Unbelievably, the translation of this book published in the Greek newspaper *Kari* gave rise to a formal protest to the French government. The Greeks took exception to a passage at the beginning of the book in which Verne describes the piratical customs of the sailors of Vitylos, a port on the eastern shore of the Gulf of Magne. The passage runs: 'If the Maniots even now, in 1884, are still semi-savages, it is easy to imagine what they must have been like fifty years ago . . . For the first third of this century they were the most determined pirates that any ship might fear to encounter on the eastern seas.' The Maniots in question were indignant, and Verne had to publish a letter in *Le Temps* in reply to these unjustified protests about a book that is all to the honour of Greece. Privately, he wrote: 'To blazes with the pirates of Vitylos! There were plenty of them then, and I'm sure there are now!'

Not surprisingly, *The Vanishing Diamond* and *The Archipelago on Fire* were only moderately successful. Hetzel almost expected as much: he told Verne outright that he did not think much of *The Archipelago*. Verne replied rather lamely that you could not astonish all of the people all of the time — or words to that effect. He definitely felt, however, that he was running out of ideas in the vein that the French call *l'extraordinaire*, and was looking for new paths within his self-imposed but rather restrictive domain of geography and science.

He returned to the big project that he had set aside in order to write *Keraban*. Ideas for this grand tour of the Mediterranean had kept bubbling to the surface of his mind while he was still at work on *The Archipelago*, with which he seems to have become a little impatient himself. He wanted to make his new novel a kind of *Count of Monte-Cristo* — a swashbuckling adventure story in the style of Dumas. But how could he keep the interest up over three volumes with the limited means at his disposal, 'without rape, adultery or heavy passion'? He told Hetzel that it was harder to do four volumes in such conditions than it was for Dumas to do twenty.

He set to work, however. The new story was entitled *Mathias Sandorf*. He was soon chafing at the bit. At the end of the first volume, he decided that he needed a rest, and was impatient to go off and be buffeted by the sea, as he put it. From April on, he was in Nantes; after that, he was at sea with Paul, Jules Hetzel and Raoul Duval, having decided to go and inspect Sandorf's projected tour for himself. 'It's not that I like the perpetual springtime down there', he told his publisher (2 February 1884). 'A bit of fog is not to be sniffed at.' The departure was set for 15 May, but it seems to have been delayed. Robert Godefroy was supposed to join the party, as was Michel ('I couldn't refuse,' said his father); but it was decided that they would meet up with the yacht in Algiers, where Honorine wanted to visit her daughter Valentine.

After this trip, which has been described earlier, Verne got down to work in earnest, full of zest and feeling restored. It was just as well he was, because that autumn Michel broke the news to him of his second elopement. He had picked out a young pianist in Nîmes, who was trying to keep her impecunious family and save up to pay for master classes in Paris. Her name was Jeanne, and she was sixteen. She could not help noticing the elegant horseman who rode under her window with assiduous regularity. It cannot have been long before they got into conversation. God alone knows what line Michel spun her with his usual brio; but he dazzled both her and her mother, though it would seem that the latter remained somewhat cool towards him. In late 1883 Michel and Jeanne ran away together. The poor girl did not find out until it was too late that her dashing young horseman was a married man. Her mother, in panic-stricken pursuit of the abductor, came running to Verne, who sent her packing in the usual way. Ironically, in the meantime he had taken in Michel's wife, and had realized that the young actress whom he had had nothing to do with previously was well-mannered, charming and cultivated. 'We all like her,' he told Hetzel. Why on earth did he not realize this earlier? If he had accepted the marriage, the atmosphere would have been very different and the couple might well have stayed together. His high-handedness had led into an impasse.

Michel, intending to remarry, behaved as if he already had. Two children were born eleven months apart, with Michel proclaiming that he wanted a dozen. Their grandfather was in despair and went to the defence of the abandoned wife, ensuring that she received a regular allowance. Fortunately, the young actress was wiser than any of them and showed proof of great generosity. Realizing that Jeanne had been even more naïve than herself, she took pity on her and consented to divorce. Michel could then marry Jeanne. Verne's anger soon subsided into a sullen glower. After all, what could he do? With Hetzel at his right hand advising him to wait and see, and Honorine at his left pointing out that things could be worse, he shrugged his shoulders and got on with his novel.

Mathias Sandorf (1885; translated 1886) goes galloping along like D'Artagnan's horses, except that instead of horses it has sleek modern ships and an array of hardware; but the pace is the same as in the stories of Dumas. Verne underlined the parentage of his yarn by dedicating it to Dumas *fils* and to the memory of Dumas *père*, to which the former replied in a touching letter that Verne was a truer son of Dumas than himself, from a literary point of view, and (the ultimate, if rather involved, compliment) that he, Dumas *fils*, had felt such affection for Verne for so long that he was very happy to consider himself his brother.

The story is long and complicated. Two villains called Zirone and Sarcany are in complicity with a crooked banker, Silas Toronthal, whose bank holds the fortune of Count Mathias Sandorf, a Hungarian exile who is plotting with his friends Professor Stephen Bathory and Count Zathmar to overthrow the Austrian hegemony. The three conspirators are treacherously denounced by Sarcany and Zirone in league with Toronthal; they are sentenced to death. Half of Sandor's fortune is granted to the informers and half is held in trust for his daughter Sava, who disappeared, believed drowned, at the age of two. Unfortunately for the crooked pair, Sandorf from his cell overhears them bragging. He and Bathory make a dramatic escape and are taken in by a Corsican fisherman called Andrea Ferrato; but they are betrayed by a Spaniard, Carpena. The wounded Bathory is caught and executed; Ferrato is sent to prison, where he dies; but Sandorf manages to swim across the Adriatic to freedom. Henceforth, his only aim is revenge.

Fifteen years later, in Ragusa, we meet the rich, famous and mysterious Dr Antekirtt, whose yacht, the *Savarena*, has put in at the Dalmatian port – which, as fate would have it, has been chosen by Silas Toronthal as his place of retirement with his wife and daughter, Sava. Stephen Bathory's widow is also living there, courageously struggling to bring up her son, Peter, with the help of a faithful retainer called Borik. The ultimate irony is that Peter Bathory is in love with Sava Toronthal, and she with him. As a further complication, Sarcany blackmails Toronthal into allowing him to marry his daughter. This marriage plunges Sava and Peter into despair; the latter is brought home with a stab wound, Dr Antekirtt intervenes: he hypnotizes Peter, who is assumed to be dead. The funeral procession passes Sava's wedding; the girl falls into a dead swoon, and the marriage has to be postponed. Antekirtt snatches Peter's body from the graveyard and restores him to life on his island of Antekirtta, where he reveals to him that he is really Mathias Sandorf; his sole aim now is to wreak justice on the three traitors.

Meanwhile, back in Ragusa, Mme Toronthal is dying. She tells Sava that she is not Toronthal's daughter, whereupon the girl is kidnapped by Silas and Sarcany and disappears. The doctor and Peter sail to Sicily on the *Ferrato*, hoping to discover a trace of Sarcany. Off Malta, they are saved from a terrible storm by a brave pilot, Luigi Ferrato, Andrea's son. Pointe-Pescade, one of Antekirtt's men, contrives to get himself signed on as a potential bandit by the Spaniard Carpena, who is acting on behalf of the Sicilian bandit Zirone, Sarcany's accomplice. The *Ferrato* sails to Sicily. On the slopes of Etna, Antekirtt's little band of hope is encircled by Zirone's bandits, but is saved by Pointe-Pescade rolling down the mountain in a snowball to alert the police. Cap-Matifou, another of Antekirtt's men, disposes of Zirone by hurling him into a crater.

The scene changes to Ceuta in Spanish Morocco, where Carpena is in prison. The doctor gets into the good graces of the prison governor and gives him a demonstration of hypnotism, the subject of which is Carpena. The demonstration is successful: Carpena jumps into the sea in the dead of night on his way back to the prison; he is thought to have drowned, but in fact he is picked up by a boat from the *Ferrato* and clapped in irons. Next, Toronthal and Sarcany are captured by Pescade and Matifou at the Trente-et-Quarante in Monte Carlo just as the latter is about to murder the former.

A letter from Borik addressed to 'Dr Antekirtt, c/o God' is delivered by the perceptive postal service. In Carthage, Mme Bathory reveals the secret she learned from Mme Toronthal: Sava is Sandorf's daughter! The slimy Silas finally reveals that Sava is in Tetuan, being held prisoner by Sarcany's devoted female spy Namir; but by the time Sandorf and Peter get to Tetuan, Sava has been removed to Tripoli by Sarcany. Mingling with the Arab crowd attending the Stork Festival, Sandorf and his companions learn that Sarcany is the guest of El Moqaddem. Pescade penetrates into the citadel at the end of a pole held by Matifou and manages to help Sava to escape. An Arab invasion of

Antekirtta led by Sarcany fails and the villain is captured. Sandorf now holds all three of the traitors. They are condemned to death by his judges and are taken to a nearby atoll to be executed at dawn. During the night, the atoll explodes when one of the prisoners sets off a land-mine while trying to escape. Sava and Peter are married and the girl recovers her fortune.

This long but by no means exhaustive synopsis gives some idea of the ramifications of this Dumas-like novel, full of twists, surprises and fortuitous encounters, some of which are rather forced. But it is the essence of this kind of literature to keep up such a pace that we have no time to be incredulous. Several of the events and settings come straight from Verne's cruise: the storm off Malta, with the brave pilot coming to the rescue; Catania and Etna; perhaps the site of Antekirtta; even the Arab attack. Sandorf is modelled on Hetzel, himself a former exile; he has Hetzel's high moral sense and fervent patriotism. Verne did not like the illustrator's notions of what Sandorf should look like: 'Benett has given the doctor a face like a convict's. It's not right at all. The young Sandorf is you at thirty-five. . . . As Dr Antekirtt, he is a mixture of you and poor Bixio [a friend of Hetzel].'

Mathias Sandorf was serialized in *Le Temps* in 1885. Before the book was out, Verne was already at work on a 'serious fantasy' about heavier-than-air flight which he expected to raise squawks of protest from the partisans of the balloon. *Robur le Conquérant* (1885; *The Clipper of the Clouds*: 1887) was the contribution of the former secretary of the Society for Aerial Navigation (founded by Nadar) to the polemic for and against the heavier-than-air flying machine. As he explained to Hetzel:

> At the present time, the question of dirigible balloons has become topical again, and experiments are taking place daily . . . I believe, or rather I hope, that all the partisans of the heavier-than-air machine will stand up for Robur against his adversaries, some of whom are vociferous; unless I am wrong, then, the book will make quite a stir.

He preferred to side-step serialization and go straight into book form.

Robur is a convinced partisan of the heavier-than-air machine, but he is neither an obsessive like Hatteras nor an avenger like Nemo. Verne had hearkened to the critics who alleged that he had started repeating himself. Robur stands on his own: he is droll, daring and cool as a cucumber. 'He is neither a mystifier nor an apostle. But that does not mean he has no feelings and remains unmoved by the sublimity of his mode of locomotion.' This attitude was much the same as Verne's own – in fact, he was over-optimistic: his novel is set in 1895, or thereabouts, whereas Ader's few feet in 1897 and the Wrights' few yards in 1903 did not really bring results until the First World War. And the modern helicopter has still got some way to go before it is as perfect as Robur's *Albatross*.

Of course, this prototype was not propounded as a real machine that actually worked, although Verne went over it word by word with his engineer, probably Badoureau, to make it sound as feasible as possible. The aim of his fantasy was to draw attention to the possibilities of heavier-than-air flight at a time when most people would only believe in the dirigible balloon, which Robur considered dangerous and un-reliable. Events have proved him right: the heavier-than-air machine has won the day. But the end of his final speech has been proved sadly wrong: 'The nations are not yet ripe for union. The secret of my inven-tion will belong to mankind on the day it is wise enough never to misuse it.'

With *Mathias Sandorf* selling well and *Robur* appearing in the *Journal des Débats*, Verne blew the dust off *Le Chemin de France,* written several years earlier, and hurried his way through *Un Billet de Loterie* while drafting out a big novel that was eventually entitled *Nord contre Sud.*

Un Billet de Loterie (1886; *The Lottery Ticket*: 1887) is a pleasant but eminently forgettable short novel set in Tellemarken. It gave Verne an opportunity to write up his trips to Scandinavia. Originally published in the *Magasin*, it was too short to stand on its own in book form; consequently, he added a short story in his Poe vein, *Frritt-Flac*, which had first appeared in *Le Figaro Illustré* in December 1884. *Le Chemin de France* (1887; *Flight to France*: 1888) is a lively tale about young Jean Keller, born in Prussia of French parents, who is called up into the Prussian army to serve against France, but who deserts to join the French troops at Valmy. The main merit of these two minor novels lies in the fact that they enabled him to fulfil his contractual com-mitments up to 1887.

In April 1885, he felt relaxed and prosperous. The big house that he had rented on the Rue Charles-Dubois in Amiens had given his wife the social standing that she felt she needed; but it would seem that something was still missing: a certain éclat, perhaps, or a dash of the high life. Whatever it was, Verne decided to throw another big party to make up for the one that Honorine had missed in 1877. This time, the fancy-dress ball would be held in their own house and not at a restaurant in town. For the occasion, it became an inn called 'The Around the World' that advertised free drink, food and dancing. Verne and Honorine were dressed as cooks. Apparently, Verne enjoyed himself; and one can be sure that his charming wife had seen to it that the caterers laid on an excellent spread to satisfy her clients.

Thus, Honorine came out at the age of fifty-five. From then on, her drawing room was a focal point in the social life of Amiens. Verne thought that it was perfectly natural that his wife should enjoy the social round; equally, he saw nothing wrong in having nothing to do with it, because it exasperated him. He always appeared at Honorine's soirées and was affable to her guests; but around ten, having shown his face, he retired to bed. Although this habit of his annoyed Honorine greatly, she made the best of it; her guests became accustomed to seeing Verne slip away earlier and earlier, leaving his wife to keep up the entertainment – which she did extremely well. He got the reputation of being asocial; but everyone agreed that Jules Verne was entitled to behave exactly as he saw fit.

His life was a life apart, centered on his desk. His social pleasure lay in taking the train to Paris for long conversations with Hetzel. After lunching together at the Café Caron, they would go to Hetzel's bookshop to continue their talk. Many years later, I heard my grandmother teasing Verne about these frequent trips to Paris: 'The part of Amiens that you know the best is the train station.' It is true that Amiens did not turn out to be the haven of peace that he had thought it would be; strangely enough, it was in Paris, which he had left because it offered too many temptations to Honorine, that he found the studious atmosphere and the intellectual exchange that he needed. His trips there were a regular thing: a cab came to collect him almost every week for the ride to the station, and met him off the train three or four days later when he returned. Sometimes he stayed with Hetzel either at Sèvres or on the Rue Jacob. But often, it would seem, he went to a place that no one knew about where he could work in peace. That place was probably the home of a friend, male or female – very probably the latter, as we have seen.

Verne's vice, his only self-indulgent extravagance, was the sea. Many years before, in 1866, he had written in reference to the *Saint-Michel I*: 'I am in love with this assembly of nails and planks, the way one is in love with a mistress when one is twenty.' Typically, when everything was going so well for him, in 1885, he took a long hard look at himself and winkled out his weakness. His cruise the year before had shown him, much against his will, how popular he was abroad. His books were selling well, his plays were packing in the audiences, he was world famous. But he had too much sense to let it all go to his head. He told himself that his situation was not as rosy as it appeared, because the more he earned, the more he spent, cluttering up his life with the impedimenta that he detested. Something had to go. Now that Honorine was happily launched into the social life of Amiens, there could be no question of cutting back on his household expenses. He saw at once that the only leak in his finances that he could plug without delay was of his own making: the *Saint-Michel III*, an infinitely more demanding mistress than the old *Saint-Michel I*. Was his lovely steam yacht worth her upkeep? His heart bled at the idea of giving up the sea. But the advantages of his ship were beginning to be outweighed by considerations of cost; and for all her horsepower she was less reliable than his old fishing-boat had been. On 15 February 1886, the *Saint Michel III* was sold to M. Martial Noe, who later resold her to the Prince of Montenegro. The price was 23,000 francs, less than half of what Verne had paid for her. She went off to finish her days in the Dalmatian waters where Sandorf had sailed. And Jules Verne, at the height of his career and at the peak of his life, deliberately turned his back on the sea.

Less than a month later, an event occurred which made this renunciation definitive. On 10 March 1886 Hetzel received a telegram in Monte-Carlo, where he was trying to reconsolidate his failing health: 'Letter from Godefroy in Amiens. In fit of madness Gaston fired revolver twice at Verne. Only one shot hit. Verne slightly wounded in foot.'

1886-1890

P AUL VERNE had three sons — Gaston, Maurice and Marcel — and a daughter, Marie, who married the industrialist Emile Gury de Faviès. Maurice and Marcel, two young blades of the belle époque, did not give him any more joy than Michel gave Jules. By contrast, the intelligent and hardworking Gaston was a brilliant student who is said to have been an auditor at the Conseil d'Etat before entering the Ministry of Foreign Affairs. Consequently, his father and uncle had the highest hopes in him.

Jules Verne was particularly fond of his nephew, whose seriousness was in marked contrast to the impulsiveness of his son and the frivolousness of his other nephews. Suddenly, Gaston's apparently level head was thrown off balance. Returning to Paris from Blois, in connection with a cousin's wedding, he took it into his head to go to Amiens. My father told me that Gaston rushed up to Verne as the latter was about to open the door of his house on the Rue Charles-Dubois, and shouted that he needed his uncle's protection. 'They're after me,' he kept saying, pointing behind him. Verne said: 'But there's no one there, Gaston.' At this, Gaston shouted: 'So! Even you won't defend me!' and shot at him with his revolver. Gaston was manifestly mad; he was taken away for observation and finally certified insane. When his father went to see him, Gaston explained his act somewhat differently but just as irrationally: he had done it to draw attention to his uncle, who was not well enough known.

A third hypothesis was suggested to Marcel Moré by his reading of *Un Drame en Livonie* (1904), in which Verne depicts a penniless fugitive who receives a large sum of money from a friend to pay for his escape. Moré suggests that this situation might parallel the one that obtained between the nephew and his uncle, and that Gaston might have shot Verne because the latter refused to give him the money he needed to run away to England. This shaky hypothesis is not very likely, because Gaston was not in need of money and because, even if he had been, his uncle was incapable of refusing to give it to him. Neither Paul nor my father, who were well placed to know the true facts in the matter, ever hinted that this might have been the case. No, Gaston was mad. The rest of his life was a long succession of psychiatric homes; he died during the First World War in a clinic in Luxembourg. In the aftermath of the event itself, Paul and Jules were immensely depressed. Once Gaston's state had become more normal, he was allowed out of the hospital for a few hours at a time; his brother Maurice often used to collect him at the home, after Paul's death in 1897, and bring him to lunch with Verne. He behaved normally on these occasions and seemed relaxed, without ever referring to the shooting incident.

More's literary psychoanalysis of this incident, suggesting that Gaston tried to kill the father figure (or the benefactor), would not hold water for a second, were it not for the very real affection that existed between the uncle and the nephew. In fact, More could equally as well have advanced a different theory based on the analogy that he himself draws between Gaston and Beethoven's nephew and would-be suicide, Karl. Like Karl, Gaston *may* have felt smothered by his uncle, not because he was over-protective but because he was famous. Like Karl, he *may* have been prey to guilt caused by his unconscious hatred of his uncle and revolt against the moral obligation to love him. But is there really any point in constructing hypotheses like these, when the facts point plainly at a persecution syndrome undetected until the attack?

The only *definite* information that we have about this attack is found in two letters, one from Paul Verne to his brother-in-law Léon Guillon and the other from Michel to his Aunt Marie. Both are in the possession of Marie Verne's grandson, Daniel Guillon. Paul's letter runs as follows:

My dear Léon:

What a frightful misfortune! I have just returned from Amiens where I saw poor Gaston, who had been taken to the hospital infirmary at the request of his uncle. The poor dear child has no consciousness of the act that he has committed. He says that he wanted to attract attention to his uncle in order to gain him a seat in the Académie — that is the only explanation that anyone has been able to get from him. The public attorney and the doctors with whom I talked have declared him totally *irresponsible*; he is going to be put in a home.

Nothing could have made us foresee such a misfortune. It was on his arrival in Paris that he disappeared. (He was returning from *Blois* with his aunt to attend his cousin's wedding.) He stopped the carriage, saying that he wanted to go to the hairdresser's, and was not seen again. We searched for him for twenty-four hours, but the first news was Jules's telegram calling me to Amiens. What a misfortune! It has driven me to distraction; and we are all as upset as you will be.

I am sending this note so that you can inform the family. I hope that you will be able to keep the horrible news from mother.

Jules is hurt in the foot – but the doctors hope that the wound will not have serious consequences; the bullet has not been extracted yet and probably won't be. He is not in pain. They are going to fit an appliance to immobilize the foot until it recovers.

Ah, my dear friend! What a cruel day! I cannot believe my misfortune!

Affectionately yours,
P. Verne

P.S. This note is for the whole family. There is nothing to hide since the papers have already spoken. Write to me c/o Mlle Meslier [his sister-in-law] at 27 Rue Caumartin, where I will probably go and stay with my wife and children.

Michel's letter is as follows:

My dear Aunt:

You have probably received a letter from Uncle Paul giving you all the details you might wish about this deplorable business. So I'm writing merely to thank you on behalf of father, mother and myself for your kind letter.

Fortunately, the latest news is not all that bad. True, he spent a fitful night, but today he is calm and the day has been a very good one. As you know, they were not able to extract the bullet. They're hoping that it will come out by itself in a few days' time, but they can't be sure. So the situation is still disquieting and serious. But I must add immediately that up till now everything has been going very well. He has no fever, or very little. May things continue that way!

If all goes well, my father will be able to get up in a month or a month and a half. But he will not be able to lead a normal life for two, three, four, or even five months, they can't tell. But that does not matter. The main thing is that he should recover.

Gaston is still at the hospital; we're still awaiting the decision of the doctors, but there is no room for doubt as to what it will be. My uncle will be

obliged to put him away in a home designated by the authorities, but he
will doubtless be able to get them to let him choose which one. The poor
man is very unhappy. It's a terrible thing for the whole family. We have to
hope that one day he will get better, as he may after all.

Please give my love to my uncle, and remember me to Edith and the other
children, whose names I confess I can't quite recall — dammit, there are so
many of them and it's been so long since I saw them that it's not surprising. Let's hope that we'll meet up again some day.

With love, from your devoted nephew,
Michel Verne

Give a big kiss to granny for me. She must be very upset by all this.

Hence, it would seem that Gaston was subject to a fit of madness that
revealed a previous but undetected mental illness, possibly aggravated
by his feeling of being suffocated by the celebrity of his uncle. There
seems to be no point in going on at further length about a family
tragedy such as everyone encounters at one time or another.

The wound in Verne's foot began to fester; the doctors gave up all
hope of extracting the bullet. While he was still bedridden, the news
was brought to him that Hetzel had died in Monte Carlo on 17 March
1886.

Verne was overwhelmed by the news of Hetzel's death. He was well
aware of his old friend's frailty, but Monte Carlo had so often proved to
be his life-line that Verne had grown used to his ups and downs, confident that a taste of his beloved Côte d'Azur would be bound to revive
him. This time, weaker than ever, Hetzel had not pulled through. Gone
was the publisher who had given his confidence in 1862, who had
guided him, sometimes restrained him overmuch, but made him what
he was — the man who had helped him, and whom he had helped in
return; what they had accomplished, they had accomplished together.
The correspondence he had kept up with Hetzel senior, he now maintained with Louis-Jules, his son. But their roles were reversed. Son
could hardly replace father, since Verne was older than Hetzel *fils*, and
had known him as a boy. Also, Louis-Jules was no writer. Fortunately
they got along well together, and a brotherly relationship sprang up
between them, in the shadow of the man who had been a father to them
both.

Shortly before the shooting incident Verne had written (25 February) a long letter to Hetzel senior, whom he knew to be ill but feeling a little better, suggesting that when he returned they could talk about a manuscript of Michel's. There might be something in it; they would have to see. Verne himself was working steadily on the second volume of *Nord contre Sud*. The relaxed tone of this letter gives little clue to the grimness of the disasters about to strike. *Nord contre Sud* was eventually seen through the press by Louis-Jules. In the meantime, Verne's bullet wound was not healing, and by June, although his general condition was much improved, the scar was still open; it was many months before he was allowed to walk again. By October he could manage a little exercise, and go to the theatre or his club. But in December he was once more forbidden to walk.

In a letter dated 9 February 1888, his sixtieth birthday, Verne declared that he felt positively 'geriatric'. His legs were giving him trouble even though the wound was partially healed. The only shoes he could wear were as big as barges; but it would seem that this did not impede him unduly, since he made plans for a trip to Paris. For the rest of his days, however, he could be seen limping as he made his way across the Square Longueville on his way to the Industrial Society, or to the town council, to the horticultural society, to the Savings Bank – or even to the circus. And yet still he worked on relentlessly (half of his output was still to be written); and in October 1886 he was already checking the proofs of *Nord contre Sud*. *Le Petit Journal* expressed interest in carrying his novel as a serial, and offered to publish a short story in its December supplement.

From then on, he devoted himself entirely to *Deux Ans de Vacances ou Un Pensionnat de Robinsons* (1888; *Adrift in the Pacific*: 1889), and this was obviously why he asked Louis-Jules for a copy of *La Vie de Collège en Angleterre* by Darryl (Grousset). This novel (*Adrift in the Pacific*) was written for the readers of the *Magasin*: a group of children encounter adversities fit to dishearten an adult. The opening chapter gives an impressive description of a violent storm. The *Sloughi*, an English schooner out of Auckland, is occupied by a group of New Zealand schoolchildren aged between eight and fourteen. The ship slips her moorings during the night; she is swept out to sea and is driven before the gale. In the absence of the officers and sailors, her makeshift captain is an inexperienced but gallant young French lad by the name of Briant, whose total crew comprises Moko, the cabin boy; between them they accomplish superhuman feats with somewhat astonishing composure, and succeed in beaching the ship on an island, where the entire troop of youngsters spend two years leading a Robinson Crusoe existence. The group is largely of English stock, the main action centering on Briant, Gordon and Doniphan, three of the older lads.

Doniphan, the elegant and well-groomed English boy, is undoubtedly the oustanding pupil of Cherman School. His somewhat aristocratic priggishness has earned him the nickname of Lord Doniphan, and his impulsiveness develops into a need to dominate; as one might expect, he is scornful of Moko, the cabin boy, who is black. Understandably, he is jealous of the influence wielded by Briant, whose gentleness, energy and highly-developed sense of loyalty have rightly earned him his position. Briant is only thirteen and a half; although quick-witted, he finds it hard to apply himself. He is fearless, practical, shrewd and alert, very obliging and obviously well brought-up, if perhaps a little dishevelled – typically French, in fact, and by that token, very different from the English boys around him. In any squabble he always sides with the underdog, and is held in high esteem by his comrades. Gordon, the American, is practical, methodical, serious-minded, and thoroughly solid. He acts as a buffer between his two friends, checking Doniphan's frequent impulses.

The description of Briant cannot fail to recall a schoolboy at the lycée in Nantes with whom Verne corresponded around 1880. This lad was from a poor family from Saint-Nazaire. His parents were separated. However, his intelligence and sensitivity impressed Verne, who invited him to spend a few days in the country with him and his family. That same schoolboy was destined to become a statesman who would be remembered as 'knowing nothing, yet understanding everything'. Even the name is the same, to all but a letter. Aristide Briand, like his fictional homonym, was the supporter of the underdog, and even if his unconventional appearance caused the odd smile here and there, his remarkable aptitude for public speaking earned him great admiration and respect. His easy-going manner made him very different from his English counterparts, who could not help but respect him all the same. He often displayed the same energy and astuteness that we see in young Briant, running the colony of youngsters on Cherman Island.

With this book, Verne persists once more in following in the footsteps of Wyss, the author of *Swiss Family Robinson*; what is worse, he merely repeats himself. *Adrift in the Pacific* reads like a rewrite of *Godfrey Morgan*, which itself is merely a feeble avatar of *The Mysterious Island*. His lack of inspiration is understandable if one considers his state of mind at that time. Added to the problems already mentioned, he was having to cope with yet another harsh loss; it seems that his old friend in Asnières died before Hetzel. It is difficult to pinpoint the exact date of her death, but it must have been around 1885, since Verne states in a letter to Hetzel at this time: 'You are aware of my sorrow.' After her death, which was a great blow to Verne, it was revealed that she had left him everything she owned. However, he declined the legacy.

Verne had entered what he called his 'black period', but he refused to let it get the better of him, obstinately working on. The 'black period' continued into 1887; his mother's death in February of that year added to his grief. Since he was now confined to the house, he could not be with her at the end, nor even attend the funeral, so Honorine went to Nantes alone. His mother's death broke 'the last link in the long family chain'. Verne owed her so much – not least, her love and encouragement when he moved from Nantes to Paris as a would-be writer. Throughout her life, it was Sophie who had provided her family manifestly with the emotional warmth that the ascetic catholic Pierre had difficulty in showing. Their difference of tone is apparent from the invaluable photograph taken in Provins *c.* 1861 and reproduced in the present work: Pierre Verne stands somewhat stern but kind in the background while Sophie peeks mischievously over the shoulder of Henri Garcet's little boy – and Jules plays the fool right at the back. Without Sophie, and with only Pierre, there can be no doubt that Jules Verne would have had less scope for clowning. As things were, his character as he aged grew away from Sophie and closer to Pierre, whose brand of dark seriousness coupled with an ironical mind dominates the later works of his son.

Verne completed *Nord contre Sud*, the novel he had begun before Hetzel's death, attempting through his work to banish all thoughts of the grey years ahead. Working on this novel enabled him to renew his acquaintance with the history of the American War of Secession, which had always fascinated him; and he escaped into his story of a pair of villainous twins who use their easily confused identities to win profit from war. The War of Secession, securing the triumph of the abolitionists and the formation of the United States of America, had ended a mere twenty years previously; the problem of slavery had been resolved, in theory, if not in practice, outside the United States. Nowadays we think of the slave trade as a thing of the past; in 1885 it was still very topical.

Nord contre Sud (1887; *North against South*: 1888) marks a renewal of vigour on Verne's part. The story provides as much drama as one could wish for. The story opens on a Southern farm, focusing on its owner, James Burbank, an abolitionist. Texar, a former slaver, is a 'dangerous evilmonger', working in his own interests rather than in those of the South. James Burbank's farm is ransacked, not by the Secessionist army, but by a 'mob of evilmongers of the worst kind' led by Texar. We are told throughout that the Texar brothers were hardened criminals long before the outbreak of war, which merely provides them with an opportunity to profiteer. Verne's apparently indulgent attitude towards the South was criticized at the time and has been attacked since. However, it is unfair to suggest that he condoned slavery. And to allege that he was racially prejudiced, simply because he has a slave-master say to an indolent young Negro that equality is more than a matter of colour and freedom, is manifestly absurd.

The controversy provoked by *North against South* proves that Verne had recovered his inspiration and vigour, a recovery which is apparent in his other activities also. He agreed to let William Burnach, the co-author of the stage version of *Mathias Sandorf*, do an adaptation of *Flight to France* and even worked on the scenario, although he could not believe that the play would ever find an audience 'in the current mood of national indifference'. He was more confident, however, in plans to adapt *North against South*; he thought that the play would need to have some comic relief written into it. He was also hoping (3 August 1887) that Rochard's production of *Mathias Sandorf* would be a success; he was convinced that the play would go well and above all that it would sharpen the focus on his name – a focus that was dimming daily.

However, a programme of public readings – his first and last – in Belgium and Holland prevented him from attending the première. On 20 November 1887, very unsteady on his legs, he left for Antwerp, returning on 1 December. He felt that his tour had been a great success; everywhere he went, the lecture halls were packed. The newspaper *L'Indépendence Belge* endorsed this, but not so *Le Figaro*. According to Cornelius Helling, in an article in the *Bulletin, Le Figaro* was right;

Verne read well, but he restricted himself to reading short stories of little consequence, and the adventures of *La Famille Raton* (1890) did not come up to his listeners' expectations.

At least he was not allowing himself to be beaten. Despite his crippled leg and his half-healed wound, he worked feverishly to counteract his sadness. He spent December in Antibes, working once again with d'Ennery on the dramatization of *The Tribulations of a Chinese Gentleman*. He found little to distract him when he was not working, since the most beautiful place on earth, as he called it, could offer nothing but torrential wind and rain.

By this stage in his life, Verne had begun to mellow. He became much closer to Michel, who lived in Paris and spent much of his time at the literary café *Le chat noir*. Michel's new wife, intelligent and clear-headed, encouraged him, but refused to allow him to use literature as a smoke-screen for an easy life. She knew how weak he was. She watched him, advised him, guided him. Under her influence he who had refused to work started to study, and showed himself to be intelligent, with a good memory and an easy assimilation of facts. Intellectually curious, he took an interest in everything. Since his wife was a musician, he studied harmony and even wrote an opera, which, however bad it was, could at least be played by an orchestra – and was, or so I was told. Slowly but surely, Jeanne brought him on to an even keel, refusing to let him impress her with his rages, which had been his main weapon until then. Jeanne gave him a home. His children got a proper upbringing. Verne let out a sigh of relief and blessed the woman who had tackled his untameable son and tamed him. In 1887 he finally recognized Michel's second marriage, and increased his allowance. In 1888 he established contact with Michel's wife, whom he found fascinating; it was refreshing to meet so much intelligence and common sense in such a compact little person. He was particularly charmed by her patience, and realized that between them they provided Michel with something of a stabilizing influence. This marked the beginning of a long and real friendship which grew over the years. One might add that Verne's passion for music predisposed him to fall for her. Like Sophie, all of his favourite women were actively musical – except Honorine. In particular, it would seem that Herminie was a talented musician.

Whilst working on *Famille sans Nom* (1889; *A Family Without a Name*: 1890) Verne wrote to Louis-Jules: 'I think our Jean [the hero of the novel] should remain nameless. Jean and Jeanne go well together, and I am very reluctant to change it.' But he was evidently obliged to do so, since Mademoiselle de Vaudreuil was not called Jeanne, but Clary.

Family Without a Name is set in Canada. For his facts, Verne read Réveillaud, and went to the Biliothèque Nationale to consult Garneau. He studied a paper by J. W. Carrié, and dipped into Russell. He quoted all these authors freely, thus giving his readers a thorough background history of Canada and the Quebec problem, which is still unresolved today.

Opinion is divided as to the value of this book; some have found it tedious – a surprising judgment, since its style is very much that of Fennimore Cooper. Younger readers are invariably enthralled by the dramatic exploits of its mysterious anonymous hero. The sceptical adult reader tends to see through the mystery fairly quickly, but can still respond to the description of the blind fury of the mob and the extremes of the repression, not to mention the documentary interest of the book.

Verne, totally involved in his historical novel and in Canada, was struck once more by an idea he had touched on in *From the Earth to the Moon*. His Amiens friend Badoureau, a mining engineer and gifted mathematician, suggested a subject backed up with research of gargantuan proportions – a series of calculations testing the hypothesis propounded by Maston, the mathematician in the earlier novel, about shifting the earth's axis. Verne bought Badoureau's work for 2,500 francs. He was 'overawed yet bursting with enthusiasm', he wrote to Louis-Jules on 18 April 1888. Not wanting to take credit for someone else's work, he insisted on Badoureau's research appearing at the end of the novel. Badoureau himself is depicted in the novel as Alcide Pierdeux.

Twenty years on, we are reintroduced to the members of the Gun Club. This time, Barbicane and Nicholl are purely instrumental; the protagonist is J. T. Maston, who comes across as a far more serious character than he was in *From The Earth to the Moon*. Barbicane and Co. have bought the northern polar ice cap, where coal deposits have been discovered. Since Mahomet cannot come to the pole, so to speak, the pole must come to Mahomet: the earth's axis wil be shifted to make it perpendicular, as a result of which the whole world will happily enjoy a temperate climate, and all the seasons of the year will melt into one. Since Maston is responsible for these calculations, no one doubts that the project will succeed. Barbicane and Co. tunnel into the side of Mount Kilimanjaro to house a gigantic cannon. From this cannon will be fired, due south, a shell weighing 400 million pounds. The recoil from the shot will flip the earth sideways and correct its axis.

The experiment takes place, but fails dismally, since Maston loses his concentration during a clap of thunder just as he is writing the number 40000000 on the blackboard, this being the earth's circumference in metres, and leaves off three noughts. He would need a trillion cannons the strength of the one inside Kilimanjaro to correct the earth's axis, and the earth's surface is not large enough to hold them all. The point that Verne is making is obvious: any interference with the balance of nature is bound to be harmful; by playing the sorcerer's apprentice, man is his own worst enemy.

By October 1888 Verne had provided Hetzel with *A Family Without a Name* and with the novel just described, which was called *Sans Dessus Dessous* (1889; *Purchase of the North Pole*: 1891). Verne informed his publisher that he had several ideas for his next book, due in 1890, a *Voyage à Reculons*, which would take place in North America and Siberia. At this time he was also working with d'Ennery on the play of *Tribulations of a Chinaman*. 'What would become of me, in heaven's name, if I didn't work six or seven hours a day?' he wrote to Jules Hetzel.

It seems indeed that he was trying to take his mind off things by taking on more and more work. At the municipal elections held in Amiens in May 1888, one of the candidates was none other than Jules Verne. There were two main electoral lists: the Conservative Unionists, led by Verne's lawyer friend Albert Deberly, and the Conservative Republicans headed by a velvet manufacturer called Frédédric Petit. There was little to distinguish between them: both were essentially middle-of-the-road parties, the former slightly to the right, the latter very slightly to the left.

Verne's interest in the town council originated with his close friend Robert Godefroy, an Amiens lawyer twenty years his junior, whose name crops up frequently in the Verne papers in the 1880s, and who took part in two of the cruises of the *Saint-Michel III*. He wrote to Petit in support of Verne's wish to stand on his list. In his letter, published by Daniel Compère in an excellent article in *L'Herne* (1974),

Godefroy leans over backwards to stress Verne's republican principles and to whitewash his associations with the Orléanists in Le Tréport.

In fact, it is clear from Verne's correspondence that he did not see the elections in a political light at all, and he said as much in a letter published in both of the Amiens papers after the first round of voting (in which he failed to secure the majority needed for outright election): 'I belong to the Conservative party; in spite of my conservative principles I joined the mayor's list with the sole aim of serving my city.' Writing to his childhood friend Charles Maisonneuve, Verne gave similar reasons for standing: he wished to be useful and to be instrumental in urban reform; his tastes were for law, life-enhancing; he was no party man.

In the second poll, Verne scraped in with 8,591 votes out of a total of 14,000. He was re-elected with a more comfortable margin in 1892, 1896 and 1900. In all, his mandate lasted for six years; and he rarely missed a meeting. He immediately became vice-chairman of the fourth committee (education, fine arts, museums, theatre, fairs and street-names). Owing to his prestige, he was put in charge of the theatre, which he attended every evening except Wednesday (Honorine's 'at home' day) alone or with his wife, always leaving before the end of the performance in order to be in bed by ten. Unimpressed by the standard of many of the shows, he tried to introduce comic operas by Bizet, Délibes and Massenet (shades of the Théâtre Lyrique!); but attendances fell off, and he was obliged to admit in his annual report that the public appeared to prefer Barnum to Bizet, referring to the indoor circus, which he had opened on 23 June 1889, and which he ran as well.

L'Ile à hélice (1895) is to a great extent a reflection of party politics in Amiens as Verne witnessed them on the town council, as we shall see. In the meantime, his activities on the fourth committee brought him into contact with all home comforts. Most of his speeches on the council were concerned with town improvements: building projects, electric lighting instead of gas, street widening, and so on. (As we shall see, *Une Ville Idéale* dating from 1875 is an amusing send-up of the absurdities of planning in the Amiens of his day.) He rarely intervened on political issues, in line with his declared intentions before the electorate in 1888; when he did so, his remarks were generally anti-Union and pro-Catholic, as in his refusal to vote for a subsidy to striking miners and his proposition of a vote of thanks to the police after a skirmish at a Catholic rally. (A group of 'anarchists' tried to break up the rally by singing the *Internationale*; but it would seem that the police hit both sides.)

Verne's interest in the Amiens circus reflects a secret admiration for itinerants, whose way of life he doubtless envied. He had already depicted travelling showmen in *Mathias Sandorf*; his novel *César Cascabel* (1890; translated 1891) is the story of an itinerant circus family who travel by caravan from Sacramento to Normandy by way of the western United States, Alaska, the Bering Straits, Siberia and Russia. Written for the *Magasin*, it is rather dull; but there is a delightful Indian girl in it called Kayete.

In the period that we are discussing (1886 to 1890) Verne was desperately fighting against depression, and this is reflected in the consistently mediocre standard of his work at this time. However, things brightened up for him from 1889 on, and he tried to forget his grief. As he says in the words of the gallant Father Rat in *La Famille Raton*, a short story which appeared in the Christmas edition of *Le Figaro Illustré*: 'We have to be philosophical about these things. For my part, as long as I can still work, I am not complaining.'

Hetzel *fils* was encountering problems on the publishing side. The public, it seemed, no longer wanted to read. Verne disagreed, but felt that the drop in sales of full-length novels was due to the plethora of novelettes on the market. He adds (19 November 1890): 'I am disappointed, if only for the few remaining works that I have still to write to complete my own vision of the world in novel form.'

With Michel, who brought Jeanne to visit him in Amiens in 1888, he wrote *In The Year 2889* (1889) for publication in America. He set aside *Le Château des Carpathes* – a very strange novel indeed, as we shall see – for publication in 1891 and set to work on one of his liveliest later works, *Mistress Branican* (1891; translated 1892). As a member of the Amiens Dickens Society, he felt justified in using the word 'mistress' in the title, in spite of unfortunate overtones that, he learned from Hetzel, the word had come to acquire. 'Dickens uses it often,' he objected sadly.

The novel opens with a description of the *Franklin*, a triple-masted sloop out of San Diego, captained by John Branican, bound for Calcutta by way of Singapore. Waiting for John's return are his wife Dolly and their infant child, Wat. Wat dies tragically, as a result of which Dolly goes mad. Time goes by, and there is still no news of the *Franklin*: she is given up for lost. After four years of continuous treatment, Dolly recovers. It is then that she learns of her husband's shipwreck, and of a vast inheritance that has come her way through a recently-deceased uncle. The news that Felton, the *Franklin's* second-in-command, has been discovered in Australia on his death-bed, gives cause for new hope. Mrs Branican duly goes to Sydney where Felton lies dying in the seamen's hospital. Felton's last breaths reveal that her husband is still alive but a prisoner of the Indas, a nomadic tribe of northern Australia. Without further ado, our invincible heroine sets out at the head of an expedition from Adelaide on the trail of the Indas.

A young newcomer joins the party, by the name of Godfrey, bearing an uncanny resemblance to John Branican; the frustrated mother feels attracted towards the child. Len Burker, the villainous husband of Mrs Branican's sister, Jane, happens rather fortuitously to cross the path of Mrs Branican and her expedition in central Australia. In her enthusiasm at seeing Jane again, Mrs Branican invites the Burkers to join the expedition.

The exhausted Mrs Branican and her followers, on the verge of success, are laid low by a sandstorm. Len Burker takes advantage of their plight to bribe the black porters, and makes off with the ransom money and the camels carrying the party's provisions. He reaches the nomads and rescues John Branican, but wastes no time in trying to kill him. However a detachment of cavalry arrives on the scene in time to catch him red-handed, having already rescued Mrs Branican and her friends. Godfrey, acting as scout, is the first to arrive on the scene, and tells John Branican of Burker's betrayal. A well-deserved pistol shot happily eliminates the villain from the action. Jane is discovered, mortally wounded by the dastardly Len. On her deathbed she reveals that Godfrey is in fact the Branicans' long-lost son, brought into the world by Dolly during her period of madness.

Possibly, this story – which contains much factual information about Australia – was suggested to Verne by his memory of Mme Sambin, his former schoolmistress, tragically widowed when her husband, a ship's captain, was lost at sea. But Verne was really only a small boy at this time. It seems more likely that the details of Mme Sambin's refusal to accept her husband's fate came to him much later on from Sophie. Dolly's ignorance of her second confinement has been found improbable, but the author does state clearly that she was unaware of herself for four years – sudden shock had caused a loss of memory. According to an eminent psychologist, this is perfectly feasible. However that may be, *Mistress Branican* is a good novel, and it is immensely readable.

In 1892 Verne published a rather bizarre and undervalued novel called *Le Château des Carpathes* (*The Castle of the Carpathians*: 1893), which I intend to discuss at some length. First the plot: Stilla is a talented singer of great renown. What is more, she is lovely to look at, 'incomparably beautiful, with long golden hair, fiery eyes, classical features, a warm complexion and a figure that even Praxiteles could not have formed more perfectly. And this same woman was a sublime artist . . .' Amongst her many admirers is one who never misses a single performance. The indescribable splendour of her voice draws him from town to town in her wake. The persistence of this man — a certain Baron Gortz — begins to trouble her. The handsome, eligible young Count Telek, en route to Naples, is, in turn, charmed by Stilla's voice, but even more attracted by her beauty. He falls hopelessly in love with her, and asks her to marry him. Stilla, 'who could so perfectly evoke tenderness or powerful emotion in her singing, and yet who had never felt the effect of either within her breast', who 'lived only for her music, and within its realms', wastes no time in accepting his offer, particularly since his vast fortune enables her to give up her career, thus escaping the obsessive presence of Baron Gortz. Rumours of her marriage spread like wildfire as her farewell performance is billed. The public is horrified; the Baron is quite beside himself with rage.

And so to her farewell performance. Her voice is more moving than ever, but Stilla is held in fascination by the odious Baron Gortz. Her emotion reaches such a pitch that during the finale of *Orlando* she breaks down at the words:

> '*Innamorata, mio cuore tremane*
> *Voglio morire . . .*'

She collapses and dies of a burst blood vessel. Baron Gortz makes good his escape but not before writing to his rival: 'You have killed her! A curse on you!' Meanwhile, Count Telek takes refuge in his family castle where he languishes with his memories of Stilla. After several years he re-emerges, and in an effort to console himself he travels far and wide. His journeyings lead him one night to the tiny village of Werst in the Carpathians. There he takes a room at the village inn, where he learns that the villagers live in terror of the nearby ruined castle, which is haunted. He decides to restore the villagers' confidence by visiting the castle himself; it is then that he learns, to his amazement, that the castle belongs to none other than his old rival, Baron Gortz, who has not been seen for years. He hesitates, but as he does so he hears Stilla's voice and knows he must carry on.

We next see him on his way to the castle ruins, which are perched on a precarious hilltop. Night falls as he approaches the outer reaches of the castle, and there on the mountain-top he sees a figure silhouetted — none other than Stilla. He is now convinced that she is alive and a captive of the Baron; the drawbridge is down, and so without further ado he makes for the castle. He has barely stepped on to the drawbridge when it is raised abruptly against the postern, imprisoning him in the castle where he wanders through the maze of dark passageways. After much stumbling around, he manages to find a slit in the wall through which he can see inside an old chapel. There he spies Baron Gortz with his loyal henchman, Orfanik, an inventor, who has constructed an intricate electrical system to keep the inquisitive villagers at bay. A secret telephone wire leading from the castle to the inn enables him to listen to the local gossip, and in turn to let the villagers hear what he chooses.

Franz learns that the two men are planning to blow up the castle and escape. In order to stop Gortz from taking the apparently demented Stilla with him, Franz manages to break into a chamber where he finds the Baron on his own, seated in an armchair, opposite a small platform where Stilla is singing the finale from *Orlando*. Our young Count rushes over to Stilla, who stares disbelievingly at him, but Gortz brandishes a knife dropped by his rival and cries: 'You'll never take her away from me!' And he stabs Stilla in the heart; there is a noise of breaking glass as Stilla vanishes. It was only a reflection! Gortz says: 'Stilla escapes you yet again, Franz Telek, but her voice is mine, and mine alone.' So saying, he seizes a box, and, clutching it in his arms, makes for the door; a shot fired by one of the villagers smashes the box to smithereens, to the distress of the Baron who rushes out crying: 'Her voice, her voice, they have destroyed her voice.' The so-called 'voice' is only a recording! The castle blows up as planned and is totally destroyed; Gortz is its one and only victim. Orfanik escapes just in time, while Franz goes mad, muttering over and over again the final words of the finale from *Orlando*. Orfanik gives him the recordings of Stilla's voice, and as he listens to the singing of the woman he loves, he slowly recovers his wits.

This is a true Victorian romance. Franz is hopelessly and passionately in love with Stilla; what he really loves is Stilla the woman, and his
final recovery is effected only because her voice evokes her person.
Rodolphe de Gortz, on the other hand, is in no way physically involved
with Stilla. He, too, is passionately in love, but with the artist in her,
her voice, without which he could no longer exist.

Beauty spurs us to discover the dual nature of love, which is both
physical and intellectual. However, the superior form of love is that
which goes beneath the surface of the physical attraction – however
beautiful that may be in itself – and discovers the inner essence, an understanding of which, in its turn, may supplant the sensual appeal entirely. Franz Telek's love is an example of the first kind of love, born of
Stilla's gaze, which is in turn a mirror of her soul. Her voice moves him,
but can be only of secondary importance to him: 'He cursed the length
of the scenes and the delays caused by the applause and curtain calls'.
Baron Gortz, ensconced in his private box, is also deeply moved, but for
very different reasons; for him, she is 'ecstatic' and 'horrifyingly pale';
yet it is because she sees him in the audience that she is seized by 'mor-
tal terror'. He, too, is in love, but Gortz's feelings, like Telek's, are for
only one side of Stilla – for him, what counts is her music. Had Telek
actually married her, it would have made little difference to the Baron;
they are only rivals in the sense that Telek would keep her from her
music, thus depriving Gortz of her voice. Nonetheless, Gortz keeps her
voice for himself alone by recording it.

More's comments on *The Castle of the Carpathians* are very pertinent. He compares it to Villiers de l'Isle-Adam's *L'Eve future*,
suggesting that Verne was influenced by Villiers. *L'Eve future* first
appeared in 1891, while *The Castle of the Carpathians* was not
published until 1892, so Verne could well have been familiar with
L'Eve future when he was working on the corrections of his own book.
On the other hand, he had already written *The Castle of the Carpathians* as far back as 1889. To be honest, even if the subject-matter
of the two differs considerably, there are certain points of resemblance.
Villiers de l'Isle-Adam visualizes his Edison capable of creating a near-
perfect female robot. Villiers is an extreme spiritualist; he tries to show
that the enduring force of love is to be found, not in sensuality, but in
the search for 'self'.

Above all, Villiers scorns the artificiality of women in general; consequently his hero is in search of a 'real' woman; in fact he is attracted

by artificiality of a different kind — a robot — which only becomes human because he imagines it to be: its 'self' is 'cogited' by himself. Yet this is still not enough; he ends up by transplanting the soul of a 'live' woman into his robot. Villiers' conclusion is a general one: imagination is more real than reality itself.

The problems raised in *The Castle of the Carpathians* are related although different. Can the identity of an artist be separated from the person who *is* that artist? Can love for a person be limited to just one facet of that person's character, however perfect it may be? Verne seems to have preferred to leave the question open: he understates Stilla's own feelings so that we can never know whether Franz's love for her is reciprocated. It seems, however, that she makes a definite choice between lover and admirer when she decides to marry Franz. Can we not carry this a little further and assume logically that the book is expressing the author's regret that even the most attractive of women rarely has the inner beauty that we expect?

The Castle of the Carpathians could well be regarded as an expression of his own attitudes, which he now realized were very complex. His relationship with his lady friend in Asnières had a similar dual nature. In *The Castle of the Carpathians* he splits this duality into two separate characters.

Baron Gortz's artistic, intellectual passion can be identified with the satisfaction Verne himself gained from his frequent talks with his close friend; his was a love not of a 'voice' but of an intelligent mind coupled with feminine intuition. By contrast, Count Telek's passion surely corresponds to the sentimental bond of mutual understanding that had grown up between Verne and his woman friend. This was still love, but personal love, which was destined to the same frustrations as that of Franz and Stilla. During his long hours of solitude, Verne must often have recalled the voice of his close friend and adviser; far more subtle than Orfanik's recording, his memory of the past enabled him to evoke the very being of the friend who inspired him. So it seems probable that his novel was a homage to the woman he had loved, with a love undeclared and possibly repressed — a love unavowed on both sides, moreover, since Stilla betrays no emotion whatsoever.

This hypothesis can be substantiated, albeit tenuously, by an unpublished play on which Verne had laboured in his youth and which shows a very profound awareness of feeling. I am referring to *Monna Lisa*, an Italian-style comedy, originally entitled 'Léonard da Vinci' and later 'La Joconde'. It depicts Leonardo painting his portrait of Mona Lisa for her philosophical if somewhat complacent husband, who has commissioned the picture. Leonardo is striving for artistic perfection in his work, and his model is full of admiration for his intelligence and talent. From this springs a bond between artist and model. She flirts with him, impatient for a declaration of the love she knows she can reciprocate. Finally, Leonardo decides to declare himself, but at that very moment his attention is diverted by the craftsmanship of a bracelet she is wearing; his concentration is broken, and he becomes absorbed in the perfection of the bracelet, which far outshines that of its wearer. Mona Lisa, somewhat vexed, is nonetheless about to yield to him, when one of his acolytes brings in a stranger, whose hideous features inspire the artist to abandon his loved one in order to sketch this new model. Furious, Mona Lisa declares that her portrait is finished and orders it to be removed if only to 'banish herself and her soul from such odious surroundings'. And so she is reunited with her husband. Leonardo for his part departs in pursuit of new inspiration for his art, creating a universe as he goes.

This, then, is the story behind the smile; tenderness mixed with scorn and even pity for the artist naïve enough to reject the love of a woman for his artistic aspirations. This *apologia* is perhaps a reflection of Verne's own love-life. One wonders if he finally realized how he, too, had refused to give up his work for a woman's smile; is this not the message of *The Castle of the Carpathians*? In a letter to Hetzel written in 1889, he implies that *The Castle* is ready for publication. Thus, the woman on whom he based Stilla must have died before 1889 or 1888, when he began working on the book, and possibly only a year or so before that. The lady in Asnières died around 1885.

1890–1900

ALTHOUGH BROKEN IN HEALTH, Verne scrupulously maintained his promised output of two volumes per year. Indeed, he was well up on his contract – so much so that it is hard to follow his work at this time; he had several books on the stocks at once: the new one and those which he was revising in readiness for publication. In 1891 and 1892, for instance, he was reworking the proofs of three books written in 1889; *Mrs Branican, Claudius Bombarnac* (a lively if somewhat far-fetched railway travelogue set convincingly in the Orient), and *Castle of the Carpathians*. At the same time he was active as a town councillor, supervising senatorial elections, sitting on the school board, and so on. Though only sixty-four, he was beset with illness and had frequent attacks of dizziness: on one occasion he almost fell from his carriage. Any kind of effort must have caused him pain, but he could not bear to remain idle. He even found time to speak at the Académie d'Amiens, the local learned society of which he became chairman.

Some bitterness crept into his outlook: his books no longer created a stir as they had done; he felt that he was becoming a has-been. 'I'll just have to accept the fact . . . I *do* live in the provinces, after all, and don't invite the critics over for dinner. Yet how could I at present?'

On the other hand, he was glad to see that his wayward son was settling down at last, and he went to stay with him in Paris. He enjoyed Michel's and Jeanne's company: his son's imagination and his daughter-in-law's good sense (and her music!) appealed to him. The long relaxed evenings spent at their house on the Boulevard Péreire did him good, and he would talk wittily for hours in an atmosphere that reminded him of his youth. Playing with Michel's two children, my brothers Michel and Georges (I was born in 1892), he felt the keen pleasure of being a grandfather. At the same time, he could not help

178

worrying about Michel's family and the responsibility he felt he had towards them. The fact is that Michel could still not make ends meet. He had gone into business, making and marketing what he called the Universal Stove — an excellent contrivance that unfortunately would not sell, despite much hard work on his part which won him his father's admiration. When the stove flopped, Michel tried to convert to the manufacture of bicycles, but once again he was swimming against the tide: his sort of bicycle — a very heavy roadster, with broad tyres and a coloured frame — came into favour many years later, whereas the bicycle that was in vogue at the time was the lightweight sort with thin tyres and a plain black frame.

As the business floundered on, prior to sinking without trace, Verne fretted over his son's temerity and took a long hard look at his royalty statements. On 23 August 1891 he wrote to Hetzel *fils*: 'I always expect my earnings to be down on the previous half year, and it can't be helped since, you tell me, the book trade as a whole is in the same pass. My half-year gross in 1889 was 25,000 francs. In 1890 it was 24,000. What, I wonder, will it be in 1891? Aye, there's the rub; but it won't stop me ploughing on.'

He was working a ten-hour day in order to finish correcting the galleys of *Castle of the Carpathians*, with which Louis-Jules had declared himself well pleased, and begin his revision of *Claudius Bombarnac*. He was worried about the former because it was 'much more romantic' than anything he had written previously. Would it go down well with the readers of *L'Illustration*? He felt that it should not be published until 1892 — it wasn't — because more than two books per year would finish him. He went on:

Michel's business is in the direst of straits . . . I have said goodbye to the whole 30,000 francs. The stove was fine, but the business was rotten and wasn't even what they wanted. Then, the money that should have been used for promotion and advertising was put into manufacturing, with the result that sales have been negligible.

Michel has worked hard, but more than that was needed . . . Who could ever imagine Michel succeeding in business? But having refused so many of his requests for help I felt I had to let him try this time. The experiment will prove to have been a disaster for us both.

His belief that business required special gifts as well as perseverance is embodied in *P'tit Bonhomme* (1893; *Foundling Mick*: 1895), a Dicken-

sian success story that he wrote at this time. After a hard start in life
(part of a puppet show at three; left to starve by the puppeteer and the
parish foster-mother; sent to the ragged school but saved by a fire;
taken in by a decayed actress who plays with him then forgets him), the
eponymous hero of this touching tale of old Ireland is eventually
adopted by a kindly farmer. He is a hard-working and conscientious lad
of nine when the famine results in the farmer's eviction for not paying
his rent. Mick is thrown on to his own resources; alone once more save
for his dog Birk, with only sixpence to his name, he sells matches in the
streets of Newmarket and does quite well thanks to his precocious
sense of business. Finding a wallet containing a hundred pounds, he unhesitatingly returns it to its owner, haughty Lord Piborne, who proffers
perfunctory thanks and engages him as his son's groom. After two
months at the castle, he has to flee because his mongrel kills an
aristocratic pointer that goes for him. Alone again, but with savings of
nearly five pounds, he takes charge of a starving boy of seven saved
from suicide by Birk, the dog.

In Cork, Mick studies the market, and the two chums go in for
newspapers, timetables, penny dreadfuls, matches and tobacco. Mick
keeps careful accounts and finds that he is worth over thirty pounds. He
buys a barrow and they work their way profitably to the brighter lights
of Dublin, where Mick sets them up with a little store which prospers
and becomes fashionable. Their ship is on the point of coming home;
but first it has to be saved from foundering by the intrepid lad determined to salvage his merchandise. After that exploit, his bank account
is so well garnished that he can rescue his childhood protectors from
adversity by buying back the house and land from which his adoptive
family had been evicted.

A touching tale indeed. I remember reading it avidly as a boy of
twelve, so it cannot be as rebarbative as some critics have found it; but
now that the years have eroded my pristine ingenuousness I must confess that I find the plot contrived and facile. The book is not to be dismissed entirely, however. It has three themes: destitute children; the
Irish question; the British mentality. Verne's treatment of the first of
these is no more exaggerated than Dickens's or Victor Hugo's. We are
told that the action is set in 1875; and if life was not quite so wretched
for these poor children as Verne makes out, it was undoubtedly
wretched enough to warrant some measure of polemical exaggeration.
On the Irish question, Verne quite naturally sides with the Irish; he

deplores the British muddle over the issues involved (social rather than political) and condemns the dual standards of the aristocracy, liberal in England and Scotland but oppressive in Ireland. The wedge of middlemen and stewards driven between tenants and landlords struck him as wholly wrong; and absentee ownership seemed to him to be the fundamental flaw in the social structure. 'Instead of letting Ireland have its head, the aristocracy tug at the reins. A catastrophe is frighteningly likely to occur, for hatred breeds rebellion.' Events have proved him right.

The third theme of this novel is the British aristocracy of the 1870s. Verne's caricature dwells heavily on their faults. Lord Piborne harks back in all sincerity to the feudal privileges of his illustrious forebears and looks down on anyone lower-born than himself. His home is run like a fief. In short, he comes across as an absurd anachronism. As for his son, he is just a silly little fool (as the mountain echo points out to him in no uncertain terms). Here, one tends to think that Verne is grinding his axe a little too coarsely. However, he does say that 'these highborn gentlemen destined to become perfect imbeciles, albeit of perfect breeding' are dying out as a race; thus, his attack is levelled at *part* of the English aristocracy; he is well aware that some English lords have brain *and* breeding. Yet his description of the highborn fool is not untrue to life; it is a type that still exists today, if less overtly.

While the foundling was going from strength to strength, Michel's business was going from bad to worse. The point was eventually reached where it had to be wound up, and the remaining stock was sold off through an insert in Hetzel's *Magasin*. A third son had just been born, which did not help matters.

Verne had worked on through attacks of dizziness and eye troubles. His draft of *L'Ile à hélice* was ready to be submitted to his brother for vetting. An hour's walking caused pain in his legs; he rarely went out any more.

In June 1893 his life was troubled by the following incident:

We have just had Michel and family here for a month. His wife is charming, and so are his children. But the Lefèvres [Honorine's daughter Suzanne had married Georges Lefèvre] refused to see them and persuaded our false friends to do likewise. Our only true friends were the Labbés and the Pinsards. Mind you, we didn't try to force the couple on any one. You know me better than that. But if the Lefèvres and the rest believe they did

their duty, we are convinced we did ours. One of the children was ill, he
needed a change of air, he came here: every liberal mind and every true
heart is with us and to blazes with fools.

This absurd and (whatever one's viewpoint) solipsistic attitude continued to weigh on future relations between the Lefèvres and the
Vernes (Honorine was particularly hurt by it) and indeed it became a
bone of contention between Suzanne and Georges Lefèvre. Suzanne's
overdose of principles in this matter squares ill with her lack of principles in passing judgment on her parents. However, all her life had
been spent in the rather fusty atmosphere of Amiens; and the true
depth of her feeling was probably no more than the resentment often
found in children whose parents remarry. Verne was not the father of
Honorine's daughters, although he had always treated them as if they
were his; the birth of Michel had stolen some of their thunder (particularly now that Verne was famous) and they felt cheated. Because
Michel had been difficult as a child, Suzanne felt the game could be won
by hiding behind a mask of strict conformism, and that seems to me to
be the real explanation of her conduct.

I was pained to find among the unpublished papers of Madame
Allotte de la Fuye a mischievous letter in the same spiteful vein from
Captain de Francy, an army supplies officer and the husband of
Honorine's other daughter, Valentine. My reason for mentioning this
family quarrel at all is that de Francy's letter gives credit to the false
rumour that our family had something to hide and that we were con-
cealing family papers. Now that what we had to hide stands revealed in
what I have just written (the busybodies will be disappointed, I fear), I
would like to point out that I am the first to deplore our lack of family
papers – for the fact is that we have none. Disgusted by the spectacle of
this nest of vipers, Verne destroyed all his personal files, considering
that anything left behind would only add venom to the bites.

In August 1893 Verne officiated at the elections and then joined
Honorine at La Fourberie, near Dinard, where Michel and Jeanne
(known as Maja) had rented a house for the holidays. La Fourberie was
not a village then: the house stood alone in its gardens, with a farm
across the way. We children loved to watch the horse plod patiently
around the threshing mill; even more we loved to go off to the nearby
beach, which in those days was completely deserted: it was only a few
yards away down a shady lane, and the sea came into view once we had

passed the villa belonging to Emile Bergerat, Judith Gautier's husband whom Verne had known in Paris in the seventies.

Our house stood next to a little cottage kept for guests. There were plenty of rooms in the house itself, and I have forgotten whether Verne slept in the cottage or just worked there. He liked La Fourberie so much that he stayed for a month, instead of the intended ten days. I have the feeling that his unreserved affection for his son's family dates from this visit. However that may be, he used his stay to complete the first volume of *Maître Antifer* (1894; *Captain Antifer*: 1895). When he left, he stopped by in Amiens and then he and Honorine took a trip to Le Havre, Caen and Saint Malo – a sign that his morale and health were at least partially restored.

However, the improvement did not last. Vexations came with the autumn. He received his royalty statement on 19 November: 'I am distressed to see from my account that the books I was counting on – *Bombarnac, Carpathians* – are not doing well. It's disheartening. True, one can't always be in vogue ... Yet I have still to complete my life's work, portraying the earth.'

Disheartened or not, he had completed *L'Ile à hélice* and *Captain Antifer* and was thinking about his volume of short stories, one of which (*M. Ré Dièze et Mlle Si Bémol*) was due for publication in the Christmas number of *Le Figaro Illustré*. What seems to have affected him most was that *Claudius Bombarnac* and *Castle of the Carpathians* had gone by unnoticed. In relation to the latter at least this is rather surprising; it represented a new departure for Verne, an incursion into a genre close to that of Lautréamont and Villiers de l'Isle-Adam, the precursors of surrealism. Admittedly, these writers were not particularly appreciated in those days. Nonetheless, one would have thought that any reviewer worth his salt would have realized at once that for an author from the *Magasin d'Education* to write a book like *Castle of the Carpathians* was an important innovation. That none reviewed it may well have been due to Verne's excessive concern with not offending the prudish clients of the Maison Hetzel: 'Herewith the galleys of *Carpathians*,' he had written on 4 March 1892. 'I have been over them very carefully. I think there is nothing that might shock the readers of the *Magasin* and I have been as reticent and brief as I could about the hero's involvement with the prima donna.'

Despite these setbacks, his pen was as alert as ever as he touched up *Captain Antifer* (a good-humoured but overlong tale of treasure-hunting set in the Middle East of Mehemet Ali, West Africa, Scotland, the Alps, and Brittany) and set to work on the books for 1895.

The good humour of *Captain Antifer* is apparent also in *L'Ile à hélice* (*The Floating Island*: 1896; *Propellor Island*, 1896), which Verne completed in November 1893. The idea of an artificial island was not new by any means; but Verne took the old idea a stage further by equipping his island with propellor screws enabling its inhabitants to live in perpetual spring: they drive it around the tropical zones on either side of the equator. As usual, Verne took care to ensure that his fantasy should appear to be reasonable and (at a pinch) feasible. He studied his idea seriously and got his brother to vet his plans for technical incongruities.

By August he was well into the book and Paul received the proofs of Part One the following summer. 'Let me say again', Verne wrote to him on 12 September 1894, 'that to my mind the second volume of *Propellor Island* is even stranger than the first. If I've got my figures wrong for the island's draught, displacement and horsepower, let me know what they should be.'

His brother's response produced the following reply (20 September):

Mon vieux Paul,

I'm writing back at once to say that I'm going to follow up on what you tell me about the displacement of Screw Island [*sic*]; I've made adjustments for the remaining passages in accordance with your instructions.

I've given up the idea of even temperature since there was nothing else I could do. Yet there was one way it could be done, by keeping the island behind the sun at a constant distance from it and backing northwards: that way, I would never have had it directly overhead. For example, with the sun over the Tropic of Cancer at 23 degrees north, I would have been at something like 40 degrees north. I would have followed it to a point where it would have been over the Tropic of Capricorn at 23 degrees south, with myself at 6 degrees south, and then I would have turned back northwards, keeping ahead of it at my constant distance of 17 degrees. But that would have been hugely inconvenient, since I would never have been able to get the island to the Tropic of Capricorn where there are several groups of islands that it has to get involved with. So I thought it best to drop the idea altogether.

When I say somewhere that the Wagnerian epidemic was on the decline, you call me an old fuddy-duddy! Let me tell you that Webor, who does the music reviews in *Le Temps* and is one of the best critics around, recently referred to *L'Attaque du Moulin, Thaïs,* and *Le Flibustier* as 'musical aberrations' – and he has the same opinion of some Wagner, the *Walkyrie* for example. But I know it's no good trying to convert you.

Your old fuddy-duddy of a brother.

When, in 1863, Verne wrote *Journey to the Centre of the Earth* he mischievously named the ship which carries Axel to Iceland via Denmark the *Walkyrie*, a dedication to the German composer, whose work of that name had first been heard privately in Paris in 1860. In *Voyage round the World (Captain Grant's Children),* written in 1865, he made his stand even clearer by referring to Wagner's 'frustrated genius'.

Verne's fondness for Wagner eventually cooled. In *Propellor Island,* he still ranks Wagner among the great composers but adds that 'the Wagnerian epidemic is on the wane'. This change of heart was no doubt not due to Wagner's attitude during the Franco-Prussian war of 1870; but it seems more likely that it was a symptom of his own changing tastes – which, paradoxically enough, got him involved in a friendly argument with his brother.

The Vernes, as we have seen, were a musical family. They all played the piano and sang. Paul composed throughout his life, and in his retirement put together two volumes of *Musical Sketches,* published in 1873 and 1891. According to the family, Jules and Paul frequently differed on musical matters; but on Wagner, it would seem that Paul was 'anti' on principle, because he was German; however, after attending a performance of *Lohengrin* at the Paris Opera in 1891, much against his will, he was forced to admit the error of his judgment, and in fact went to see the work no less than seven times running. His new-found enthusiasm, the object of the correspondence quoted earlier, grated against Verne's more mellow Wagnerianism; Verne, after all, had been a disciple from the outset.

In connection with *Propellor Island,* Marcel Moré points out that Verne must have been impressed by his reading of Nietzsche's *Der Fall Wagner,* translated by Daniel Halévy and Robert Dreyfus in 1893, and even more impressed by Gounod's essay on Mozart's *Don Giovanni.* This is substantiated in the novel, which was the subject of much discussion beforehand between Verne and his brother. Verne's eulogy of Mozart, spoken by the King of Malecarly (the governor of the island), is

a straightforward résumé of 'the inspired study by Gounod', whom
Verne regarded as 'the greatest French composer of the end of the
nineteenth century'.

Malecarly's list of approved composers includes Reyer, Saint-Saëns,
Ambroise Thomas, Gounod, Massenet and Verdi, as well as Berlioz,
Meyerbeer, Halévy, Rossini, Beethoven, Haydn and Mozart. No mention is made here of Wagner; he is referred to later by Calistus Munbar
who considers his music 'therapeutic', but who by the same token
reserves Berlioz for those of 'anaemic temperament' and Mendelssohn
and Mozart for those of more full-blooded nature. So once again
Wagner is in good company.

I was not surprised to find Reyer at the head of the list; according to
the family, Verne supported him from his début; certainly he was one
of his admirers by the time of *L'Anneau de Cakantéla* (1858). But the
inclusion of Verdi's name comes as a surprise, especially after the
Voyage en Ecosse, in which *Il Trovatore* gets rather rough treatment.
Nonetheless, Verdi's work had evolved considerably over the years,
and by the time *Otello* appeared Verne may very well have revised his
opinion. Had he not written in *The Castle of the Carpathians* in 1892 that
the Italian school was once again dominant in the field of musical composition? Therefore it seems very probable that he was won over by a
production or a score-reading of Verdi's *Otello*. I even suspect that here
we have the source of Stilla's death-aria, the finale from *Orlando*, an unknown opera. Moré's research confirms this.

Verne to Hetzel (23 October 1894):

> My brother Paul has read the galleys [of *Propellor Island*, Part One] and
> sent them back with his corrections from the mechanical and nautical
> viewpoint. So we have made this unfeasible-sounding machine as feasible
> as possible. And since Paul is extremely punctilious, I like to think that
> even the hair-splitters will accept it.

At the close of the year, he was correcting the page proofs (and completing one of the novels due in 1898, *Seconde Patrie*).

Propellor Island begins with four French musicians travelling from
San Francisco to San Diego, the next stop on their tour. Their train has
been stopped fifty miles short of their destination owing to damage on
the track, and the stagecoach that they have taken to complete their
journey has overturned in the dead of night. They reach a sleeping
village, after escaping from a bear by charming it with their in-

struments, and they attempt to attract attention to themselves by playing Onslow's *Suite in B flat*. When nothing happens, the quartet strike up furiously and improvise 'a cacophonic sonata sounding like Wagner played backwards'. The villagers wake up and give them a great welcome.

At this point, Calistus Munbar, a jovial and talkative American dilettante who has admired their rendition of the Onslow piece, descends from an electric charabanc and takes them under his wing. Here the story really gets under way, as Munbar takes them by ferry to a fantastic city.

This ideal city has broad streets and avenues. Its palatial buildings in varied styles have balconies that project over moving sidewalks. The magnificent stores are crammed with wares but have few customers, since orders are taken by the 'teletograph' system, which enables the citizens to sign cheques, marry and even divorce without leaving their homes. The streets are paved with rotproof parquet, and people move about in electric cars, except in the opulent districts where they drive in carriages drawn by teams of horses. This city for millionaires is known as Milliard City. Like any other city, it has its rich and its poor, because 'there is always someone richer than oneself'. It is split between the Protestant district on the port side and the Catholic district on the starboard side, although all church services are held by telephone.

Milliard City is the capital of an artificial propellor-driven island, Standard Island, composed of 270,000 steel caissons covered with soil forming a total area of 15 square miles. The buildings are made of unconventional materials such as aluminium, artificial stone and hollow glass bricks. They are rented out at fabulous prices to none but Americans: the Northerners on the port side, the Southerners on the starboard side. The ten thousand inhabitants include few lawyers (making for few lawsuits) and even fewer doctors (making for a low death rate).

The port and starboard propellor systems are driven at 2,000 volts by two 5-million horsepower generating stations fired by solidified oil. The island's extremely sophisticated phonographs and theatrophones provide superb concerts (there is even a piped muzack service!); however, now that the time has come for 'palpable virtuosi in flesh and blood' to take the place of the machines and give the millionaires 'the thrill of real performance', Calistus Munbar has been instructed to engage the famous French quartet at any price.

They agree to take part in the island's next trip, but first they visit
the museum where all the world's greatest masters from Raphael and
Leonardo da Vinci to Yon and Cabanel (*sic!*) are represented (but no
impressionists, no *angoissés*, no futurists – though the time will come,
says Verne, when Standard Island will be invaded by 'that decadent
horde').

The library is just as richly endowed, but those who frequent it
prefer the phonographic books: they press a button and an excellent
elocutionist reads to them. The newspapers, magazines and
broadsheets are printed in chocolate ink on edible paper; after being
read, they can be eaten for breakfast. As an added convenience, some
are laxative and some astringent.

The quartet's first concert – of works by Mendelssohn, Haydn,
Beethoven and Mozart – is a sell-out at $200 a seat, and is a triumphant
success. Thereafter, however, disturbing signs of dissension break out
on the island. The port community led by the tycoon Tankerton wish
to transform the island into an enormous business precinct, whereas
the starboard community led by the tycoon Coverley wish to lead a
quiet civilized existence *à la française*.

The island visits successively the Marquesas Islands, the Society
Islands, Tahiti, Tonga, and is on the way to Fiji when an unknown
vessel comes alongside undetected in a night of storm and blackness
and lets loose a cargo of wild animals. No one doubts that the vessel
came as an agent of the British Government, whose policy of hostility
towards the island is well known. The hunt after the animals is
dangerous and gripping. Tankerton's son Walter is within inches of
death but is saved by Coverley; Coverley in his turn is saved in the nick
of time by Tankerton: general reconciliation ensues and Walter
Tankerton and Dy Coverley can at last own up to their secret love and
get engaged.

However, the idyll is interrupted by an invasion of islanders from the
New Hebrides. The inhabitants of Standard Island defend themselves
heroically and the pirates are repulsed with the aid of French settlers
from Sandwich Island. All would be well were it not for the fact that the
governor of the island has been killed during the skirmishing and there
is therefore no official available to marry Walter and Dy. A mayor has
to be elected. Unfortunately, the electoral campaigns reopen the sores
of discord between the port and starboard communities: the wedding is
called off, and in the absence of a consensus each side elects a mayor of

its own. The port mayor commands the port machines, the starboard mayor the starboard machines; since their orders contradict one another, the island is tranformed into a gigantic spinning top and eventually breaks apart. But, rid of all their millions, Walter and Dy can go off and marry simply in New Zealand.

If we have gone to such great lengths in our discussion of this apparently slight novel, it is because in our opinion *Propellor Island* is in some sort Verne's aesthetic (and social) credo. Benett's full-length portrait of the King of Malecarly for the illustrated edition is perhaps the key to the book's importance: the regal figure got up as a bourgeois, with neat beard and black frock-coat, is said to be none other than Verne. Jules Verne, the bourgeois king – that is what we get in *Propellor Island*: his so-called *pompier* tastes, his conservative prejudices, his disappointed utopianism, his baffled hopes in science. But do not let us forget the other Jules Verne – the man in Nadar's wonderful photographic portrait made just after the award of the Légion d'Honneur; the man with a shrewd eye lined with sadness and laughter.

His island's peregrinations provide his readers with an introduction to the geography and history of the Pacific islands – and with a handy checklist of his hobbyhorses during this period of his life: music; American-type 'progress'; town planning; government; technology; art; the British Empire; and so on. Furthermore, the microcosm that he depicts allows him to play philosophical variations on the passions of the eternal human comedy. No material cares impinge on the lives of the islands' inhabitants. Yet through stupidity and passion they destroy the source of their happiness: their rivalry, pride, vanity and ambition bring about their armageddon. Beyond Verne's critique of American gigantism and the weight of the dollar lies a critique of western society. His book is not quite a masterpiece, because its impact is diminished by its being stretched out into two volumes; but it is fun to read; and it is good to find Verne recovering the use of the faculties that made him so original in the first place.

In a sense, humour was part of Jules Verne's trademark as a writer. In his youth, it came naturally to him, but as he grew older it seems that he had to make a deliberate effort to cultivate the slightly mocking tone found in his best work – to such an extent that it would be possible to chart his true state of heart from his narrative style. When the humour rings hollow, or is lacking altogether, Verne was not well.

As an example of Verne's humour at its best, I would like to mention a talk that he gave at the Académie d'Amiens on 12 December 1875. (I have not paid much attention in this book to the speeches that Verne made at local societies for the simple reason that they are relatively unimportant.) On this occasion, his subject was 'An Ideal City'.

In fantasy, the speaker is astonished to find Amiens transformed overnight into the city that its inhabitants would like it to be: the trains to and from the city are through-corridor trains (requests for which had been ignored by the railway company for years); the thoroughfares are lined with comfortable benches and lighted at night (another bone of contention). Toll charges have been abolished and the muddy streets repaved with cubes of porphyry. Ladies' fashions have reached the supreme heights of refinement (a familiar target for Verne's satire). Marriages have boomed owing to the introduction of a Bachelor Tax — and births have become so numerous that 'a five-hundred nursepower baby-feeding machine' has had to be installed. The city has a tram network (another grievance satisfied) and a posh department store; and a telegraph hook-up enables 'a Polish pianist in the employ of the Emperor of the Sandwich Islands to be heard simultaneously in London, Vienna, Paris, St Petersburg and Peking'. The Scientific, Commercial and Technical High School has four thousand students: Latin has, of course, been removed from the curriculum. Because all the doctors in the town have adopted Chinese medical techniques and their patients pay only so long as they keep well, hardly anyone falls ill any more. 'The music of the future', in the form of a *Reverie in A minor on the Square of the Hypotenuse*, is dispensed by the Band of the 324th Regiment; it is 'neither human nor celestial — no lilt, no beat, no melody, no rhythm: quintessence of Wagner, audio-mathematics, cacophonomania — like an orchestra tuning up'. But from fantasy the speaker is brought back to firm reality by the sight of the mini-geyser spouting as usual from the burst water main in the middle of the square; as usual, the station clock is slow; and the ministerial delegate at the annual Agricultural Show makes his usual boring speech.

How could this be anything but a gentle send-up of life in Amiens? At any rate, the humour in this talk is typical of Verne's jaunty, mocking vein which he found increasingly difficult to write up to. After the mid-nineties, in particular, the sombre face beneath the mask appears and brightens only momentarily in novels such as *The Will of an Eccentric, Bourses de Voyage* and *The Chase of the Golden Meteor*.

Although he could barely hold his pen from writer's cramp, he worked on as hard as ever. While correcting the proofs of *Propellor Island* in August 1894, he wrote to Hetzel:

> I have been weeping for something for 1898. As you know, 1895 is *Propellor Island*, 1896 is *Drame en Livonie*, 1897 is *L'Orénoque* and they're all ready. I finished *L'Orénoque* a week ago, which means that it will stay on the shelf for thirteen months and I will revise it when I have to send it in.

Propellor Island did appear in 1895, but *Un Drame en Livonie* was not published until 1904 and *L'Orénoque* came out in 1898. The first was replaced by *Clovis Dardentor*, which was followed in 1897 by *Le Sphinx des Glaces*.

He was worried sick, so worried in fact that the only way he could cope was by working round the clock. 'You always did manage to be cheerful', he wrote to Paul on 8 August. 'I rarely am these days. With all my responsibilities, I'm very frightened of the future. Michel has no work, can't find any, has lost me 200,000 francs and has three sons — and all their education is going to fall upon me. In short, I'm coming to a bad end.'

His worry was not for Michel (who was at that time dabbling in journalism and fiction writing); he was just as worried about his grandchildren. His way of being a grandfather was not expansive. As in everything else, he kept his feelings to himself and it was a surprise to his family when he was discovered at his window discreetly but attentively watching over his youngest grandson (who was then about four) playing in the garden below.

It was doubtless feelings like this that made him hasten the publication of *Clovis Dardentor* (1896; translated 1897), which he dedicated to his grandsons. It is hard to understand why he wrote this story at all. An unmonied young man decides to get himself adopted by the rich bachelor Clovis Dardentor by saving him at the peril of his life. In fact, it is he who is saved by his future adoptive father, along with his less ambitious cousin whom he has dragged along to further his plot. Clovis himself is saved by a girl, whom he adopts, who marries the cousin, who thus becomes the son-in-law and thus becomes the heir. As Verne admitted, the thing is pure vaudeville with a dash of Majorca and other exotic spots thrown in for good measure.

In the same year Verne published another, much livelier book, *Face *au Drapeau* (1896; *For the Flag*: 1897), which got him involved in a lawsuit with Turpin, the inventor of melinite. This powerful explosive was adopted by the French army, but Turpin did not receive the recognition that was his due; and when the secret of its manufacture was leaked to a foreign power he protested so loudly and for so long that he was eventually brought to trial for having leaked the secret himself to draw attention to his claim. He was found guilty of treason and not pardoned until many years later. In the meantime, his case had developed into a veritable *affaire* and all the papers in France had taken up the cudgels for or against him. Understandably, he felt rather bitter about the whole business.

His story, that of the unrecognized genius at war with society, was right up Verne's street, and there can be no doubt that it provided him with the original idea for his novel. Indeed, Turpin's name crops up in the penultimate chapter; and in a letter dating from November 1895 Verne refers to him explicitly: 'In a few days I will send you the proofs of my new novel – you know, the one about Turpin that I told you about.' Nonetheless, Verne's hero Thomas Roch is *not* Turpin and their stories are not the same.

Roch is a monomaniac. His only moments of lucidity come when he is concerning himself with his invention, which has monopolized all of his thinking life. His explosive is much more powerful than melinite – more like an atomic bomb – and comprises a fuse material that foreshadows the V2s and ICBMs. Roch does not hand over his invention to a foreign power, nor does he reveal state secrets to a possible enemy; he sells his brainchild to the highest bidder, who unscrupulously takes advantage of his diminished faculties to get his hands on it. When Roch is ultimately faced with the colours of his fatherland fluttering at the mast of a ship that he is supposed to destroy, he refuses to act and patriotism triumphs over all.

Not so Turpin, whose disposition was as explosive as his cherished invention. He seized upon Verne's book – all in all an excellent vindication of unrecognized genius – and used it as a passport to more publicity by suing its author for libel. The suit dragged on until 1897 (Verne's lawyer was Poincaré, the future French President; Verne went to see him in Paris on what was to be his last trip to the capital); and eventually Turpin, who really did not have a leg to stand on, lost yet again.

Verne's health was going from bad to worse: distension of the stomach, rheumatism, vertigo. He no longer dared to go out alone. And he was very upset by the death of Dumas *fils* following that of Frédéric Petit, 'a true friend and an irreplaceable mayor'. However, he continued to fulfil his duties on the town council and played an active (honorary) role on the boards of the local savings bank and agricultural society.

Even though he thought of himself as a finished man, he cannot have lost all of his remarkable energy; in spite of all his ancillary obligations he continued to write with boyish enthusiasm. Writing to his brother in October 1895, he said:

> I'm terribly excited about my continuation of the Poe novel and almost into the second volume already.

Yet at the same time:

> I still have much difficulty with my writer's cramp, but that hasn't stopped me working as much as ever. I never go anywhere: I've become as great a stay-at-home as I was a gadabout. Age, illness and worry are conspiring to turn me into someone whose backside never leaves his chair.

On 1 September 1896, he sent Hetzel Part One of *Le Sphinx antarctique*, subsequently published as *Le Sphinx des Glaces* (1897; *An Antarctic Mystery*: 1898):

> It will be a kind of counterpart to *Captain Hatteras*, although there is nothing in the two books – plot or characters – to make them alike. It will come at the right time, since people are talking about voyages and discoveries at the South Pole. My point of departure is one of Edgar Poe's strangest novels, *The Narrative of Arthur Gordon Pym*, but it will not be necessary to have read Poe's novel to understand mine. I have used everything that Poe left in suspense and have developed the mystery surrounding certain of the characters. I have one particularly good *trouvaille*: one of my heroes who, like everyone else, thought that Poe's novel was entirely fictitious, comes face to face with a matching reality. Needless to say, I go much further than Poe did. Let me know what you think; I hope that my readers will be very interested.
>
> I am so taken with the extraordinary side of a work like this that I wish to dedicate it to the memory of Edgar Poe and to our friends in America. I'm very excited about this novel; we shall see whether it gets the public excited too . . . In my opinion, it's another *Gordon Pym*, but more true to life and I think more interesting. Tomorrow I'm going sailing to get myself shaken around a little.

He corrected the proofs the following January. His violent attacks of

dizziness had returned and his doctors irrigated his stomach several
times ('would that the surgeons had perfected a technique for gastrec-
tomy!'). His writing hand was getting worse all the time, he had
bronchitis now in addition to his rheumatism, and he could barely drag
himself around his room. Worst of all, he received word that his brother
had had a series of heart attacks; and then came the terrible news of his
death, on 27 August 1897. Verne was so crushed and so ill that he could
not attend the funeral.

And the saga of Michel continued. In March 1897, Verne had asked
Hetzel to do him a great favour ('almost on my bended knees') and use
his influence to help Michel get a job, presumably on the railways. This
was an idea of Charles Bourdon, Michel's cousin; it came to naught,
but Charles had got Michel to apply elsewhere as well and I assume
that this worked, since my father was in fact employed by the
organizers of the Universal Exhibition held in Paris in 1900.

An Antarctic Mystery purports to be the journal of one Jeorling, who is
convinced that Pym's journal is a fabrication foisted upon the world by
Poe. 'It is unadulterated fantasy — delirious into the bargain.' Jeorling
sets sail from Christmas Harbour bound for Tristan da Cunha on the
schooner *Halbrane* whose captain, the taciturn Len Guy, is convinced
that Pym's story is authentic and that the survivors of the *Jane* are still
alive somewhere. He has even made an unsuccessful attempt to trace
Pym and his companion Dirk Peters. 'Not surprising that he failed,'
Jeorling writes. 'They don't exist.'

At the time Verne was writing there was good reason to believe that
the Antarctic continent was split by a sound. Today we know that this
'sound' is in fact a stretch of open sea, the Weddell Sea, and that Antarctica is a single continent; but in his day Verne was quite justified in
using the hypothesis of the sound and the divided continent, particularly in a fantasy that explicitly sets out to out-Poe Poe.

In the *Narrative of Arthur Gordon Pym*, Poe's heroes land on the
island of Tsalal, a strange place if ever there was one. There is no point
in trying to understand the weird things that happen, because their sole
raison d'être is to disorient the reader and confront him with a world of
irrationality. The only signpost to comprehension that Poe gives us is
the leitmotiv of the opposites black and white. His new race of men
with jet-black skins and black teeth are terrified of white, which they
seem to regard as the colour of death. In their world, white represents

the cold, the ice and snow that lie as a permanent menace around their temperate little universe. This, surely, is the meaning that must be given to the series of abysses on the island that form a pattern that spells the Arabic word for 'to be white', the Ethiopian word for 'to be shady' and the Egyptian word for 'the region of the south'. We can suppose that for these blacks mysteriously cast away on the island, perhaps while en route from Africa, some feared white creature lives in the south. This 'white terror' (which may explain why the blacks have always massacred any white men setting foot on their island) is the focal point of Poe's fantasy.

It is at this juncture that Verne's narrative links up with Poe's. Jeorling's journal provides no explanation of the strange nature of the island of Tsalal. The tortured terrain prevents the narrator from verifying vague descriptions of the island's weird geography. In any case, the expedition encounters no sign of man or beast apart from an inexplicable heap of bleached human bones and the skeleton of a dog with a collar bearing the words 'Tiger Arthur Pym'. Captain Guy decides to call the search off. At this point Hunt, a member of the crew signed on in the Falklands, utters the words: 'Ah, Pym! Where are you now?' When asked to explain himself, Hunt claims that Poe never met Pym: his entire narrative was based on notes given to him by Dirk Peters. Hence the novel could be a figment of his imagination. When pressed for further explanations, Hunt admits that he is in fact none other than Dirk Peters in person.

The *Halbrane* enters a zone of icebergs, one of which overturns and sweeps the ship to its destruction. Henceforth the crew is trapped on this floating mountain swept along through thick fog by a violent gale. They eventually run aground short of the Pole. Thirteen of the crew led by Hearne (who has incidentally discovered that Dirk Peters is a murderer) mutiny and set out in the salvaged lifeboat to attempt to cross the ice field. The remaining ten resign themselves to braving out the winter. One day, four men found drifting in a boat turn out to be the captain and three sailors from the *Jane*. They tell how they escaped from the collapse of the mountain on Tsalal and spent three weeks cut off in a crevasse. One day they heard a great panic among the natives who were being pursued by a large white animal with a foaming mouth that leapt at their throats. It was none other than Tiger, mad and rabid. Most of the natives fled in terror; the rest died of rabies. In Pym's narrative, Tiger makes a single reappearance aboard the *Grampus* in order to eliminate the few remaining mutineers and then disappears from the story – until Verne, positing his survival rather than his death (Pym leaves the issue open), makes good use of him as a *deus ex machina* to take the story a step further towards his own stupendous, but suitably Poesque, dénouement.

The castaways embark in the boat that brought the four men from the *Jane*; it is a native boat with no metal in its construction. Like Pym, they are swept along by the current. Their speed increases without apparent reason and the huge figure seen by Pym grows before their astonished eyes into a rock in the form of a sphinx. As they get nearer, all the iron objects on board go spinning off towards this rock, including their anchor which drags them along on the end of its taut cable until it finally breaks and the boat slows down. Jeorling and his companions examine the sphinx and discover that all the iron objects that flew from their boat are stuck against the rock. They conclude that the sphinx is a 'mass of iron magnetized by the electrical currents in its base stemming from the discharges of clouds hurtling past on the north wind'. Then, the dénouement: with a shock that kills him, Dirk Peters sees the corpse of Arthur Gordon Pym plastered against the rock, hanging from the strap of his rifle which had got caught up in the irresistible force of the magnetic sphinx.

Why carp at this ending, which is perfectly in key with the phantasmogorical narrative of Poe? Whether such a magnet could exist or not is an issue as academic as the issue of a divided Antarctica. *An Antarctic Mystery* is a fantasy; the novelist's role was merely to give it a semblance of verisimilitude, and leave things at that.

Verne's assertion, in a letter to Hetzel (9 November 1897), that he was still working regularly, like a well-oiled machine, and 'still stoking up the fires' was no exaggeration. He sent in the manuscript of *Le Superbe Orénoque* (1898; no translation) which he had completed in 1894; a few weeks later, towards the end of 1897, he was correcting the galleys with the intention of adding further revisions, and indeed at the beginning of March the following year he was still sending in corrections to the map of the Orinoco.

The theme of the novel (a daughter, disguised as a boy, searching for her lost father) is merely a pretext for what is in fact just a lively travelogue – interesting and instructive but hardly indispensable.

As proof that he was 'still stoking up the fires' he sent Hetzel, in July

From the Earth to the Moon: interior and exterior of the projectile, by de Montaut. The astronaut was named 'Ardan' (an anagram for Nadar); the space vehicle was the same weight and height as that used one hundred years later in the Apollo 9 moon expedition, and it was launched from the same place —Florida

The famous 'splashdown' picture (by Bayard), in *From the Earth to the Moon*, which proved to be so prophetic when – one hundred years later – the American astronaut Frank Borman landed in the Pacific after the Apollo 9 moon expedition – about two-and-a-half miles from the point mentioned in the novel. Borman, in a letter to the author, wrote that he—like other space explorers—had as a schoolboy been fascinated by Jules Verne's books: 'In a very real sense he is one of the great pioneers of the space age'

Jules Verne aged 60. Engraving by Guillaumot

The steam yacht *Saint Michel III*, which Jules Verne sailed at various times to North Africa, Scotland, Scandinavia and the Mediterranean

The Amiens municipal council. Jules Verne is second from the right and mayor Petit third from the left in the front row

Honorine and Jules Verne in old age

Jules Verne's house in the Rue Charles-Dubois, Amiens, his wife's home town, where he lived throughout his last fifteen years. Jules Verne is in the foreground with his dog Follette; Honorine is in the doorway

Jules Verne's study-bedroom (*above*) at 44 Boulevard de Longueville, Amiens, which communicated with his library (*below*)

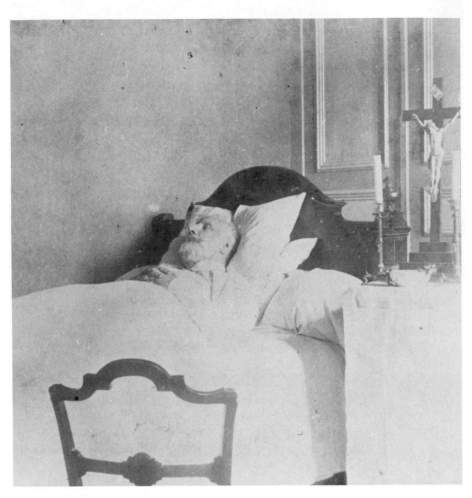

Jules Verne's death-bed

1898, the first volume of what he called ('for lack of a better title') *The Testament d'un Excentrique* (1899; *The Will of an Eccentric*: 1900).

The immensely rich Mr Hypperbome, a member of the Chicago Eccentrics' Club, 'who had never been known for his eccentricity', decides to be eccentric at least once in his life – at the time of his death. He makes arrangements for his funeral to be a kind of fairground sideshow: under the terms of his will, a huge fortune will go to the winner of a board game played by six citizens of Chicago plus a seventh, to be known as XYZ. After throwing the dice, the players move their counters forward by a corresponding number of squares and must then visit the state shown in the square before playing again. 'In short, when they've read that, they'll know the USA in detail.'

It was an amusing idea, and the book itself is good-humoured enough, but the narrative gets bogged down in excessive detail. For once, Verne's scrupulous accuracy hampers him. The book is too long (one volume would have sufficed, in lieu of two) and the description of Hypperbome's funeral, coming as it does at the start of the novel, is frankly tedious and holds up the action: where one chapter would have sufficed, Verne gives us three. Also, there is far too little fun in the novel and far too much travelling.

> I don't need to tell you, my dear Jules [Hetzel], that I'm sick and tired of children searching for their fathers, fathers searching for their children, wives searching for their children and wives searching for their husbands. *Orénoque* is the last of that lot. I'm through with castaways as well, except for my two-volume sequel to *The Swiss Family Robinson*, which I think is more interesting than Wyss's original.

It is strange that Verne should have taken it upon himself to write a follow-up to a book that he implies is weak. In his own stories he had always avoided drawing explicit moral conclusions, preferring to leave that to the reader if he was so inclined. By contrast, the Swiss book is so obviously edifying that it is positively stifling. The only explanation I can think of for Verne's interest is that he was getting old and, as often happens, looking back nostalgically at his childhood heroes.

In truth, it would seem that Verne was losing heart. In addition to his permanent bad health, he felt unable to understand the period he was living in. His own intellectual climate was that of the 1848 revolution, the liberal principles of which had stuck with him throughout his life. He could not come to terms at all with the unprincipled gaiety of the belle époque; and a nation in pursuit of pleasure had little time for books rooted in a world whose moral premises appeared outmoded.

Nonetheless, Verne's position on the Dreyfus affair seems incomprehensible. From his sedentary and bourgeois old age in Amiens he was apparently incapable of understanding what was really at stake. For him, as a good republican, a judge's decision was sacrosanct. Yet if he had been clearer sighted, he would have realized that the real moral anarchy of the belle époque lay not so much in the loose living that he complained about, as in the government's determination to destroy a man's life with the sole purpose of covering up a scandal.

From the outset his son Michel, a so-called reactionary with royalist tendencies, was violently outraged by the injustice of the Dreyfus case. I remember that what upset him most was the deliberate procedural error whereby documentary evidence was produced in court without being shown beforehand to the defence – particularly since the document concerned turned out to be a forgery. Obviously, Michel's visits to Amiens at this time could not help being stormy ones. They might well have resulted in a momentary breach with his father; but fortunately their affection for each other was by now such that their relationship emerged unscathed. In any case, Verne's judgment was too sound for him not to see eventually that his son's indignation was justified; but to admit that much he had to sweep aside a good many beliefs that he had always regarded as inviolable.

This made him all the more disposed to listen to the opinions of his prodigal son, who had turned out to have a cultivated and alert mind with which Verne could communicate. Michel had managed to find a job; in that respect, his father felt more reassured. His role in the preparations for the Great Exhibition had enabled him to show what he was capable of. He had made several trips to Russia, Siberia, Silesia and Rumania to start up mine workings. His prosperity enabled him to give a free rein to his contemporary tastes; and he became an habitué of the salon of Mme de Loynes, where he and his wife Maja (Jeanne's nickname) met such brilliant and famous figures as Jules Lemaître, Ernest and Léon Daudet, Maurice Barrès. Many other well-known people frequented the Loynes salon: doctors, engineers, scientists. Michel was part of this scene until the Dreyfus affair split it up.

We had moved our summer quarters from La Fourberie in Britanny to

Les Petites-Dalles in Normandy. Verne came there 'for a week or thereabouts' in August 1899; in fact, his visit must have been longer than he intended, for I remember that my father rented a tower facing the sea, the Tour Pelletier, specially for his stay. It was right next to our house.

A letter dating from October 1899 informs us that he was 'deep in the heart of the Klondike'; hence, he must have been writing *Le Volcan d'or*, which was not to appear until 1906. He suspected that he would not be alive when it was published: 'As you know', he wrote to his publisher (27 August), 'I have quite a few volumes ready for publication, the fruits of my continual labour. Probably some of them will be posthumous.' In point of fact, sixteen further volumes were published while he was still alive, including *Le Volcan d'or*; seven more were published posthumously.

He fought old age and illness with all his strength. 'It won't stop me from working. It won't stop me from slaving. What could I do without my work? What would become of me?' This cry from the heart sounds very much like a cry of despair.

Seconde Patrie, as Verne's sequel to *Swiss Family Robinson* was called, appeared in 1900. As late as May of that year, Verne was still sending in corrections to the map. He had decided to leave 'the big, cold, oppressive house' on the Rue Charles-Dubois, where he had lived for eighteen years, to move back to the nearby house at 44 Boulevard Longueville where he and Honorine had lived for eight years before their move up in the world. Repairs to the new house took a long time to complete: at the end of the year he was still 'removal-bound'.

Honorine was seventy; the time for worldly show was over. She must have had no regrets about leaving the over-large house that was so hard to heat. She was glad to return to the house that she had left in such a joyful flush of ambition; Verne happily went back to his work table in his monkish cell.

Honorine's last fling was to go up to Paris to see 'Michel's exhibition'; she came back delighted. Verne contented himself with staying at home in Amiens well away from all the fuss. He had dreamed the dream of a society in which industry would be a benefactor of all mankind; what he heard of the festivities and fireworks in Paris was not made to reassure him. This hunger for amusement which favoured only the few while the others gathered up the crumbs could not help resulting in disheartenment. Living fifty years ahead of his time, Verne could perceive the social upheavals and wars that would be the price of this one-sided and illusory prosperity.

When Michel, now quite well-off and very much the man of the twentieth century, came up to Amiens from Paris wearing a brand-new fur coat (still a sign of wealth in those days), he felt obliged to justify his purchase to my grandfather, whose modesty of dress was well known.

'I really got a bargain when I bought this coat. Fur is very economical: I paid a thousand francs for it and it will last for ten years. That's a mere hundred francs a year.'

'Oh, but I agree with you!' said Verne. 'A good bargain indeed. I'm the same. *I* have a coat made every ten years. It costs me a hundred francs and at the end of ten years I have it turned!'

Although he answered all his fan mail, which was considerable once people realized that 'Jules Verne, Amiens' or 'Jules Verne, France' was a sufficient address, he never spread himself; his recipe for admirers' correspondence was a simple one: 'Never turn over the page'.

His life was as regular as clockwork. Up at dawn or earlier, he went straight to work; around eleven he took a short walk, moving slowly on account of his bad legs and declining eyesight. After a frugal lunch, he would smoke a small cigar, meditating silently in his armchair with his back to the light in order to spare his eyes, which were generally shielded by a peaked cap. Later on, he would go limping off to the Société Industrielle for a look at the papers and technical reviews before moving on to the town hall. After that he might call at the Cercle Universitaire or the Cercle de l'Union before walking home down Boulevard Longueville. Then he would eat a light meal before retiring for a few hours' rest; if he was unable to sleep he would do crossword puzzles – he got through more than four thousand of them over the years.

Friends occasionally called to see him. Always affable, he brightened up as soon as the conversation turned to something that interested him: then he spoke brilliantly. The striking thing about him was his simplicity and his lack of regard for convention: if he got tired in the street he would unhesitatingly sit down on the nearest doorstep. In ordinary life he appeared taciturn; he liked to retreat into silence, avoiding useless verbiage as if he was afraid that it might disturb his peace of mind: when he gave an opinion, it was trenchantly to the point, but he avoided sterile discussion like the plague. In the face of disagreement, he would never attempt to argue; he was tired of disputes, having suffered too deeply from family quarrels, and life had taught him that preconceived ideas led almost invariably to a truncated view of the truth. He was a peaceful man and, better still, a man of peace.

His contact with the world outside Amiens and his family was minimal. Now it was Hetzel who took the train to come to *him*. ('I could barely make out what you were saying,' Verne wrote to him after receiving a surprise telephone call at the Société Industrielle in 1894. Typically, Verne did not like this newfangled contraption, while admiring it.) Even in Amiens, he was rarely seen after 1898. To the chairman of the Académie d'Amiens, excusing his absence, he wrote in 1902: 'Words flee me, and ideas no longer come.' But his interest in the world remained active until the end. Only a few months before his death he agreed to lend his name to a newly-founded Esperanto Society, and promised to write a novel about this artificial language designed to break down national barriers; but he did not have time to put his promise into practice.

The years had caught up with him and he knew that he did not have much longer to live. He could no longer trust his body, and felt more than ever that his life depended on his mind. Having reached the age at which a man balances up his life in terms of success and failure (the latter receiving more weight than is warranted by the facts), he had forgotten nothing of his childhood and youth: the ghost of Caroline reminded him of his first failure in love which his literary ambitions had only partly expunged from his memory. Dumas, *Les Pailles rompues*, the Théâtre Lyrique – how far away all that was, and yet so near. What had possessed him to try and succeed as a playwright? The theatre had never brought him anything but a handful of favourable reviews. And what a fool he had been to imagine that he could make a successful stockbroker when he had nothing but contempt for the world of money. Why on earth had his father ever agreed to help him commit the double folly of going into the Stock Exchange and getting married to Honorine? He was quite incapable of giving a young and pretty woman like her the amusements that she aspired to. Hadn't he said that the marriage was impossible? Poor Honorine had had to count every penny while he left the bank to its own devices and spent all his time scribbling.

All the work that he had managed to accomplish over the years had
certainly satisfied his own curiosity. But what did it all amount to?
Hetzel had believed in him; eventually, it appeared that he had invented a new genre, the scientific romance. That, at least, was
something to his credit. But what were *Hatteras, The Centre of the
Earth, Twenty Thousand Leagues,* and the rest, when all was said and
done? Bestsellers! He had got caught up in his own success and had
tied himself down to the *Magasin d'Education.* How much of his life
lay in ruins around him through none of his fault! With the death of his
mother, 15 February 1887, the focal point of the family had disappeared for ever. His father, whose wise counsel and help were always
unstintingly given, had died twenty years before her. Hetzel, who had
replaced him as Verne's friend and mentor, had passed away on 17
March 1886. Then Verne's best friend, his brother Paul, had died in his
turn on 27 August 1897. Verne felt the world moving away from him,
taking a new turning which he did not understand and which left him
grimly alone. Michel and his family lived away in Paris and he still
could not entirely forgive his step-daughters for their attitude to his
son's marriage. Everyone was at war with everyone else, and there was
no sign that an arrangement would ever be possible. Verne consoled
himself by thinking of his readers, people he had never met but in some
sense friends to him – his young readers in particular, for it was to them
that he had devoted his life. They were his real family.

His solitary life had been a full one: his ambition had been to write
and he had written millions upon millions of words, becoming world
famous in the process. He had lived off his writing and he loved his
profession since all he needed to earn his living was paper and pencil.
My father told me that Verne once exclaimed: 'What a fine profession
I have! I'm a free man. I get a pencil and some white paper, go
off by myself and there I am sitting on the slopes of Popocatepetl
or paddling in Lake Titicaca.' He hadn't exactly filled his coffers
with gold; but he had at least managed to support his family; and
money for its own sake held no interest for him. Yet this undoubted
success seemed to have a taste of failure about it, for it lacked the
one thing that Verne desired more than any other: the esteem of his
fellow-writers.

Most of them were indifferent towards his work, even though
Charles Baudelaire, Théophile Gautier, and the popular authors Jules
Clarétie and Georges Bastard all stood up for him at different times in

his career as a writer. As Charles Raymond pointed out in an article in the *Musée des Familles:*

> Verne is the undisputed ruler of the kingdom that he has conquered, but strictly speaking he is not a novelist, since, in his works, love, the basis of all novels, is conspicuous through its absence. Women are almost always made to take a back seat . . . his heroes have no time to waste on the sweet nothings of the cunning little god.

Clarétie concludes his essay on Verne in his book *Célébrités contemporaines* (1883) by saying:

> I know that refined writers with loftier ambitions as regards the analysis of human nature say of him: He is a story-teller. Yet a story-teller who can enchant an entire generation as he has done is a man to be reckoned with, mark my words.

By contrast, the great critic of the day, Emile Zola, attacked Verne's scientific novels. For his part Verne criticized Zola for wallowing in descriptions of human turpitude; he thought it preferable to exalt man's resources rather than his deficiencies. This opposition of views did not prevent Verne from admiring Zola's talent, even though his vulgarity shocked him. In 1877 he had written to Hetzel the elder:

> Read Zola's *L'Assommoir*: it's foul, obsessive, terrifying, repugnant, nauseating – and prodigious! How in the blazes will he ever do better than this? It's the great epic of the working-class drunkard. Should such things be recounted? But I repeat: it's prodigious.

Hetzel cannot have shared Verne's admiration, in spite of his reservations, for we find Verne writing again in more detail:

> Good heavens, don't read *L'Assommoir* if you don't want to. What I am talking about is Zola's talent for amazing detail which is far above anything I've seen in the same vein. But he depicts two things which should not be depicted in that way. I'm not trying to learn anything from it; all it can do is show me a series of amazing photographs – forbidden photographs.

Fifteen years later, he wrote to the younger Hetzel:

> *La Débâcle* is a boring novel and I'll never read it again, though I have often returned to the others. I don't care what Zola says, it's trite and boring, that's what I think. To my mind, Chatrian [properly, Erckman-

Chatrian, a largely forgotten tandem of novelists and playwrights]
produces more unforgettable true effects in twenty lines than Zola in twenty pages.

This criticism of *La Débâcle* proves that Verne read Zola over and over
again, even though Zola had been unkind about Verne's books. On the
more moderate exponents of naturalism Verne's opinion was more
nuanced. To Louis-Jules, he wrote:

> I've already mentioned having read Stendhal's Roman writings after my
> trip there. That led me to read the *Chartreuse de Parme* for the twentieth
> time. How it still grips me! And how much better it is than anything being
> done nowadays! I have read *Sapho* – an amazing piece of writing, I read it
> in one sitting. All the same, the influence of Zola is always there, along
> with certain intentional vulgarities. I don't like the ending and anyway
> Sapho is far from being a model of womanhood – a former lesbian, if you
> please! The hero really deserves better. Daudet dedicates it to his sons for
> when they're twenty. I know where they'll go when they've read it! But it's
> undeniably full of talent.
>
> How much talent, too, in Guy de Maupassant: never vulgar, he recounts
> the most libidinous things one could imagine. Read his latest short stories,
> the *Contes de la Bécasse* and *Les Sœurs Rodani*, but don't let your wife
> read them (*4 May 1884*).

We do not know whether Maupassant's opinion of Verne was as
favourable. At all events Verne could count on the support of the
French academicians Sardou, Labiche, Ducamp, Camille Roussel,
Legouvé, Augier and Sarcey. At the same time it was true that the
critics no longer paid any attention to him. He complained to Louis-
Jules (30 August 1894):

> When I read all that is written about any old thing that gets into print, I
> sometimes feel jealous even though I do live in the depths of the provinces
> . . . I expect you sent review copies to *Le Figaro* and the other papers.
> Let's wait and see what they say, if they have *anything* to say.

And again (28 May 1895):

> I discovered that the first volume of *Propellor Island* was out when I saw it
> in the shops. Are you waiting for a better time of year to publicize it? I read
> almost all the papers but haven't seen an advertisement or review in any of
> them. The most lightweight of novels get publicity.

As early as 1893, Verne evidently felt that his publisher was not doing his best by him (6 August):

> I am always upset to see that all the papers carry reviews of just about anything. Even if in some cases the reviews are only a few lines long, the books we publish don't even get that, except around Christmas. *Bombarnac* in particular hasn't had the grace of a review, which upsets me but doesn't stop me from ploughing on.

Even though he had become world famous, he had been hurt by the indifference of his peers. Already in 1869 Hetzel had unwisely suggested his standing for election to the Académie Française. Verne's reaction was unambiguous: how could an author whose works were published in a magazine for the young aspire to such heights?

> I regard your idea as a fond dream. Anyone without a great deal of money or without political standing has no hope of getting in. I'm referring to the Académie Française. As for the Académie des Sciences, can you imagine old Verne sitting next to a Bertrand or a Deville? I'd look a proper fool.

A few years later, Dumas *fils* took up Hetzel's 'fond dream' and convinced Verne that it was not so far-fetched as he thought. He had never had any such ambition himself, but when Dumas realized that his lobbying would not succeed Verne was mortified. The wound healed quickly but it left its mark. Dumas had spontaneously urged him to apply for election; Hetzel had told him to think about it seriously in 1873 (Verne had replied, 'There's an awful lot of people who should get in before me – in particular, a certain Stahl'); in 1877 Verne still thought that his candidacy would be 'shrugged off' on account of 'the relative unimportance of books for the young' and because 'the study of the human heart is more literary than any adventure stories are'. The matter was brought up again in 1883, 1889 and 1892 without his being seriously bothered about it: 'I ask for only one thing: to be allowed to live in peace in the depths of the provinces and finish my job as a novelist, if finished it can ever be.'

1900–1905

L E VILLAGE AÉRIEN (1910; *The Village in the Treetops: 1961*) was originally given the working title of *La grande Forêt* – 'the great forest' – after its setting in central Africa. Two big-game hunters, the American John Cort and the Frenchman Max Huber, cross this supposedly impenetrable virgin forest encountering evolution at work but above all discovering a moral: adversity forces men to cooperate in order to survive; but their cooperation ends as soon as the danger is removed.

Towards the end of his life, Verne seems to have been reaching the same point in belief as his father, whose strict religiosity was really a symptom of acute metaphysical anguish. Pierre's view of humanity was restricted to considering (and preaching) virtue as the only way man could unflinchingly climb Jacob's ladder. Jules had placed *his* hope for this ascension in scientific research. But man was still his own worst enemy. Following a different process, Verne was reaching the same conclusion as his father: there was no greater virtue than charity.

The past, as we have seen, was very much alive for him: looking for a title for a sea-serpent story (planned a long time before, but not sent in for publication until April 1901), he hit upon a name remembered from his boyish escapade as a would-be runaway on the *Coralie* – Jean-Marie Cabidoulin. However, instead of *Les Histoires de Jean-Marie Cabidoulin* publishers have preferred the doubtless more intriguing title *Le Serpent de Mer* (1901; *The Sea Serpent*: 1967), despite the fact that Verne's chosen title emphasizes that only the atmosphere created by the superstitious sailor Cabidoulin could make anyone believe in the existence of the fabulous beast. In fact, three-quarters of the novel is not about the serpent at all but describes the normal workings of a typical whaler of the period, the *Saint Enoch*. One must admit that this is not one of his best books.

Was *any* of the numerous manuscripts he was hoarding for the *Magasin* likely to be one of his best, once revised? Certainly not the next one in line, at all events. Verne got the idea for *Les Frères Kip* (1902; no translation), which is also a transposition of his own feelings for Paul, from another of France's many *affaires* which made the headlines in 1893. Two brothers called Rorique (Degraeve) had hijacked a French schooner, the *Niuorahiti*, after killing the captain, the owner's agent, four crew and a passenger. Brought to trial, the brothers claimed that they were innocent and that the deaths had occurred while they were putting down a mutiny. Even though the prosecution rested on the testimony of one man, the ship's cook, they were found guilty and sentenced to death. After a public outcry, however, the sentence was commuted to life imprisonment with hard labour. Subsequently, the President himself intervened, possibly to allay charges that his regime was tolerating a miscarriage of justice, and reduced the sentence again to twenty years.

Les Frères Kip is a poor novel, but it contains an interesting *trouvaille*: an enlargement of the face of the dead Captain Gibson reveals the image of his murderers, Flig Balt and Vin Mod (irresistible names!), imprinted on the pupils of his eyes.

It seems that on death the retina retains an image of the last thing a person sees. Verne probably got this information from La Grange and Valude, *Encyclopédie d'ophtalmologie*, as Moré points out; it is also probable that he was led to seek this information after reading *Claire Lenoir*, a short story by Villiers de l'Isle-Adam written in 1867 and reprinted in *Tribulat Bonhomet* in 1887, Verne's copy of which (dated 1887) has come down to me as an heirloom. The image retained on the retina of Claire Lenoir was a hallucination; Verne has none of that, but goes straight to his reference books and reads up on the facts. La Grange and Valude would have informed him of the work of Giraud-Teulon, who fixed retinal images after death by removing the eye and submerging it in a bath of alum. Moré points out that Verne makes a mistake that Villiers de l'Isle-Adam did not make, namely that Captain Gibson's photograph dates from the day after his death, by which time (as Verne himself earlier implies) the image would have faded. A worse mistake, it seems to me, is that Verne omits to have the eye submerged in alum, a process which we are told is essential if the image is to be fixed for any length of time.

Verne revised the manuscript of *Les Frères Kip* in September 1901, and it was published the following year. In the meantime, the Dreyfus affair had been drawing to an end: the cover-up operation collapsed and Dreyfus was pardoned. The time seemed ripe for the publication of *Un Drame en Livonie*, originally planned for 1896 but held back presumably because Verne and Hetzel thought that its publication at the height of the Dreyfus affair would be too controversial. (Its subject is judicial error – a concept which Verne had vigorously repudiated in conversations with his son but which seems to have occupied his mind increasingly, since his plan for the book dates from 1894, the year Dreyfus was sentenced, and the book itself is a sign that Verne's thinking on the implications of the affair underwent a radical change between then and the year it was published, almost a decade later in 1904.)

On 7 June 1894 Verne had written to a young Italian correspondent, Mario Turiello, saying that with seventy volumes behind him he still had thirty or so to do. On 5 May 1897 he told his correspondent that he was so far ahead in his work that he was writing his novel for 1903. On 10 July 1899 he claimed to have twelve volumes completed and stashed away for the years to come. By 15 January 1902 the hoard had not dwindled but actually increased to fourteen, despite the fact that several books had been published in the meantime. *Les Frères Kip* was his eighty-third book; when it was published, he was working on his one-hundredth and was 'attacking the one hundred and first' by the end of the same year!

At all events, in 1902, three years from his death, he was delving into his voluminous bottom drawer for *Un Drame en Livonie*. However, two other books came out first: *Bourses de Voyage* (1903; no translation) and *Maître du Monde*. The former is a lightweight schoolboy cruise around the Lesser Antilles complete with pirates (Wil Mitz appears half-way through the second volume to defeat dastardly Harry Markel); it would seem that publication of this story was brought forward to coincide with rumours of a possible annexation of the Danish Antilles by the United States. For once, Verne is fair to England: he approves of English efforts to work the barren island of Antigua by installing huge water tanks, after the French had given the place up and gone home.

Of his remaining novels, Verne was to see the publication of only three. In *Maître du Monde* (1904; *Master of the World*: 1914), Robur reappears: not as the great figure we knew but as a success-crazy maniac. It may well be that Verne originally planned this book as a kind of detective novel, with Robur appearing just to clear up the mystery: an early title was, in fact, *Avatars d'un Policeman américain*.

Un Drame en Livonie (1904; *Drama in Livonia*: 1904) was probably written before *Les Frères Kip* but not revised until 1902. It is a lively, well-written novel with some fine descriptive passages; and it has several echoes of the Dreyfus machination.

A quieter tale followed: *L'Invasion de la Mer* (1905; no translation), in which a surveying expedition harassed by Tuaregs attempts to find a canal route to link the Gulf of Gabès with the parts of the Sahara lying below sea-level. Work on the canal begins but an earthquake breaches the Gabès ridge and the sea rushes in, to accomplish in a few days what would have taken men years. The moral seems to be that man needs to be taught humility.

In the middle of March 1905 Verne fell seriously ill, as a result of his diabetes. At first there were hopes that he would pull through, as he had done on a similar occasion the year before. But after a few days he himself announced to Honorine that he felt the attack would prove fatal. Michel, who was in the process of moving his family to the south of France, arrived immediately with his second-eldest son, Georges. Michel and Jean were summoned by telegram from Toulon. Marie Guillon, his youngest sister, rushed up from Paris, where his condition was headlined in the evening papers. The news agencies broke the story with top priority on 20 March; by the morrow, the world knew that Jules Verne was dying. Malecarly, Verne's ideal bourgeois realm in *Propellor Island*, was losing its old king. The century was turning with a vengeance.

Jules Verne died on 24 March 1905 at eight in the morning, aged seventy-eight.

> When he saw that we were all there, he gave us one fond look that clearly meant: 'Good, you are all here. Now I can die'; then he turned to the wall to await death bravely. His serenity impressed us greatly and we wished that we might have as fine a death ourselves when our time came. According to Marie Guillon, his beloved little sister, who sat with him for five days until the end, he remarked to the priest who came to see him every day: 'You have done me good. I feel regenerated.' More significantly, it seems to me, he asked that any disagreements that might have arisen among the family should be forgotten.

He was buried in the cemetery of La Madeleine in Amiens on 28 March, very simply, as he would have wished. Two years later, a sculpture by Albert Roze (depicting Verne rising dramatically from the tomb) was placed over his grave by Michel; the stone reads 'Towards immortality and eternal youth'. The same sculptor was responsible for the monument inaugurated in 1909 and paid for by public subscriptions from all over the world: it stands close to Verne's house on Boulevard Longueville, near a bench where he was wont to sit on fine afternoons. Honorine died on 29 January 1910, five years after her husband, at the age of eighty. She was buried alongside him.

On Verne's death his estate came under the administration of Michel, who contracted with Hetzel to publish the remaining novels, eight in all (a ninth 'posthumous' novel, *L'Invasion de la Mer*, was at press when Verne died). In addition, Michel sought to protect the estate by publishing in *Le Figaro* and *Le Temps* (May 1905) a list of all Verne's surviving works: sixteen plays, three short stories, an untitled novel, the *Voyage en Ecosse*, and a piece entitled *Paris in the Twentieth Century*, plus the eight novels. Of the novels, some were completed and ready for press in typewritten form (an idea of Michel's, this: since Verne's writer's cramp and failing eyesight made normal work almost impossible after 1902, Michel sent him a girl to take dictation); others were inked over in the old way ready for typesetting; and two were in draft form necessitating revision prior to publication.

Michel's business interests had expanded to include nickel mines, paper mills and banking. This versatility had distressed Verne, whose entire life had been one hard single-minded grind; it seemed to him that Michel was trying to do too much at once and might well let business turn him into that abhorrent creature: the businessman. There was only one solution: get out while the going was good. There was a great deal of arguing before my father made his decision; but he eventually wound up his affairs and we left Paris just before Verne died, doubtless happier because of our move.

In 1905 Michel had plenty of time on his hands. A paper mill that he had run successfully for a few years after the Exhibition of 1900 had regrettably burnt down. After that, he had gone into banking, but had resigned when called upon to endorse illegal transactions. As Verne's sole heir, together with his mother, he felt it his duty to ensure that his father's works be preserved for posterity. Therefore he set to work in his house at Les Maurillons, near Toulon; and books by Jules Verne continued to be published by Hetzel until 1910. (The final novel was published by Hachette in 1919.)

In the postwar years, he formed a one-man company called Les Films Jules-Verne to make cinematograph versions of his father's books. We were regaled with stories of his work on location: three hundred extras signed on in Marseilles, thirty black men in a dug-out canoe on the Verdon (a wild river in a magnificent site above Grasse), Michel doing apparently everything else himself: script, production, direction, costume, supervision and the rest. He shot *Les Cinq Cents Millions de la Bégum*, *Le Destin de Jean Morénas*, *L'Etoile du Sud*, and *Les Indes Noires*. But he never had enough backing to do things properly, even in those heroic days of the cinema. When his company was wound up, the film rights were sold out of the family.

Michel died in 1925. He had been an honest man, and that is the main thing. Cultivated and imaginative, he had done much in the course of his life. Fair-minded in everything, he had been one of the first and most passionate of the Dreyfusards. A child of the belle époque, he had been one of the last of the big spenders. His wife Maja, by keeping him on a tight rein, had succeeded in restraining his violence and in bringing him round the course without mishap – which was no mean feat.

The first of the novels seen through the press by Michel, *Le Phare du Bout du Monde* (1905; *Lighthouse at the end of the world*: 1923), had been written in pencil and then inked over in a very legible hand, presumably in preparation for imminent publication. Hence it could come out almost immediately. It is quite desolately and unusually humourless – as harsh as the landscapes it describes. The book is set on Isla de los Estados off Tierra del Fuego, from which it is separated by the twenty-mile Le Maire Strait used by ships rounding Cape Horn. A new lighthouse built on the island in 1859 is guarded by three men, who are depicted in their isolation during the harsh Atlantic winter and coping with a gang of wreckers. Good triumphs over evil eventually, even though the tally of corpses is unduly weighted in favour of the villains.

Le Volcan d'Or (1906; *The Golden Volcano*: 1963) is set in the Klondike where two cousins from Montreal, Summy Skim and Ben Raddle, are investigating a claim bequeathed to them by their uncle. On their way to the Klondike, Summy and Ben encounter two young women, Jane and Edith, who are cousins also and bent upon an expedition similar to their own. Understandably, the four find that they have something in common and decide to join forces. However, the prospectors' hopes are dashed by an earthquake which floods their claims and they are about to abandon everything when a dying man appears and tells them how to get to a golden volcano in the far north. When they arrive, Ben decides to hasten the volcano's eruption by blasting a hole in the side of the mountain. Unfortunately, things get held up by the arrival of an adventurer called Hunter: there is a fight, Jane is kidnapped, Summy rescues her. Thereupon Ben dynamites the volcano, but things go disastrously wrong: the eruption that he provokes is so violent that all the nuggets fall into the sea and explode in a shower of gold dust. Hunter is killed by a falling lump of gold and everyone beats a hasty retreat through the crashing golden consummation as 'the gold goes up in smoke, like so much else in this vile world'. But there is a happy ending.

L'Agence Thompson (1907; *The Thompson Travel Agency*: 1907) is an entertainment. As such, it reminds us of the comedies of manners that Verne wrote for the stage as a young man. At the same time, it provides Verne with an opportunity to satirize the dishonest selling methods that flourish on people's willingness to be drawn by proposals that are too good to be true.

Robert Morgand is a young Frenchman working for an English travel agency whose disreputable practices have enticed on board a dangerously old cruise ship a group of English and American tourists. The cruise goes laughably wrong, and ends in a peaceful shipwreck; but Morgand and the young American Alice Lindsay fall in love and all ends happily, particularly when Alice learns that young Morgand is in fact the impoverished Marquis de Gramond (she is a little snob) and not, as she suspected, an unscrupulous fortune hunter.

In its sentimentality, this love story is untypical of Verne, who generally preferred action to sentiment; but the fact that all the characters in the story are stock characters without any typically Vernian idiosyncrasies suggests that this book was merely a bow to the prevailing fashion. His critique of sharp business may well have been his way of giving vent to some of his feelings about his son's business interests.

The next book to be published, *La Chasse au Météore* (1908; *The Chase of the Golden Meteor*: 1909), is more in Verne's usual vein. It is an extrapolation of the latest scientific theories. Zéphirin Xirdal, an inventor, has devised an extraordinary machine that can create an 'energy void'. The 'neutral helicoidal ray' beamed out by his machine will cause a solid gold meteorite discovered by two amateur astronomers to fall on to an island off Greenland which he buys for the purposes of the experiment. His uncle, a banker, gleefully buys up gold-mine shares as the prices plummet when the news gets out; but Zéphirin is so revolted by the international disputes that arise over possession of the gold meteorite that he changes its course at the last minute and causes it to fall into the sea. With all the fuss over, he goes back to his attic and continues working at his inventions.

There can be no doubt that this book is intended to be a critique of the social system as Verne saw it: corrupted by the pursuit of wealth. The tone that he adopts is raillery, but the humour is rather forced – there are some dreadful puns – even though the caricature of the absent-minded inventor is fairly well done. Mrs Hudelson is Verne's idea of the perfect wife: kind, understanding, considerate, never nagging, respectful, interested and encouraging. 'Unfortunately, wives like this are rarely found outside novels.'

Le Pilote du Danube (1908; *The Danube Pilot*: 1967) is a fair-to-good detective story. It was written in one continuous sitting over the space of a few weeks; in this case, the indispensable process of revision that all Verne's books went through just prior to publication had to be done by his son. Between 1898 and 1902, Michel had travelled on the Danube, visiting Austria, Hungary, Rumania and Bulgaria. Verne had always been interested in the turbulent history of the Balkans. Conversations with his son jogged his alert imagination and he had decided to write a novel about the Danube, following its course from the Black Forest to the Black Sea.

Michel did not care much for *Le Secret de Wilhelm Storitz* (1910; translated 1965) and presumably the decision to postpone its publication was his. (Verne had wanted it published during his lifetime.) Michel held that H. G. Wells's novel on a similar theme (*The Invisible Man*, 1897) was a much better book, because in real life invisibility was more likely to be a nuisance than an advantage: allowing Storitz to use invisibility as a ploy to frustrate the marriage of a girl who spurned him was banal. Now it seems to me that this criticism misses the point of both the novels and it is not even accurate. True, Storitz does use his father's discovery to further his nefarious ends; but for Myra, his innocent victim who is rendered invisible in her turn, invisibility is a positive curse – as it is for Wells's hero Griffin until the plot turns to murder, at which point it is as useful to him as to Storitz. Verne is quick to point out that invisibility is not exactly conducive to making friends and influencing people: he has Storitz's manservant Hermann appear to be terrified at the prospect of being 'forever cut off from his fellow men' when pressed into service as a *particeps invisibilis*. And he says explicitly that the discovery 'had no practical use and brought out the worst in men'. It would seem, then, that Verne was just as sceptical as Wells was about the positive advantages of invisibility. This is not to suggest that either author was seriously proposing that invisibility could actually be achieved: both novels are fantasies and Wells deliberately suspends credibility through the use of humour (Griffin can disappear, but his clothes can't) while Verne sets his novel in the familiar gothic landscape of eighteenth-century central Europe.

In any case, it is surely a mistake to read these two fables at such a superficial level. Wells used his story as a pretext for dealing with the social questions of his day. Verne saw the plot as a chance to express his poetic feelings towards Hungary. *Storitz* is not so much an adventure story as a descriptive prose poem, and this is where Michel seems to have gone wrong in his judgment of it, impressed as he no doubt was by the 'scientific' genre of his father's previous novels.

The description of Myra's house seems to have been drawn from Verne's recollections of his own house on the Rue Charles-Dubois:

> The main gate and the little tradesmen's entrance next to it give into a paved courtyard, beyond which extends a large garden bordered with elms, acacias, horse-chestnuts and beeches that overhang the enclosure wall. Facing the doors are the servants' quarters smothered with aristolochia and Virginia creeper. From there to the main house runs a corridor with leaded windows of coloured glass that joins the house at the foot of a round tower about sixty foot high containing the main staircase. A glassed-in gallery runs along the front of the house; from there, doors hung with old tapestries lead to Dr Roderich's study, the drawing-room and the dining-room . . .

Jean Chesneaux, in *The Political and Social Ideas of Jules Verne*

(1972), refers to Captain Nemo as 'an implacable rebel who combines the *quarante-huitard* dream of national liberty, the fight against colonialism, and the libertarian rejection of all authority'. I tend to think that this was in fact the standpoint of Verne himself, whom the author and critic Pierre Louys once called 'that underground revolutionary'. His early propensity towards revolt is obvious from the lively series of letters he wrote to his father in his twenties. Later on, the necessities of life intervening, his plays reflect a certain compromise as Verne contents himself with merely lampooning the society of his day. Finally, in his novels, he caresses the dream of progress, only to admit to himself in 1886 that 'science must not move faster than morals'. Robur represents the future of science, a future in which science will be capable of changing the social and political face of the world; he says: 'We must wait for the day when mankind will be sufficiently learned and wise never to misuse it.'

Verne was extremely sensitive to the social problems of his times. In the early days, industrialization had seemed to him to be a worthwhile means of improving living standards; as he grew older, however, he had grown increasingly fearful of industrial development because it went hand in hand with the rise of finance – a tentacular and dark world far removed from its original purpose: investment in human progress.

By temperament he was an anarchist, in the real sense of the word; but he was not blind to the inevitable fragility of any system based on goodwill alone; and as a republican he was horrified by the prospect of democracy sliding into demagogy. He loathed the creed of get-rich-quick; for him, the way to happiness was patient, methodical work.

In their discussions together, Michel would cleverly argue the case for socialism. Verne was not unaware of the advantages of socialism, to which he readily acceded; at the same time, his mind was sharp to its drawbacks. How could any social theory take into account the whole complexity of life, however attractive that theory might appear in terms of logic? Experience had shown that, by necessity, theories excluded from their basic propositions vital human needs – needs as precious to human life as liberty. Satisfying man's material needs was one thing; satisfying his moral needs was another. In any case, what was the point of constructing systems of government? Weren't they all destined to collapse sooner or later as part of a natural process of action and reaction beyond man's control?

Mankind had not become markedly wiser by 1894, the year in which

Verne sets *Les Naufragés du Jonathan* (1909; *The Survivors of the Jonathan*: 1909). On the contrary, the gap between science and morals had never stopped widening. At the end of his life, Verne was terrified to think of what was going to happen as the unavoidable result of this gap: already the state of scientific knowledge indicated that, through misuse, science would lapse into moral bankruptcy and give mankind power of such scope that wisdom would no longer be able to control it. This is the theme of his last manuscript, written with such urgency and haste just prior to his death that Michel was left with a difficult job of revision.

In *The Survivors of the Jonathan* Verne portrays a pure anarchist, a dreamer of the earthly paradise: a world without laws and therefore without crime. This devotee of absolute liberty lives far from 'civilization' and governments on an island in the Tierra del Fuego archipelago. Society as such does not exist there; the only other inhabitants are a few families of Fuegians whom he encounters only as a helper – hence their name for him: Kaw-Djer, or benefactor. His friendship for a Fuegian and his son, his fishing companions, has given him a perfect knowledge of the dangerous straits around the archipelago. One day, an emigrant ship, the *Jonathan*, runs ashore on the island and Kaw-Djer organizes the rescue operation. All the emigrants are drop-outs of one sort or another; faced with the challenge of 'the eternal problem of life' they count on Kaw-Djer to get them out of their predicament. When he suggests that they go in for a little self-help and salvage what they can from the foundering *Jonathan* disputes break out, from which Ferdinand Beauval, a failed politician, makes personal capital. But the cargo is salvaged and Kaw-Djer finds himself the unwilling leader of a little colony. 'This wretched population looked to him for help, advice and decisions.' But if a leader was needed, why should it be him, the anarchist? 'Because you're the only leader we've got,' says the quartermaster.

On the pretext that 'nothing belongs to anyone' the hard-line communist Dorick and his followers 'grab all the best places and imperturbably take whatever suits them'. The capitalist Patterson exploits a drunk. Selfishness and 'latent mutual hatred' become evident in the course of the winter:

> Kaw-Djer was struck by the baseness of his companions . . . They were docile slaves who did what they were told and no more. They did nothing on their own initiative, preferring to hand over the responsibility for their

security to someone else. What cowardice it was to allow the few to dominate the many. Was this the way men were? Could they not do without laws and authority to make them think? Laws to compel them to use their minds against the brute forces of nature, to restrict the despotism of some and the slavery of others, and to check hate? . . . He was discovering that men are very different in reality from the ideal he had assembled in his imagination. This being so, there was nothing essentially absurd in admitting to oneself that men needed protection against themselves, against their weakness and greed and vices; and that, since each individual required protection in his own interests, laws were merely a formal expression of *individual* aspirations, like the sum of divergent forces in mechanics.

In the old days, before he had freed himself from the net of legislation that is cast over the old world . . . Kaw-Djer had seen only the drawbacks of government. The incoherence and the frequently irritating incursions of the tentacular mass of laws, decrees and what-have-you had blinded him to the higher necessity of the principles behind them. At present, however, surrounded by people whom fate had placed in conditions close to the primitive state, he felt like a chemist at work in his laboratory, observing some of the incessant reactions that take place in the melting pot of life . . . Nonetheless, his old beliefs struggled for a hearing. He was cruelly torn between his libertarian ideals and the dictates of reason . . . What astonished him more than anything else was the imperfection of men, their inability to break with their accustomed routine . . . The notion of property was a particular article of their creed. Not one of them could avoid saying as the most natural thing in the world: 'This is mine'. And not one of them was aware of the high comedy, so glaring in the eyes of a libertarian philosopher, of such a fragile and perishable creature's claiming to monopolize, for himself alone, ever so tiny a fragment of the universe. . . His friends the Fuegians . . . would have been greatly surprised by such theories, for the only possessions they had ever had were themselves.

After Ferdinand Beauval has made himself governor of the island but shown himself to be incompetent — he 'copes' with a famine by inciting the crowd to ransack the more prosperous farms; whereas the communist Dorick raises a riot — Kaw-Djer is forced to intervene at the head of a small troop of armed men and proclaim himself their leader. Following his coup d'état, the anarchist finds himself in the bitterly ironic situation of having to promulgate laws and organize a society: food is requisitioned, landgrabbers are evicted, work is made obligatory, property is recognized. A law court is established along with a police force; there is even a prison. Kaw-Djer is on the point of retiring from public life when gold is found on the island and the economy is ruined by everyone rushing off to the hills to become prospectors. Outsiders move in and crime breaks out on a vast scale. A mob attacks the capital and Kaw-Djer is forced to order the police to open fire; in despair, he contemplates the pile of corpses caused by the shooting. Whereupon Chile sends a gunboat to filch the gold by imposing a protectorate on the island. Kaw-Djer resists, proves that the islanders can stand up for themselves, and then signs away the gold rights in exchange for self-government. After that, he steps down in favour of a younger man whom he has groomed to take his place and sails off secretly to become the keeper of a lighthouse that he has had built on Horn Island.

> Far from everyone, useful to everyone, he was going to live alone, free for ever . . . Nowhere else could he have found the strength to bear the burden of living. The most poignant dramas are the dramas of the mind . . . when a man has known them . . . he feels exhausted, at a loss, unseated from the foundations on which he has built . . .

The note of despair in these words is surely an echo of Verne's own thoughts. A slightly earlier passage sounds equally personal:

> Rejecting all restrictions on his own conduct, he found it just as cruel to impose restrictions on others . . . Obliged to abandon his ideals and bow to the facts, he had gone through with his sacrifice courageously; but in his heart the dream that he had abjured protested.

Kaw-Djer's sympathy with communist theory is manifest; but he has little time for the communists themselves because they are all too fallible and out for themselves. His government has much in common with socialist collectivism: the gold deposits are regarded as state property; electricity supplies are a public service; the boat plying around the archipelago is publicly-owned. Private property is tolerated as a necessary evil, not for reasons of dogma but because it stimulates the economy. In short, his system of government, arrived at pragmatically and not by choice, is a kind of socialist liberalism not unlike the guidelines behind Lenin's New Economic Policy inaugurated fifteen years later.

People are often surprised by the dark pessimism of the late works; in fact, if they had been reading carefully, they would have realized that in all Verne's books the hero succeeds through a constant and courageous struggle against adversity and that passages of disillusionment and even despair are to be found throughout the works. True, the note of despair emerges more distinctly as time goes on. In 1895, *Propellor Island* propounds a scathing critique of American gigantism, opportunism and petty politicking; but also it implies that science is beginning to overreach itself. In 1896, the inventor Thomas Roch misuses his invention; and in 1904 the power-crazy Robur goes completely mad. *The Survivors of the Jonathan* of 1909 expresses the anguished fears for society that Verne felt at the end of his life. His last manuscript, *Voyage d'Etudes*, which Michel published in 1919 as *L'Etonnante Aventure de la Mission Barsac*, goes one stage further along the stony road of disillusionment. The mixture of good and evil fermenting in the human soul is more than likely to result in the perversion of science; and mankind, intoxicated by superlatives, may well commit its knowledge, which is its glory, to an ignominious destruction of all that it has achieved.

In the latter part of Verne's life, Michel had grown very close to him — not only emotionally but also intellectually. I can remember the two having long conversations at 44 Boulevard Longueville about the book that Verne was currently writing. The old man was delighted to be able to submit his plans to someone whom he evidently regarded as a valid interlocutor and critic. Jean Chesneaux is correct in thinking that Michel's influence was much more important than that of Paschal Grousset, the left-wing socialist, who wrote under the name of André Laurie. Verne had told Hetzel exactly what he thought of Grousset when ghosting the novel that became *The Begum's Fortune*: 'Writes well, thinks wrong.' And the other book that they did together, *L'Epave du Cynthia* (1885), is a dreary thing in which Verne seems merely to have interpolated a few passages of polar geography to pad out Grousset's boring string of non-events.

Obviously, Verne and Grousset knew each other; and Verne probably sympathized with much of what Grousset had to say. But bearing in mind that Verne found Grousset muddle-headed, though definitely talented as a writer, it is hardly conceivable that Grousset could have influenced Verne except superficially. Michel's influence was much more profound. From him, Verne got clear and stimulating ideas that rapidly turned a conversation into a discussion. Michel was

Verne's confidant in the latter part of his life, and no one was better placed to be his literary executor.

The manuscript with the working title *Voyage d'Etudes* is a rough and fragmentary first draft. Michel had to edit it fairly extensively and round out the narrative with matter that he wrote himself. He did not undertake this task lightly; but he could not bring himself to destroy the last thoughts that his father had committed to paper. He was helped in his job by his recollection of the talks that he and Verne had had about the book as it was taking shape. In any case, this indispensable editing that he did was no more drastic than the kind of thing that Hetzel had gone in for on more than one occasion; true, the author was not around any longer to give his final approval, but all things considered only minor changes were involved that might have been made by someone less qualified than Michel.

The results of his labours were published as *L'Etonnante Aventure de la Mission Barsac*, serialized by the newspaper *Le Matin* in 1914. Publication in volume form was delayed by the outbreak of war; once the war ended, however, the book appeared under the imprint of Hachette, who had taken over the Hetzel list in 1914.

Lewis Buxton, younger son of the ageing Lord Buxton, is compromised in a bank hold-up a few years after his brother George has allegedly disgraced himself in Niger by deserting from the army and leading his men into banditry. We know from the start that Lewis is innocent, since he has been kidnapped by the bank robbers who intend his disappearance to imply his involvement in the robbery; but Joan Buxton, the daughter, is bent on proving George's innocence to sweeten the last years of her old father's life. We meet her in Conakry, French West Africa, where she is working with a commission of enquiry engaged in determining whether the natives should be given the right to vote. The commission runs into trouble: the officer commanding their military escort is replaced by a deserter with false orders. All the villages they come to have been devastated. Finally, when Joan has just determined that George was in fact murdered, the members of the commission are abducted in gliders near Kubo and taken to an unknown town called Blackland in the depths of the desert ruled by a tyrant, Harry Killer.

Blackland stands on the banks of a river. On one side of the river, three semi-circular compounds house respectively Killer's private army, a colony of hardcore criminals whom he uses for bank robberies in Europe and a huge force of slaves. On the other bank stands Killer's fortress with the laboratories and workshops of his tame scientist, Marcel Camaret. This mild-mannered monomaniac has allowed himself to be inveigled into producing his inventions without knowing to what use they are put by Killer. He makes rain by increasing the charge of electricity in the clouds by means of shortwave radio beams, thereby transforming the desert around Blackland into lush countryside. He makes remote-controlled aerial torpedoes with warheads propelled over vast distances by rather unconvincing electric motors – what happens to the wires? – and variable-wing gliders that take off and land vertically, the thrust being provided by engines working on the compressor-burner principle (like turbojets) driving helicopter-style rotors. The variable-wing mechanism has come in for some learned criticism which I am not competent to answer, particularly since Camaret's explanations are very vague; but I would like to point out that the purpose behind the mechanism (faulty or not) was to 'provide these machines with a system of reflexes', like that of a bird in flight whose nervous system informs it of a need for a change in configuration: an early step in the direction of the modern science of cybernetics, and not an accidental one since Verne has Camaret invent as well what he calls his 'wasps'. These are cylindrical machines with three rotors and a propellor; they operate in swarms from a kind of hive, alternately loading and discharging case-shot, and homing automatically onto targets charted on a 'cycloscope' that gives a vertical view of the surrounding terrain.

The gullible maniac who has invented and built these terrifying marvels discovers their cost: crime, murder, tyranny. He rebels and entrenches himself in his workshops, defended by the wasps that swarm loaded with shot and carbonic acid. But Killer starves him out. Whereupon the slaves revolt and a frightful carnage takes place. Joan Buxton discovers her brother Lewis in Killer's dungeons and it transpires that Killer is in fact none other than Ferney, the son of Lord Buxton's second wife. Ferney hates his stepfather most bitterly and for years has been seeking to undo him utterly: it was he, Ferney, who murdered good George Buxton, usurped his command, and led his men into banditry; and it was he again who robbed the Buxton bank and kidnapped Lewis to cast a slur on the family name.

So much for thrills. But of course *La Mission Barsac* is more than a thriller, as Blackland and Camaret are there to remind us: the real subject of the novel is science in the service of evil. Camaret has a rather inflated opinion of himself: 'I made this town out of nothing, the way God made the universe!' When he learns the dreadful cost in terms of human lives and misery of his single-minded experiments, his reason wavers. 'My work is dead!' he cries. He hesitates, then pounding his chest says (in reference to himself); 'God has passed sentence on Blackland!' And he rushes off to blow the town to bits with a series of carefully calculated explosions set off by remote control. The commission is saved *in extremis* by the duped Captain Marcenay, who is called in by experimental wireless telegraphy and asks Joan to marry him. She accepts.

Despite this happy ending, the warning in this book, the last that Verne wrote, is clear enough. Throughout the nineteenth century, science had brought such a continual stream of improvements into men's lives that the question as to whether an inventor can be held responsible for the way his invention is used would have appeared odd indeed. However, by the end of the century it had become apparent that the new discoveries were not all beneficial. After having Captain Nemo say that it was not new continents the earth needed, but new men, Verne seems to be saying that the world needed not new science, but new morals – or at least that the former should not be allowed to progress faster than the latter.

There still remained the collection of short stories that Verne had been trying to get published for years. It came out in 1910 under the title *Hier et Demain*. Most of the stories are minor. *La Famille Raton*, originally published in *Le Figaro Illustré* in 1891, is a fairy tale for which Hetzel did not much care. *M. Ré Dièze et Mlle Si Bémol*, which Théophile Gautier asked Verne to write for the Christmas number of *Le Figaro Illustré* in 1893, is half fairy tale and half fantasy in Verne's usual vein. *L'Histoire de Jean Morénas* is another of Verne's heroic brother stories, and not one of his best. And *Le Humbug* is a full-blooded farce about American advertising and its willing victims. However, two of the stories are worth looking at more closely: the novellas *La Journée d'un Journaliste américain en 2889* and *L'Eternel Adam*.

The first is a science fiction story written in collaboration with Michel, who held the pen, and was originally published in *The Forum* in 1889. Transportation is provided by aircars. Over longer distances, air-trains are available; and transatlantic travel operates smoothly and comfortably via a system of pneumatic tubes. The telephone system works in conjunction with a television device known as the telephoton enabling the parties to a conversation to see one another; the same network broadcasts news and entertainment. Hibernation and electrically-induced hypnotic sedation are available as a public service. Electric calculating machines like our computers go through the most complicated calculations in seconds. The press (i.e. our mass media) is all-powerful. Its opinion polls give rulings on peace and war and guilt and innocence, obviating the need for governments and law courts. The *Earth Herald* draws its revenue from advertising carried on clouds. Its editor, Francis Bennett, behaves like a head of state. Great Britain is an American colony. Accumulators and solar generators maintain a constant climate; there is talk of melting the polar ice. Moving sidewalks, food pipelines, artificial daylight are all part of the everyday lives of people in 2889.

This mixture of banality and originality is followed by a novella that critics have found to be pessimistic: *L'Eternel Adam*, the date of which is unknown. Zartog is an archaeologist living several thousands of years from now. He discovers a tube containing a manuscript which he deciphers and translates. It is the story of the seven sole survivors of a catastrophe that occurred in the twentieth century, when the earth's crust collapsed and the world was flooded. These survivors were the founders of the new race to which Zartog belongs. As he reads on, Zartog learns that the vanished civilization had reached a higher point of development than his own of which he is so proud: all knowledge disappeared in the flood, and mankind had to struggle back from a new point zero. The Adam and Eve of his civilization, whom he has always believed to be the founders of the human race, are revealed to be two survivors of the catastrophe whose names have become deformed by centuries of tradition. And when Zartog returns to his excavations he discovers traces of a civilization that is older still: Atlantis, no less.

Zartog finds this lesson in relativism hard to take; and so have some of Verne's critics. But it seems to me that their arguments ignore the facts. We do not need to go into theories about the nature or origin of the universe to know that our world, a little ball of relatively unstable mud, has gone through great upheavals in the distant past, and that entire civilizations nearer to us in time have disappeared in the space of a few generations — not because of entropy but because of human turbulence. And there is no way that science can convince us that such up-heavals will not happen again, because it just does not know whether they will or not.

In any case, Zartog does not give in: he goes on working; and that in itself indicates that any pessimism to be found in *L'Eternel Adam* is not directed against man's endeavours as such, but against his lack of wisdom. (In this, *La Mission Barsac* is much more pessimistic, since there the scientist is led to destroy what his science has unwisely created.) But in any case, even in his so-called optimistic period Verne stresses the necessity for caution in action: if none of his heroes get dis-heartened and give in, none of them cast caution to the winds – far from it, they are forever checking their guns and machines and plans and routes and strategies. Verne's optimism was never uncritical and never cosy: the example of his heroes tells us always to be prepared for the worst.

'If Jules Verne and his *voyages extraordinaires* are still alive today, it is because they and their century pose the problems that are ineluctably ours a century later.' To this admirable remark of Jean Chesneaux's we should add that Verne also proposes a way of coping with the problems; courageously and cautiously, like his heroes, with a con-fidence mitigated by a fear of the worst that can be caused by our im-providence and selfishness. 'Fortune smiles on the brave, on those who dare' – but not on the reckless. The true worth of man is measured not in terms of material success but in terms of the effort required to succeed.

L'Eternel Adam, *Les Naufragés du Jonathan* and *La Mission Barsac* have overtones of disillusionment that appear to clash with the op-timism of Verne's work as a whole. There is nothing abnormal in the fact that this disillusionment coincided with the end of his life, for none of us die with the enthusiasm of our youth. But in fact his thinking did not vary all that much in the course of his life. His optimism was always qualified: 'great achievements are built on high hopes'; but 'we can attempt to achieve without hope, and we can persevere without success'. His heroes have to surmount apparently insurmountable obstacles; when they fail, they are not discouraged; and when they succeed, they do so only because they persevere. They lose out only to the forces of nature: here, their only possible move is to come in at a tangent and turn the natural forces to their advantage by a kind of ruse

– which is what science is all about. When their plans contradict natural laws, Verne's heroes invariably fail: their islands explode or sink and their machines fall apart. Verne's optimism as a novelist is less his doing than the reader's: his protagonists are *expected* to bring their plans to fruition; they are forever pursuing a happy ending.

In the late novels, success merely becomes more elusive: plans go awry. Men's greed is thwarted as the nuggets from the golden volcano are turned to dust and the golden meteorite falls into Baffin Bay. Dreams of liberty and a perfect society explode in the riots on Hoste, as Kaw-Djer is forced to face the facts:

Deprivation, passion and pride are not alone in making men fly at one another's throats. There is also madness, the madness that lurks within every crowd and drives them on, once they have tasted violence, until they are drunk with destruction and carnage. This is the madness . . . that makes the terrorist shoot down pointlessly the inoffensive passer-by, that in revolutions makes an undifferentiated hecatomb of the innocent and the guilty – and that inflames armies and wins battles.

And Verne's despair is surely as great as his hero's when he writes:

To see the idol that you have worshipped in your heart smashed at your feet and tell yourself that you were building on a lie, that nothing you thought was true and that your life has been a stupid sacrifice to a chimera – what utter failure.

Over the years, caution became Verne's watchword in everything. He lost his blind faith in unlimited progress. The conquest of nature was dependent on the conquest of wisdom – and mankind had no wisdom. Men's pride made them forget the ephemerality of their existence and the worldly possessions they were so eager to acquire. In order to gain momentary possession of a fragile fragment of a precarious world, pride made them continue to indulge in the absurd and cruel strife from which they were the first to suffer. Why persist in trying to build on thin air? Civilizations are transitory and collapse in a day after centuries of effort. What good was anything we did in a world destined to die?

Having reached the deepest depths of nihilism, he saw a glimmer of hope: the narrator of *L'Eternel Adam*, whose heart freezes with horror at the discovery that his view of nature is completely false, recovers sufficiently to say:

The real superiority of man does not lie in dominating or conquering nature. For the thinker, it lies in understanding nature, in making the immense universe lodge in the microcosm of his brain. For the man of action, it lies in remaining serene when faced with the revolt of matter, in saying to it: 'Destroy me if you like; but impress me – never!'

These brave words are reminiscent of those spoken by Professor Lidenbrock in 1864 during the eruption of Stromboli. They are repeated by Kaw-Djer during his musings on human destiny:

The efforts made by this strange, insignificant creature who is capable of containing within his tiny brain the vastness of an infinite universe . . . are not in vain, because his thoughts are thus commensurate with the world, their neighbour.

And it is Kaw-Djer again, going off to bury himself in solitude, who provides the optimistic answer to our anguish:

We die but our acts do not die, because they are perpetuated in their consequences, which go on forever. We pass briefly here; yet our steps leave their imprints on the sand for all eternity. Nothing occurs without having been determined by what preceded it; and the future is composed of the unknown prolongations of the past.

BIBLIOGRAPHY

The main primary sources for an account of the life of Jules Verne are as follows:

Bibliothèque Nationale, Paris, Manuscrits Fonds Hetzel, 1° série, Nos. 73–80, comprising 1187ff of correspondence of Jules Verne to P. J. Hetzel and his son, 183ff of correspondence of the Hetzels concerning Jules Verne, 505ff of contracts, receipts and accounts, 226ff of documents concerning Jules Verne, 413ff of correspondence of Michel Verne. The whole donated by Hetzel's grand-daughter and biographer, C. Bonnier de la Chapelle.

Nantes Public Library, Collection Guillon. (Donated by Maxime Guillon-Verne, son of Jules Verne's sister, Marie Guillon.)

Nantes Public Library. (Mainly the residue of papers used by Jules Verne's biographer Marguerite Allotte de la Fuye.)

Private collection of Jean Jules-Verne. Includes the MSS of Jules Verne's plays and juvenilia.

Private collection of Mme Dumoret, grand-daughter of Jules Verne's brother, Paul Verne.

Private collection of Mme Vaulon, grand-daughter of Jules Verne's sister, Marie Guillon.

A. Parménie and C. Bonnier de la Chapelle, *Histoire d'un Editeur et de ses Auteurs, P. J. Hetzel*, Paris, 1953.

Marguerite Allotte de la Fuye, *Jules Verne, sa Vie, son œuvre*, Paris, 1928.

Bulletin de la Société Jules Verne, Paris (19 rue des Petits Champs).

Unpublished family memoirs.

Jules Verne's personal files were destoyed by him in 1898. His library was largely dispersed during the hostilities of 1939–45.

A   WORKS BY JULES VERNE (except very minor ones)

The works are listed in chronological order of publication or performance. For each entry, the English-language translation indicated is the earliest known; where no translation is indicated, none has been traced. For entries whose titles vary significantly in translation, the most recent translations are listed also. Names of translators are given where known. Works never published or performed are entered with the mention MS; dated holographs are not queried as to date, other MSS are. All MSS are in the possession of Jean Jules-Verne, unless otherwise indicated. The place of the first performance of plays and libretti is Paris in all cases; names of theatres are indicated. First French publication of the works is by Hetzel & Co., Paris, unless otherwise indicated. First English-language publication is by Sampson Low, Marston & Co., London, unless otherwise indicated.

All titles are novels, unless indicated otherwise.

Arco { Arco Publications, London
{ Associated Booksellers, Bridgeport, Conn.

(With A. d'Ennery) indicates co-author. (1867–Riou) indicates date and designer of illustrated edition.

Alexandre VI. Play. MS (1847)
La Conspiration des Poudres. Play. MS (1848?)
Le Coq de Bruyère. Play. MS (1848?)
Don Galaor. Play. MS (1848?)
Une Promenade en Mer. Play. MS (1848?)
Le Quart d'Heure de Rabelais. Play. MS (1848?)
Abdallah. Play. MS (1849?)
Un Drame sous Louis XV. Play. MS (1849?)
La Guimard. Play. MS (1850?)
La Mille et deuxième Nuit. Libretto. MS (1850) (Music by Aristide Hignard)
Les Pailles rompues. 1850 Play. Théâtre Historique

De Charybde en Scylla. Play. MS (1851?)

Les Premiers Navires de la Marine mexicaine. 1851 Short story in
Musée des Familles, Paris
—— *The Mutineers; a romance of Mexico.* W. H. G. Kingston,
trans., 1877

Quiridine et Quidinerit. Play. MS (1851)

Les Châteaux en Californie ou Pierre qui roule n'amasse pas mousse.
1852 (With Pitre-Chevalier) Play in *Musée des Familles,* Paris

Martin Paz. 1852 Short story in *Musée des Familles,* Paris
—— *Martin Paz.* E. Frewer, trans., 1875

La Tour de Montléry. Play. MS (1852?) (With Charles Wallut.)

Colin Maillard. 1853 Libretto. Théâtre Lyrique (With Michel Carré.
Music by Aristide Hignard.)

Maître Zacharius ou l'horloger qui a perdu son âme. 1854 Short story
in *Musée des Familles,* Paris
—— *Master Zacharius.* 1876

Au Bord de l'Adour. Play. MS (1855?)

Les Compagnons de la Marjolaine. 1855 Libretto. Théâtre Lyrique
(With Michel Carré. Music by Aristide Hignard.)

Un Fils adoptif. Play. MS (1855?) See below, *Un Fils* 1950. MS in
Bibliothèque de l'Arsenal

Guerre aux Tyrans. Play. MS (1855?)

Les Heureux du Jour. Play. MS (1855)

Un Hivernage dans les Glaces-Histoire de deux fiancés dunquerquois.
1855 Short story in *Musée des Familles,* Paris
—— *A Winter amid the Ice, and other stories.* 1876

Mona Lisa. Play. MS (1855?) See below, *Monna Lisa,* 1974

Un Voyage en ballon. 1856 Short story in *Musée des Familles.* See
below, *Un Drame dans les Airs,* 1874

Les Sabines. Libretto. MS (1857?) MS incomplete

M. De Chimpanzé. 1858 Libretto. Bouffes-Parisiens (With Michel
Carré. Music by Aristide Hignard.)

Voyage en Ecosse. Non-fiction. MS (1859?)

Auberge des Ardennes. 1860 Libretto. Théâtre Lyrique (With Michel
Carré. Music by Aristide Hignard.)

Onze Jours de Siège. 1861 Play. Théâtre du Vaudeville (With Charles
Wallut.)

Cinq Semaines en Ballon. 1863 (1867-Riou)
—— *Five Weeks in a Balloon.* Chapman & Hall, London, 1870

Le Comte de Chantelaine. 1864 Short story in *Musée des Familles,* Paris

Edgar Poe. 1864 Non-fiction in *Musée des Familles,* Paris

Voyage au Centre de la Terre. 1864 (1867 – Riou)
—— *Journey to the Centre of the Earth.* Griffith and Farran, London, 1872

De la Terre à la Lune. 1865 (1872 – Montaut)
—— *From the Earth to the Moon direct in 97 hours 20 minutes; and a trip around it.* L. Mercier and E. C. King, trans., 1873

Les Forceurs de Blocus. 1865 Short story in *Musée des Familles,* Paris
—— *The Blockade Runners.* 1876

Les Aventures du Capitaine Hatteras. 1866 2 vols (1867 – Riou)
(I. *Les Anglais au Pôle Nord.* 1864
II. *Le Désert de Glace.* 1866)
—— I. *English at the North Pole.* Routledge, London, 1874
—— II. *Field of Ice.* Routledge, London, 1876

Les Enfants du Capitaine Grant. 1867–8 3 vols (1868–Riou)
—— *Voyage round the World.* Routledge, London, 1876–7
—— *Captain Grant's Children.* (I. *The Mysterious Document.* II. *Among the Cannibals.* III. *On the Track.*) Arco, s.d.

Géographie illustrée de la France et de ses Colonies. 1868. Non-fiction. (With Théophile Lavallée)

Autour de la Lune. 1870 (1872 – Neuville and Bayard)
—— *From the Earth to the Moon . . . and a trip around it.* L. Mercier and E. C. King, trans., 1873

Histoire des Grands Voyages et Grands Voyageurs. 1870–3 Non-fiction. (Benett et Philippoteaux) (With Gabriel Marcel)
—— *Celebrated Travels and Travellers.* Dora Leigh, N. D'Anvers, etc., trans. 3 vols 1879–81

Vingt Mille Lieues sous les Mers. 1870 (1870 – Riou and Neuville)
—— *Twenty thousand leagues under the Seas.* 1873

Une Ville flottante. 1871 (1872 – Férat)
—— *A Floating City.* H. Frith, trans., Ward, Lock, London, 1876

Aventures de Trois Russes et de Trois Anglais. 1872 (1872 – Férat)
—— *Meridiana; the Adventures of three Englishmen and three Russians in South Africa.* 1873

Une Fantaisie du Docteur Ox. 1872 (1874 – various) Short story.
—— *Dr Ox's Experiment, and other stories.* 1874

Un Neveu d'Amérique ou les deux Frontignac. 1873 Play. Théâtre Cluny (With Edouard Cadol and Charles Wallut.)

Le Pays des Fourrures. 1873 2 vols (1873 – Férat and Beaurepaire)
—— *The Fur Country; or, seventy degrees north latitude.* (I. *The Sun in Eclipse.* II. *Through the Bering Strait*) N. D'Anvers, trans., 1873

Le Tour du Monde en quatre-vingt jours. 1873 (1874 – Neuville and Benett)
—— *Around the World in Eighty Days.* G. M. Towle, trans., 1874

Un Drame dans les Airs. (*Un Voyage en Ballon.* 1856) 1874 Short story.

L'Ile Mystérieuse. 1874–5 3 vols (1875 – Férat)
  I. *Les Naufragés de l'Air.*
  II. *L'Abandonné.*
  III. *Le Secret de l'Ile.*
—— *The Mysterious Island.* W. H. G. Kingston, trans., 1875

Une Ville idéale. 1875 Discourse in *Mémoires de l'Académie d'Amiens*

Le Chancelor. 1875 (1877 – Riou and Férat)
—— *Survivors of the Chancelor.* E. Frewer, trans., 1875

Michel Strogoff. 1876 2 vols (1876 – Férat)
—— *Michael Strogoff, the Courier of the Czar.* 2 vols, W. H. G. Kingston, trans., 1876–7

Hector Servadac. 1877 2 vols (1878-Philippoteaux)
—— *Hector Servadac.* (I. *Anomalous Phenomena.* II. *Homeward Bound.*) E. Frewer, trans., 1878

Les Indes Noires. 1877 (1877 – Férat)
—— *Child of the Cavern; or, Strange Doings Underground.* W. H. G. Kingston, trans., 1877
—— *Black Diamonds.* Arco, s.d.

Un Capitaine de quinze ans. 1878 2 vols (1878 – Meyer)
—— *Dick Sands, the Boy Captain.* E. Frewer, trans., 1879

Les Enfants du Capitaine Grant. 1878 Play. Théâtre de la Porte Saint-Martin (With Adolphe d'Ennery.)

Les Cinq Cents Millions de la Bégum. 1878 (1879 – Benett)
—— *The Begum's Fortune.* W. H. G. Kingston, trans., 1880

Les Révoltés de la Bounty. 1879 (1879 – Benett) Short story.
—— *The Mutineers of the Bounty.* W. H. G. Kingston, trans., 1880

Les Tribulations d'un Chinois en Chine. 1879 (1879 – Benett)
—— *Tribulations of a Chinaman.* E. Frewer, trans., 1880

Le Tour du Monde en quatre-vingt jours. 1874 Play. Théâtre de la Porte Saint-Martin (With Adolphe d'Ennery.)

—— *Around the World in Eighty Days.* C. Clarke, trans., S. French, London, 1875

La Maison à Vapeur. 1880 2 vols (1880 – Benett)
—— *The Steam House.* (I. *Demon of Cawnpore.* II. *Tigers and Traitors.*) A. D. Kingston, trans., 1881

Michel Strogoff. 1880 Play. Théâtre du Châtelet (With Adolphe d'Ennery.)
—— *Michel Strogoff.* E. Philippe, trans., S. French, London, 1881

La Jangada. 1881 2 vols (1881 – Benett)
—— *The Giant Raft.* (I. *Down the Amazon.* II. *Cryptogram.*) W. Gordon, trans., 1881

L'Ecole des Robinsons. 1882 (1882 – Benett)
—— *Godfrey Morgan: a Californian mystery.* W. J. Gordon, trans., 1883
—— *School for Crusoes.* Arco, s.d.

Le Rayon Vert. 1882 (1882 – Benett)
—— *The Green Ray.* M. de Hauteville, trans., 1883

Un Voyage à travers l'Impossible. 1882 Play. Théâtre de la Porte Saint-Martin (With Adolphe d'Ennery.)

Kéraban le Têtu. 1883 2 vols (1883 – Benett)
—— *Keraban the Inflexible.* (I. *The Captain of the Guidara.* 1884. II. *Scarpante the Spy.* 1885)

Kéraban le Têtu. 1883 Play. Théâtre de la Gaîté

Frritt-Flac. 1884 in *Le Figaro Illustré*, Paris (1886 – Willette)
—— *Frritt-Flac* Short story in *Yesterday and Tomorrow*, Arco, s.d.

L'Archipel en Feu. 1884 (1884 – Benett)
—— *The Archipelago on Fire.* 1886

L'Etoile du Sud. 1884 (1884 – Benett)
—— *The Vanished Diamond, a tale of South Africa.* 1885
—— *The Southern Star Mystery.* Arco, s.d.

L'Epave du Cynthia. 1885 (With André Laurie.)
—— *Salvage of the Cynthia.* Arco, s.d.

Mathias Sandorf. 1885 3 vols (1885 – Benett)
—— *Mathias Sandorf.* 1886

Robur le Conquérant. 1886 (1886 – Benett)
—— *The Clipper of the Clouds.* 1887

Un Billet de Loterie. 1886 (1886 – Roux)
—— *The Lottery Ticket: a Tale of Tellemarken.* 1887

Le Chemin de France. 1887 (1889 – Roux)
— — *Flight to France.* 1888
Nord Contre Sud. 1887 2 vols (1887 – Benett)
— — *North Against South: a Tale of the American Civil War.* (I. *Burbank the Northerner.* II. *Texar the Southerner.*) 1888
Mathias Sandorf. 1887 Play. Théâtre de l'Ambigu (With William Busnach and Georges Maurens.)
Deux Ans de Vacances ou Un Pensionnat de Robinsons. 1888 2 vols (1888 – Benett)
— — *Two Years Holiday.* (I. *Adrift in the Pacific.* II. *Second Year Ashore*) 1889
Une Famille Sans Nom. 1889 2 vols (1889 – Tiret-Bognet)
— — *A Family Without a Name.* (I. *Leader of the Resistance.* II. *Into the Abyss.*) 1890
Sans Dessus Dessous. 1889 (1889 – Roux)
— — *Purchase of the North Pole.* 1891
In the Year 2889. 1889 Short story in *The Forum*, New York (With Michel Verne.)
César Cascabel. 1890 2 vols (1890 – Roux)
— — *Cesar Cascabel.* (I. *Travelling Circus.* II. *Show on Ice.*) 1891
La Famille Raton. 1891 Short story in *Le Figaro Illustré*, Paris
Mistress Branican. 1881 2 vols (1891 – Benett)
— — *Mistress Branican.* 1892
Les Tribulations d'un Chinois en Chine. 1891 Play (theatre?) (With Adolphe d'Ennery.)
Le Château des Carpathes. 1892 (1891 – Benett)
— — *Castle of the Carpathians.* 1893
Claudius Bombarnac. 1892 (1892 – Benett)
— — *Claudius Bombarnac.* 1894
M. Ré Dièze et Melle Si Bémol. 1893 Short story in *Le Figaro Illustré*, Paris
— — *Mr Ray Sharp and Miss Me Flat.* In *Yesterday and Tomorrow*, Arco, s.d.
P'tit Bonhomme. 1893 2 vols (1893 – Benett)
— — *Foundling Mick.* 1895
Maître Antifer. 1894 2 vols (1894 – Roux)
— — *Captain Antifer.* 1895
L'Ile à hélice. 1895 2 vols (1895 – Benett)
— — *The Floating Island.* W. J. Gordon, trans., 1896

— — *Propellor Island.* Arco, s.d.
Clovis Dardentor. 1896 (1896 – Benett)
— — *Clovis Dardentor.* 1897
Face au Drapeau. 1896 (1896 – Benett)
— — *For the Flag.* Mrs C. Hoey, trans., 1897
Le Sphinx des Glaces. 1897 2 vols (1897 – Roux)
— — *An Antarctic Mystery.* Mrs C. Hoey, trans., 1898
— — *The Mystery of Arthur Gordon Pym.* Arco, s.d.
Le Superbe Orénoque. 1898 2 vols (1898 – Roux)
Le Testament d'un Excentrique. 1899 2 vols (1899 – Roux)
— — *The Will of an Eccentric.* 1900
Seconde Patrie. 1900 2 vols (1900 – Roux)
— — I. *Their Island Home.* 1923
— — II. *Castaways of the Flag; the Final Adventures of the Swiss Family Robinson.* 1923
Le Serpent de Mer (Les Histoires de Jean-Marie Cabidoulin). 1901 (1901-Roux)
— — *The Sea Serpent.* I. O. Evans, trans., Arco, 1967
Le Village Aérien. 1901 (1901 – Roux)
— — *Village in the Tree Tops.* I. O. Evans, trans., Arco, s.d.
Les Frères Kip. 1902 2 vols (1902 – Roux)
Bourses de Voyage. 1903 2 vols (1903 – Benett)
Un Drame en Livonie. 1904 (1904 – Benett)
— — *Drama in Livonia.* Arco, s.d.
Maître du Monde. 1904 (1904 – Roux)
— — *Master of the World.* 1914
L'Invasion de la Mer. 1905 (1905 – Benett)
Le Phare du Bout du Monde. 1905 (1905 – Roux)
— — *The Lighthouse at the end of the World.* 1923
Le Volcan d'Or. 1906 2 vols (1906 – Roux)
— — *The Golden Volcano.* (I. *Claim on Forty Mile Creek.* II. *Flood and Flame.*) Arco, 1963
L'Agence Thompson. 1907 2 vols (1907 – Benett)
— — *The Thompson Travel Agency.* (I. *Package Holiday.* II. *End of the Journey.*) I. O. Evans, trans., Arco, s.d.
La Chasse au Météore. 1908 (1908 – Roux)
— — *The Chase of the Golden Meteor.* Frederick Lawton, trans., Grant Richards, London, 1909
— — *Hunt for the Meteor.* Arco, s.d.

Le Pilote du Danube. 1908 (1908 – Roux)

—— *The Danube Pilot.* I. O. Evans, trans., Arco, 1967

Les Naufragés du Jonathan. 1909 2 vols (1909 – Roux)

—— *The Survivors of the Jonathan.* (I. *Masterless Man.* II. *Unwilling Dictator.*) Arco, s.d.

Hier et Demain. 1910 (1910 – Benett-Myrbach and Roux) Short stories

M. Ré Dièze et Melle Si Bémol (1893)

La Destinée de Jean Morénas (1855?)

Le Humbug (1863)

La Journée d'un Journaliste Américain en 2889 (In the Year 2889, 1889)

L'Eternel Adam (1900?)

—— *Yesterday and Tomorrow.* I. O. Evans, trans., Arco, s.d.

The Fate of Jean Morénas

An Ideal City

Frritt-Flac

Gil Braltar

The Day of an American Journalist in 2889 A.D.

Mr Ray Sharp and Miss Me Flat

The Eternal Adam

Le Secret de Wilhelm Storitz. 1910 (1910 – Roux)

—— *The Secret of Wilhelm Storitz.* I. O. Evans, trans., Arco, 1965

L'Etonnante Aventure de la Mission Barsac. 1919 2 vols Hachette, Paris (1919-Roux)

—— I. *Into the Niger Bend.*

—— II. *City in the Sahara.* I. O. Evans, trans., Arco, 1965

Un Fils Adoptif. 1950 Play. French TV (With Charles Wallut.)

Monna Lisa. 1974 Play in *L'Herne*, Paris

B FULL LENGTH STUDIES OF VERNE

Allott, K. *Jules Verne.* London, 1940

Allotte de la Fuye, M. *Jules Verne.* Erik de Mauny, trans. London, 1954

Bastard, G. *Verne, auteur des Voyages Extraordinaires.* Paris, 1883

Beeker, B. *Jules Verne.* New York, 1966

Bitelli, G. *Giulio Verne.* Bescia, 1955

Born, F. *The Man who invented the Future.* J. Biro, trans. Englewood Cliffs, 1964

Chesneaux, J. *The Political and Social Ideas of Jules Verne*. T. Wikeley, trans. London, 1972

Chini, L. *Guilio Verne*. Florence, s.d.

Diesbach, G. de. *Le Tour de Jules Verne en quatre-vingts livres*. Paris, 1969

Escaich, R. *Voyage au monde de Jules Verne*. Paris, 1955

Evans, I. O. *Jules Verne and his Work*. London, 1965

Frank, B. *Jules Verne et ses Voyages*. Paris, 1941

Franquinet, E. *Jules Verne en zijn Wonderreizen*. The Hague, 1964
—— *Jules Verne, zijn Persoon en zijn Werk*. Eindhoven, 1942

Freedman, R. *Jules Verne, portrait of a prophet*. New York, 1965

Huet, M.-H. *L'Histoire des Voyages Extraordinaires*. Paris, 1973

Lemire, C. *Jules Verne*. Paris, 1908

Marcucci, E. *Guilio Verne e la sua opera*. Milan, 1930
—— *Les Illustrations des Voyages Extraordinaires de Jules Verne*. Paris, 1956

Martin, C.-N. *Jules Verne, sa vie et son oeuvre*. Lausanne, 1971

Metral, M. *Sur les pas de Jules Verne*. Neuchâtel, 1963

Moré, M. *Le Très Curieux Jules Verne*. Paris, 1960
—— *Nouvelles explorations de Jules Verne*. Paris, 1963

Popp, M. *Julius Verne und sein Werk*. Vienna, 1909

Vierne, S. *Jules Verne et le roman initiatique*. Paris, 1973

Waltz, G. H. *Jules Verne, the biography of an Imagination*. New York, 1943

C   ESSAYS ON VERNE

Audouard, O. 'JV' in *Silhouettes parisiennes*. Paris, 1883

Amicis, E. De 'Una visita a Jules Verne' in *Memorie*. Milan, 1900

Barthes, R. 'JV' in *Mythologies*. Paris, 1957

Bridenne, A. 'JV' in *Portraits intimes*, Paris, 1899

Bridenne, J.-J. 'JV' in *La Littérature française d'imagination scientifique*. Paris, 1950

Butor, M. 'JV' in *Portraits de l'artiste en jeune singe*. Paris, 1965

Clarétie, J. 'JV' in *Célébrités contemporaines*. Paris, 1883

Drougard, E. *Villiers de l'Isle Adam, les trois premiers contes*. Paris, 1931.

Goupil, A. 'Le Personnage du savant dans l'œuvre de Jules Verne.' D.E.S. dissertation. University of Cacn, 1965

Jeune, S. 'JV' in *De F. T. Graindorge à A. O. Barnabooth*. Paris, 1963

Macherey, P. 'JV, ou le récit en défaut' in *Pour une théorie de la production littéraire*. Paris, 1966

Parmenier, A. and Bonnier de la Chapelle, C. 'JV' in *Histoire d'un éditeur et de ses auteurs: P. J. Hetzel (Stahl)*. Paris, 1953

Turiello, M. 'JV' in *Causeries littéraires*. Naples, 1895

—— 'JV' in *Mélanges littéraires*. Naples, 1908

D   PERIODICALS (Special Numbers on Verne)

'Arts' (Paris), no. 341, January 1952

'Arts et Lettres' (Paris), no. 15, 1949

'Bibliothèque de Travail' (Cannes), no. 502, 10 October 1961

'Bulletin de la Société Jules Verne' (Paris), nos. 1–13, 1935–8. New Series, nos. 1–25, 1967–73

'Désiré' (Paris), no. 26, 1970

'Europe' (Paris), no. 112–3, April–May 1955

'L'Arc' (Aix-en-Provence), no. 29, 2nd trim. 1966

'L'Herne' (Paris), 1974

'Les Lettres françaises' (Paris), no. 561, 24–31 March 1955

'Les Nouvelles Littéraires' (Paris), no. 2012, 24 March 1966

'Livres de France' (Paris), no. 5, May–June 1955

'Magasin d'Education et de Récréation' (Paris), no. 248, 15 April 1905

'The Times Literary Supplement' (London), 7 December 1940

E   SELECTED ARTICLES AND REVIEWS

Amis, K. review in the *Observer*, London 1 December 1961

Barjavel, R. 'Sans lui, notre siècle serait stupide.' in *Les Nouvelles littéraires*, Paris, no. 2012, 24 March 1966

Butor, M. 'L'image du monde au XIXe siècle.' in *Arts et Loisirs*, Paris, March 1966

—— 'Homage to JV.' in *New Statesman*, London, 15 July 1966

Barthes, R. 'Par où commencer?' in *Poétique*. Paris, no. 1, 1970

Bellemin-Noël, J. 'Analectures de JV' in *Critique*, Paris, no. 279–280, 1970

Belloc, M. 'JV at home' in *The Strand Magazine*, London, February 1895

Bory, J.-L. 'Le Voyage intérieur: JV' in *Les Nouvelles littéraires*, Paris, no. 2983, 24 July 1969

Buissière, F. 'A propos du vol d'Apollo: JV ou la vérité du roman' in *Europe*, Paris, no. 482, June 1969

Chesneaux, J. 'L'invention linguistique chez JV' in *Langues et techniques*, Paris, 1972

Courville, L. 'Bas les masques' in *Les Nouvelles littéraires*, Paris, no. 2012, 24 March 1966

Dorléac, B. 'Une imagination jamais absurde' in *Arts et Loisirs*, Paris, March 1966

Golding, W. review in *The Spectator*, London, 9 June 1961

Guérard, F. 'Trois romans de JV portés à l'écran' in *Image et Son*, Paris, no. 120, March 1959

Laissus, J. 'JV, l'extraordinaire voyageur' in *Comptes rendus du 91e congrès national des Sociétés savantes*. Paris, 1967

MacKenzie, N. review in *New Statesman*, London, 15 September 1956

Moré, M. 'Hasard et providence chez JV' in *Critiques*, Paris, May 1962

Orwell, G. review in New Statesman, London, 18 January 1941

Pyrce-Jones, A. review in *Horizon*, London, January 1941

Serres, M. 'Un voyage au bout de la nuit' in *Critique*, Paris, no. 263, 1969

—— 'Oedipe-messager' ibid., no. 272, 1970

Slonim, M. 'Revival of JV' in *New York Times Book Review*, New York, 22 May 1966

Sprout, M. 'The influence of Poe on JV' in *Revue de littérature comparée*, Paris, March 1967

Vierne, S. 'L'authenticité de quelques œuvres de JV' in *Annales de Bretagne*, Rennes, no. 3, 1966

—— 'Les refuges dans les romans de JV' in *Circé*, Paris, 1971

INDEX